# THE MARKET APPROACH TO EDUCATION

# THE MARKET APPROACH
# TO EDUCATION

## AN ANALYSIS OF AMERICA'S FIRST
## VOUCHER PROGRAM

*John F. Witte*

PRINCETON UNIVERSITY PRESS    PRINCETON, NEW JERSEY

**Copyright © 2000 by Princeton University Press**
Published by Princeton University Press, 41 William Street,
Princeton, New Jersey 08540
In the United Kingdom: Princeton University Press, Chichester, West Sussex
All Rights Reserved

**Library of Congress Cataloging-in-Publication Data**

Witte, John F.
The market approach to education : an analysis of America's first
voucher program / John F. Witte.
p.    cm.
Includes bibliographical references (p.   ) and index.
ISBN 0-691-00944-9 (cloth : alk. paper)
1. Educational vouchers — Wisconsin — Milwaukee Case studies.
2. School choice — Wisconsin — Milwaukee Case studies.   3. Education,
Urban — Wisconsin — Milwaukee Case studies.   I. Title.
LB2828.85.W6W58   2000
379.1'11 — dc21                                               99-28151

This book has been composed in Sabon

The paper used in this publication meets the minimum requirements of
ANSI/NISO Z39.48-1992 (R1997) (*Permanence of Paper*)

http://pup.princeton.edu

Printed in the United States of America

10   9   8   7   6   5   4   3   2   1

## For My Mother, Willene Witte Winn ⸻

SHE TAUGHT ME MUCH MORE THAN SHE WILL EVER KNOW

# Contents

List of Figures     ix

List of Tables     xi

Preface     xiii

Acknowledgments     xv

1. Introduction     3

2. The Enduring Controversy over Educational Choice     11

3. Educational Choice and the Milwaukee Voucher Program     29

     Appendix to Chapter 3
     *Historical MPS Achievement Test Data*     49

4. Who Participates in Choice Programs?     52

5. The Milwaukee Choice Schools     83

6. Outcomes of the Milwaukee Voucher Program     112

     Appendix to Chapter 6
     *Modeling Selection Bias*     152

7. The Politics of Vouchers     157

8. Implications and Conclusions     190

References     211

Index     219

# List of Figures

3.1 MPS Student Enrollment, Percent by Race, 1968–97     37

3.2 Concentration of African American MPS Students, 1997     38

3.3 Concentration of Hispanic MPS Students, 1997     39

3.4 Public and Private School Enrollment in Milwaukee, 1960–97     42

6.1 1990 Cohort Math Scores (NCEs)     142

7.1 Asay's View     176

7.2 Memorandum from PAVE Director Daniel McKinley to School Administrators, August 4, 1995     187

## List of Tables ————————————————

| | | |
|---|---|---|
| 2.1 | Critical Distinctions between Public and Market-Based Schools | 13 |
| 2.2 | Personal and Institutional Choice Paradigms | 16 |
| 3.1 | School Choice in America, by Income, 1993 | 32 |
| 3.2 | The Milwaukee and Cleveland Voucher Program Requirements | 45 |
| A3.1 | Iowa Test of Basic Skills, Grade Equivalents, 1959, 1965, and 1970 | 49 |
| A3.2 | MPS Metropolitan Achievement (1975) and Iowa Test of Basic Skills (1981, 1985), Median National Percentiles | 50 |
| A3.3 | Survey Sample Sizes and Response Rates | 50 |
| A3.4 | Race and Income Response Rates | 51 |
| 4.1 | Participation and Attrition from the Choice Program, 1990–95 | 56 |
| 4.2 | Household Demographics, 1990–94 | 60 |
| 4.3 | Factors Affecting Decisions to Participate in the Choice Program, Applicants, 1990–94 | 63 |
| 4.4 | Scale Data — Means, Standard Deviations, Reliability, and Sample Sizes | 64 |
| 4.5 | Significance Levels of Differences in Scale Means | 66 |
| 4.6 | Prior Test Scores | 67 |
| 4.7 | Choice v. MPS Logit | 71 |
| 4.8 | Chapter 220 v. MPS Logit | 80 |
| 5.1 | Teacher Seniority and Certification in Choice Schools, 1990–95 | 94 |
| 6.1 | Experimental and Control Groups for the Milwaukee Voucher Program | 121 |

6.2    Mean NCEs, Iowa Test of Basic Skills, 1990–94          124

6.3    Estimated Iowa Test of Basic Skills, 1991–94, Student
       Record Data Base Variables Only                        126

6.4    Estimated Iowa Test of Basic Skills, 1991–94, Full
       Variables Set                                          127

6.5    Estimated Iowa Test of Basic Skills *Reading* Score,
       Including Student Choice Year: 1991, 1992, 1993, 1994   129

6.6    Estimated Iowa Test of Basic Skills *Math* Score,
       Including Student Choice Year: 1991, 1992, 1993, 1994   130

6.7    Regressions Results, 1991–94, *Choice* (Treatment) and
       *Rejects*                                              135

6.8    Logistic Regression on Rejects Having Any
       Postapplication Test, 1991–94                          138

6.9    Regression Results, 1991–94, *Choice* (Treatment) and
       *Rejects* — Excluding Lowest Scoring Students (NCE < 5)  140

6.10   Regression Results, 1991–94, Rejects (Treatment) and
       MPS                                                    141

6.11   Mean Differences between Continuing and Attrition
       Choice Students, 1990–93                               145

6.12   Test Scores of Leaving and Returning Choice Students,
       Spring 1991 and 1992                                   146

6.13   Why Choice Students Left the Choice Program,
       1991–94                                                148

A6.1   Ordinary Least Squares, 1991–94, Choice (Treatment)
       and Low-Income MPS Students                            153

A6.2   Heckman Two-Stage Results, 1991–94, Choice
       (Treatment) and Low-Income MPS Students                155

In policy, politics, and social science, there are two intellectual approaches to problems and debates. The first begins with an answer and then works back to evidence and the construction of a supportive logical argument. The second begins with a question and then searches for evidence and data to prove or disprove the proposition behind the question.

Both approaches are legitimate. The former guided many of the most important political writings that affect the modern world. For Americans, *The Declaration of Independence* and *The Federalist Papers* come immediately to mind. In the early twentieth century, the latter form of inquiry, characteristic of the hard sciences as early as the eighteenth century, was enthusiastically adopted by the social and behavioral sciences. But in the latter half of the twentieth century, with challenges from linguistic theorists and postmodernist critics who questioned the ability of any objective social science, the question-oriented approach to research came under fire. The snarling cynical label of "positivism" was the battle cry of opponents.

I hope that this study is viewed primarily as being of the second, positivist form. Looking back on the last ten years, I wish that I could have begun with an answer rather than a question. This book would have been written sooner, it would have been simpler, and my life would have been much easier. But then how could I say to my students, who usually come to me with a "dissertation argument," that dissertations start with a question, not a conclusion?

Unfortunately, while my devotion to positivism is not diminished, this study may not be the finest example of that intellectual genre. Although this book is replete with quantitative and other systematic evidence, much of what I have come to know, or believe, has not been based on hard scientific research. Rather it is based on carefully listening and observing and questioning in an offhanded manner. And some of the most strongly presented conclusions of this book are based on pulling together strands of actions, results, and inferred motives — not quite the stuff of hard science.

And, in the text that follows, although I am rarely present except in the third person or expert mode, I have been a part of this. I was appointed in September 1990 as the State of Wisconsin evaluator of the Milwaukee voucher program, which was the first voucher program in America. The State Superintendent of Public Instruction, Bert Grover, whom I hope still considers me a friend, appointed me. That appointment is described later, but because Grover was an outspoken critique of vouchers, some pro-voucher supporters assumed I was a voucher opponent from the beginning. I believe that a thorough reading of my prior work would actually indicate I might have leaned the other way. That was Grover's opinion when he agreed to my conditions of independence as an evaluator, shook my hand, and said: "You're going to screw me on this one, aren't you?"

My evaluations and the data we collected have played a role in the political history of the voucher movement. And I have been flattered by and contributed with enthusiasm to the media attention given the program, what I refer to in chapter 7 as "choice theater." However, I sincerely believe that my role in terms of events was modest—the course would not have changed absent my involvement. I am more concerned about my reaction to my role—especially the temptation to turn against educational choice because of vicious attacks on my character and my work by voucher advocates.

To mitigate that possibility I have tried to present the arguments and conclusions in a very old-fashioned way that distinguishes facts from theoretical speculation or value-based conclusions. I realize the great difficulty and at times impossibility of doing that. However, I have made every attempt to present "the facts" as such—in a positivist form. And when I have drawn conclusions or inferences from those facts, based on theoretical propositions and normative judgments, I have redundantly pointed that out to the reader. Phrases such as "reasonable people can of course reach other conclusions" are included on numerous occasions. If nothing else comes of this book, I hope the reader gains an appreciation for the importance of trying to distinguish normative evaluations from factual material and the effort required to do so. I do not agree with postmodernist assumptions that such efforts are completely hopeless.

The messages of this book are complex due to reliance on varying intellectual approaches combined with a set of diverse results. I doubt that anyone who reads further will walk away fully satisfied. I certainly have not. What I do hope is that the reader finds slivers of ideas that encourage further thought. And, that in an area of education policy that evokes the most grandiose rhetoric, the reader develops an appreciation for the need to filter the rhetoric through a tough screen of reality.

# Acknowledgments ─────────────────────────────

THIS BOOK and the research on which it is based could not have been completed without the aid of many people and several organizations. Initial funding and continuing assistance were provided by the faculty and staff of the Robert La Follette Institute of Public Affairs of the University of Wisconsin–Madison. Major funding and intellectual support were provided by grants from the Spencer Foundation, with special appreciation for the help of Donna Shalala and Pat Graham. The Wisconsin Department of Public Instruction provided me the opportunity to study the Milwaukee voucher program, offering support without interference of any kind. I especially thank Bert Grover, Steve Dold, Bambi Statz, Sue Freese, Bob Paul, and Bert Adams. The Milwaukee Public School System was also extremely cooperative; special thanks to Gary Peterson, George Reineke, Mary Lamping, and Tim McElhatton. I am also grateful to the faculty, staff, and students of the private schools who participated in the program. They opened their schools, their minds, and their hearts to people they could have viewed with suspicion. I also thank the dozens of people, mostly students, who worked on this project over the years. For lasting contributions I give special thanks to Mark Rigdon, who began this project with me back in September 1990, and Chris Thorn, who contributed mightily over the years even after he officially had moved on to better things. Alice Honeywell not only aided greatly in the production of this book, but also helped produce the yearly reports on which much of this book is based. Andrea Bailey, Julie White, Troy Sterr, Kim Pritchard, Mark Cassell, and Peter Ballard also contributed beyond what would have been reasonable to expect. Very useful commentary on the project and manuscript was made by Henry Levin, Jennifer Hochshild, and Gary Orfield. The time and peace to complete this manuscript came through a year-long sabbatical first at the Public Affairs Research Center of the Budapest University of Economic Sciences and later at the Center for Educational Research at the London School of Economics. I thank my friends and associates at both of those wonderful universities. Finally, for seeing me through some very trying times during this study, and never leaving my side, I thank my wonderful wife, Mary, and my children, David and Amy.

# THE MARKET APPROACH TO EDUCATION

# 1

## Introduction

I AM SEATED in the basement of a sixty-year-old school in the spring of 1991. The room is painted grayish green and it is clean, but clearly the space has been improvised for the music class I have been watching for twenty minutes. Twenty-three first-grade students sit on folding chairs. All are African American; there are nine boys and fourteen girls. The girls wear clean, white blouses and blue plaid, pleated skirts. The boys wear white dress shirts and blue pants. The teacher is a black woman who I have heard has had problems showing up for work. She is not having any problems today. The class is quiet as they listen to her sing and talk. They love this class.

She begins talking about a verse they have just sung. She says the song is a black spiritual: "Lord Help Me Lay My Burdens Down." She asks the class if they know what "burdens" are.

An overly eager boy shoots up his hand as his mouth opens: "Burdens are heavy things!"

"Well, yes, they are sort of, but in the song they refer to worries," responds the teacher. "Can anyone tell me about worries they want the Lord to help with?"

A compatriot of the first boy: "Like when I go home with my report card." [Laughter]

A tiny girl in the second row, hair in pigtails, with a voice so small it is hard to hear from ten feet away: "To make the shooting over my house stop."

Another girl, sitting next to her: "So the fighting will stop at home."

The first boy [laughter gone]: "To keep the gangs and the druggers away."

The teacher looks at me, shakes her head, and says: "Let's try the second verse."

The exercise was not for my benefit. I had been following the class all day and I was only a modest curiosity by early afternoon. And our research team had been around the school for three days. The school was one of the seven schools that had been certified in the summer of 1990 to participate in the Milwaukee Parental Choice Program—the nation's first voucher program. This book is the story of the first five years of that program.

At the time, this school had been in existence for twenty-three years as a nonsectarian school. Formerly it was a Catholic school, and the uniforms, students silently walking in halls in pairs, and the willingness to discuss spirituality were reminiscent of that Catholic past. But the replies of those tiny people were not reminiscent of that past — a past of white, working-, and middle-class Catholics.

As I observed this school in the spring of 1991, the nation was engaged in intense and confusing debates over the crisis and need for reform of American education. The most recent call for reforms, in a nation that goes through waves of education reforms, began in 1993 with the White House release of a strongly worded report entitled *A Nation At Risk* (National Commission on Excellence in Education, 1983). That was followed in subsequent years by reports from the National Governors' Association, *Time for Results* (National Governors' Association, 1986) and the National Commission on Children, *Beyond Rhetoric: A New American Agenda for Children and Families* (National Commission on Children, 1991). Added to the crisis mentality, which promoted numerous and diverse calls for reform, were a string of studies indicating that American children were considerably behind the children of many other countries, particularly in math and science education (OECD, 1989, 1990, 1992). While there has since been a revisionist metanalysis of this crisis (Berliner and Biddle, 1995), few would argue that education in our inner cities was satisfactory. Indeed, in Milwaukee a series of reports was published in 1985 that highlighted the dismal results in terms of achievement scores and dropout rates (Witte and Walsh, 1985; Witte, 1985). The study also emphasized that the gap between the Milwaukee Public Schools (MPS) and surrounding suburbs was enormous — characterized as "two worlds separated by a few miles" (Governor's Study Commission, 1985).

In 1991, however, the private school I was visiting was touted as a school that worked, at least by inner-city standards. It was considered among the best of the private schools in the choice program. By that time the Milwaukee voucher program had already attracted an avalanche of national political and media attention. Various political officials, including numerous governors, U.S. senators, cabinet secretaries, and the vice president of the United States, had visited the school. It was also featured on several network news shows, including a segment on *60 Minutes*. The school boasted that students in its eighth-grade graduating classes almost all graduated from high schools — and some of the best high schools in the area (most prominently, the two Catholic ones). In citing these numbers, they of course did not acknowledge that their eighth-grade class was about one-third of their kindergarten or first-grade classes, thus begging the question of what happened to those who slipped away. But again, by most standards, to those familiar with inner-city schools, this school was a success. It was orderly, clean, and disciplined. Parents were constantly around the school, and classrooms were, for the most part, competently staffed. Yet when both the teacher and I heard the voices of those small children, we were once again reminded of the constant intrusion of the outside world into this and other inner-city schools. And it is an outside world that is rough, especially rough for young and fragile children.

I bring this emphasis on reality to the surface early on because much of the debate over educational choice is couched in rhetorical flourishes that simply do not face the reality of education in our inner cities. Supporters of choice are quick to praise competition. Make schools compete with each other and the schools from which all families can choose will be better. But where else has competition worked in our inner-city neighborhoods? Has it worked in housing? In grocery stores? In health care? In retail clothing? Most Americans take many things for granted in their communities that cannot be taken for granted in most inner cities in America. For example, you probably cannot buy a new car and maybe not even a used one in most inner cities. You probably cannot buy a bicycle or even get a hinge for a door. You cannot see a non–X-rated movie. You cannot shop in a large, well-stocked, reasonably priced grocery store. You can buy liquor, but the prices will be high. Why does the market fail to provide these things? Does the government have a monopoly on movies? On car sales? On grocery stores?

Why then do so many business and political proponents of educational choice have such blind faith in competition as the salvation of education in our cities? There are a number of possible answers. Proponents may be simply naïve. Many, after all, have very limited experience with life in the inner city. They may not really think about what they are saying—having relied on slogans so long that the slogans become self-fulfilling prophecies. And, of course, they may not be supporting choice with the education of inner-city youth in mind at all. They may see choice as a way to retaliate against educational bureaucracies and teachers' unions that they loathe. Or they may simply support private schools in general.

On the other side of the debate, the rhetoric is equally strident, and the motives may be equally suspicious. Opponents argue that if choice prevails, it will spell the death of public education, the common school tradition, integrated education, and the general commitment of the nation to education for all Americans. Those conclusions seem equally as bewildering to me. We have a hundred-year tradition of limited private schooling in the United States. Approximately 12 percent of our population, with very little variance, has been enrolled in private schools since 1940. And the vast majority (approximately 85 percent) is en-rolled in relatively low-cost religiously affiliated schools (see chapter 3). Most students remain in the public schools, and most are not in failing inner-city school districts. There is also considerable evidence that parents of those children are quite happy with their children's public schools (*Phi Delta Kappan*, 1996).

Given that most children attend private schools for religious reasons, and most public school families are satisfied with the schools their chil-dren attend, will vouchers radically change this pattern of demand? It seems unlikely. The one available study, a simulation in New York State, concluded that a voucher equivalent to what is spent on public school students would at best double the private school population (Lankford and Wykoff, 1992; Lankford et al., 1995). For other states without the private school tradition of New York, this estimate would undoubtedly be lower. I argue in the final chapter that if limited voucher programs such as Milwaukee's are expanded to offer vouchers to every-one, a possible result may be that public school districts simply absorb private schools. Thus fears that vouchers will destroy public education seem unfounded.

Although some of the schools I describe in this book are indeed racially segregated, they are usually not more segregated than some neighboring public schools. In fact, some of the schools have used the choice pro-gram explicitly to diversify their student body. Moreover, the issue itself may be something of a red herring. In systems like New York, Detroit, Washington, D.C., or Los Angeles (where the nonwhite percentage of students is close to 90 percent), we need to ask if it is realistic to focus on integration as a priority goal and to judge choice — pro or con — based on its marginal effect on integration. In short, the current damage to our inner-city schools in terms of learning environments, educational outcomes, and segregation has been done without choice.

The messages of this book reflect reality. The first message is that choice can be a useful tool to aid families and educators in inner city and poor communities where education has been a struggle for several generations. If programs are devised correctly, they can provide mean-ingful educational choices to families that now do not have such choices. And it is not trivial that most people in America, and surely most read-ing this book, already have those choices. But choice is not a tool that can be expected, by itself, to change dramatically the educational out-comes of the majority of inner-city students — even in the long term. Just as private entrepreneurs have not invested in car dealerships, movie the-aters, and grocery stores in the inner city, without massive subsidies it is unrealistic to expect new schools to be generated which in turn will perform some sort of magic to offset the gunfire, drugs, and difficulties of family life found there.

Can choice provide alternatives for some students who would not otherwise have them? Yes. Can choice support existing private schools with long traditions, but no further source of financial support? Yes. Can it provide different educational alternatives that may be the answer for some children? Yes. Will it, or could it, transform the overall status of inner-city education in the next generation? Probably not.

Second, if choice is extended beyond the inner city, as has been proposed many times, and as some suspect is the ultimate motive of many promoting targeted choice programs, the results are unlikely to be favorable to the poor. I will use the term "universal voucher programs" to indicate unrestricted use of educational vouchers within a state or the nation at large. Policy makers may want to support universal vouchers on different grounds than aiding failing students in poor districts, as is done in some other countries. However, that support must take into account the expectation that those currently attending or expected to attend private schools are most likely to choose and be admitted to private schools. Thus, in the absence of governmental constraints, Catholics will be more likely to choose Catholic schools, and their baptismal records will be relevant data for admission. The same will be true for other denominations. Most of those schools will not be in the inner city, and most will be attended by middle-class white students. The policy transition this represents, from a need-based, targeted program to a more universal, redistributive program, indicates a sharp and radical transformation.

If these points are correct, the policy debate over education choice can never be general. For the debate to have any meaning, the specific context and conditions of the choice arrangements must always be defined. This book tells the story of the first private school voucher program in the United States. My intent is to describe and analyze that program for what it was, not for something its supporters or detractors often tried to make it into.

The chapters that follow begin with a discussion of the theoretical and political issues surrounding choice. The enduring and intense controversy surrounding choice is traced to four phenomena. The first is that education involves statutory arrangements designating both the institutional structure and the arrangement of family choices concerning schools. Increasingly in the last decade, a market model of education has been promoted as an alternative to the nineteenth-century model of publicly defined, regulated, and assigned schools. That model significantly challenges the traditional institutional arrangements and is thus vigorously opposed by those dependent on the status quo. The second phenomenon is the growing belief among those in our worst educational environments that the choices they have are not equal to the choices most middle-class Americans have for their children. That normative position not only keeps the issue alive, but also provides the most compelling rationale for choice. Third, a considerable amount of money may be at stake, especially if the policy being promoted is full-cost vouchers for all children. Finally, the voucher issue is very likely to be decisive in federal court cases challenging the general First Amendment interpretation of the separation of church and state.

The third chapter provides background on education in Milwaukee and the Milwaukee Parental Choice Program (hereafter referred to alternately as the MPCP, the Choice program, or the voucher program). It describes (1) the range of educational choice programs prior to the MPCP; (2) the historical conditions of education in Milwaukee; (3) the politics of education leading up to the creation of the MPCP; (4) the 1990 Choice program, with subsequent court challenges; and (5) the research issues and design.

The fourth chapter analyzes the question of who chooses to participate in the MPCP and other choice programs throughout the country. The ideal research design for a choice program involves both a random assignment experiment to determine outcomes and a natural selection experiment to determine what types of families are naturally inclined to enroll in private schools under the constraints of the Choice program. The results of the latter provide a very consistent and interesting picture of MPCP families. The interpretation of those results is not completely parsimonious, however. Moreover, other choice programs without the constraints of the MPCP attract quite different sets of students.

The fifth chapter is devoted to describing the private schools in the Choice program — against the historical context of private school education in America. Much of the material in this chapter is drawn from extensive case studies of the schools in the program through the first four years. These studies included school histories; classroom observations; in-depth teacher and administrator interviews; student interviews; descriptions of curriculums and pedagogy; and statistical analyses of teacher qualifications, turnover, and demographic characteristics. Finally, the failure and bankruptcy of a number of choice schools are noted, again reinforcing the importance of not letting rhetoric obscure reality when it comes to educational choice.

Chapter 6 presents the outcomes of the MPCP. The more positive findings on parental attitudes and involvement and the effects of the program on the private schools are first addressed. The less positive findings, including attrition from the program and achievement test

scores, are then described and, with the help of appendices for technically minded readers, quite rigorously analyzed. For the most controversial findings on achievement test scores, a series of econometric estimates are reported. However, the results—that private schools at best
do as well as public schools—are consistent using a number of procedures. The limitations of both reliance on achievement tests and the
estimation procedures are discussed. I also critically examine a common
assumption that, without the benefit of selection, inner-city private
schools will produce dramatically more positive educational outcomes
than public schools. That was clearly not the result of the MPCP, and, I
will argue, does not make sense given the family environments shared
by public and private schools and the modest resources of the private
schools.

The final chapters assess the politics of educational vouchers and the
likely results of expanded voucher programs. I begin in chapter 7 by
describing the continuing politics of the MPCP and the voucher movement in general. This discussion is set against a theoretical background
attempting to explain the transition of a program from a substantive
program targeted for a needy population to a more universal program
with clearly redistributive effects. I examine what appears to be the
most likely path for Milwaukee and other voucher programs in following this transition—that a program originally intended to target choice
on poor inner-city families is manipulated over time to produce the opposite results—subsidies for middle-class, non–inner-city families to
make choices they would have made on their own.

I then analyze why educational choice seems to have such a riveting
effect on the media and on the politics of education. I refer to this
political/media obsession as "choice theater." I suggest that the metaphor of a play best describes the media presentations of educational
choice. I also portray how the politics of vouchers fit well with media-
constructed plays. Finally, the chapter examines the role of the courts
and how both the politics of vouchers and choice theater are directed
toward court decisions. With particular reference to the First Amendment of the U. S. Constitution, I note the potential importance of the
normative and political beliefs of the justices in deciding religious freedom cases. The vagueness of key concepts in First Amendment law and
the flexibility to pick and choose between precedent cases make the
issue of vouchers highly political, so that the justices become an important audience for choice theater.

The final chapter draws together the various strands of the study. It
examines what we can learn from voucher policy and politics that is
relevant to theories of policymaking and the experimental approach to
policy design. I carefully examine the differences between targeted and

universal voucher systems, supporting the former but not the latter. Last, based on the assumption that educational choice and vouchers represent a crossroad in American education, I examine what type of education pure market-based approaches to education would produce. They are not ones of which I approve.

In the end, this book is primarily about a single, five-year educational experiment involving only a few thousand children. Its importance lies partly in its uniqueness. But as I present it — and others may disagree — its importance is also a symbol of the frustration of trying to improve inner-city education and the confusion over how that should be accomplished. I hope this study adds a note of realism in terms of the limitations of schools, be they public or private. That schools have serious limitations may be a terrible reality that we need to face. When faced with conditions of abject poverty, with families that have great difficulty focusing resources on education, and with students who are immersed in a culture that often undervalues education, schools fight an uphill battle to provide top-quality, equal education for the majority of children.

# 2

## The Enduring Controversy
## over Educational Choice

CONSIDERABLY MORE VERBIAGE has been expended than action taken concerning private school choice in American. Modern discussions of education vouchers date to 1955 when Milton Friedman first suggested them as a way to reduce the inefficiencies and monopolistic character of public schools (Friedman, 1955). Until 1996, however, the MPCP was the only example of a voucher program or any other kind of program that provided substantial public monies to private primary and secondary schools. One other program in Cleveland began in 1996. So why does the issue remain so controversial and on the political agenda in so many states? What is its appeal, and why is it so fiercely opposed? This chapter suggests four explanations: (1) educational choice offers a radical institutional change over current public school practice; (2) it invokes powerful normative arguments and images involving freedom and equality; (3) it potentially involves a considerable amount of money; and (4) it is at the heart of a legal and constitutional struggle over First Amendment religious rights and protections. These explanations imply a number of theoretical and research issues that guided this study and which serve as the organizational focus of this book.

### Why Educational Choice Remains So Controversial

*Choice and Institutional Theories of Education*

Most debates over educational choice, be they theoretical or policy oriented, occur at a confusingly abstract level. Arguments in support of choice often focus on the failings of the public system, which they characterize either as a monopoly with attendant externalities (Friedman, 1955), or as politically controlled bureaucracies that feed political constituencies (Chubb and Moe, 1990). The latter produce shirking and bureaucratic surpluses, which are not applied to education achievement (Manski, 1992).

Less attention is often paid to the underlying market model that would replace the public school system. The new market system is often not spelled out in any detail, nor are the assumptions concerning individual

and institutional behavior that would be required to produce the anticipated efficiency gains. In addition, few if any theorists factor in the
current private school system, which, as we will see in chapter 3, has
been dominated by religious institutions and presumably a religious motivation on the part of consumers and providers.

Policy debates are often as abstract, simply invoking images of competition, innovation, and vague references to accountability. We shall
return to some of the more extreme examples of this in the final chapter.
Several scholars, however, especially John Coons and Stephen Sugarman, a number of years ago provided very detailed policy alternatives
for voucher programs (Coons and Sugarman, 1978). They have subsequently refined these proposals into a single alternative written as if it
were a state ballot initiative for California (Coons and Sugarman, 1992,
1993). John Chubb and Terry Moe also provided a quite detailed model
of a voucher program in their widely cited and debated 1990 book. A
number of authors have highlighted the fact that the exact programmatic definition of choice and voucher plans is critical (Murnane, 1986,
1990; Levin, 1990, 1991; Witte and Rigdon, 1993).

Opposing arguments are also often stated in grand generalities invoking images of choice as the destruction of the public schools or at least
the resegregation of schools by race, class, and ability. Equality is to be
sacrificed on the altar of free choice and opportunity. Both the academic
and policy positions often ignore how far along those roads the mostly
public education system has already taken us in many of our inner-city
school districts. This battle of words is highly repetitive but intense.

Given the intensity of the debate, remarkably little has been produced
in terms of policy changes — at least policies that include subsidies
for private schools. Yet choice seems to endure and remains a highly
charged and controversial issue. One explanation lies in the clash of
institutional models implied by a voucher system. Each model has its
appeal and rationale, but the models differ both in terms of institutional
structure and organization and in terms of the structure of choice for
families and schools. The first of these variables is crucial to the design
of our basic institutional arrangements concerning the delivery of education; the second describes how citizens interact with those institutions, and on what basis in terms of choices and rights.

As depicted in table 2.1, all of the important dimensions that define
an educational institution exhibit major differences in the theories behind public and private education in America. The differences begin
with fundamental differences in the institutional purposes of public and
private schools. Public schools were created in this country to provide a
"free," universal education for all children. Most state constitutional
provisions defining public education include the words "equal" or "uni-

**TABLE 2.1**
Critical Distinctions between Public and Market-Based Schools

| Attribute | Public: Democratic/ Collective | Market: Independent/ Private |
|---|---|---|
| *Purpose* | Universal, equal education "Civic" education Community satisfaction Family satisfaction | Internal organization Family satisfaction Profit or Equivalent |
| *Statutory construction* | Democratically controlled Public organization Highly regulated | Independently controlled Private organization Very little regulation |
| *Organizational control:* personnel, budgets, work rules, physical plant, etc. | External: by political and bureaucratic authorities | Internal: by board, staff, and parents |
| *Product:* grade structure; curriculum; pedagogy; classroom organization; schedule | External: by political and bureaucratic authorities | Internal: by board, staff, and parents |
| *Accountability* | To the public; Means: external assessment | To families; Means: family satisfaction |

form." As such, states are obligated to provide a suitable education for all students regardless of ability or disability status. Private schools, on the other hand, were primarily developed by the Catholic church to provide a suitable education that included religious training. Independent private schools often have a mission or image that distinguishes their methods, curriculum, or clientele from public schools. They may follow theories of Maria Montessori or Rudolph Steiner, provide boarding schools, or simply offer a place apart for the sons and daughters of the rich. In any event, their purpose is internal, providing a choice that their clients desire.

A unique aspect of American education is that the laws governing public and private schools are primarily state statutes and state constitutional provisions. Although they may differ somewhat from state to state, the main outlines are uniform. Because most private schools are religiously affiliated, the First Amendment of the U.S. Constitution prevents states from providing anything other than minimal regulation of private schools. Similarly, state constitutions also almost always have some form of an antiestablishment clause, which provides similar barriers to state regulation of religious organizations, including schools (Kemerer, 1995, forthcoming; Kemerer and King, 1995). Typically states require only a minimum period of instruction (e.g., contact hours or days per year), a sequential curriculum, and observance of health and safety laws. Public schools, on the other hand, are highly regulated at both the state and district levels. Although there may be considerable variation from state to state, the locus of regulatory power has been at the school district level. That changed somewhat in the 1980s and 1990s with an increasing role of states in curriculum, standards, testing, and assessment.

Both the control of the organization and the design of the education "product" are very different in public and private schools. In public schools, control is vested in democratically controlled bodies — state legislatures, state departments of public instruction, school district boards, and school district appointed officials and administrators. It is the responsibility of those bodies to design and alter the organizational arrangements in schools and to determine the form of education they produce. In the main, for private schools these tasks are highly decentralized. Although there may be a non–school-level governing system in some circumstances (e.g., Jesuit-run high schools), for the most part, private schools are usually connected to churches and church districts and are highly independent. This does not mean that they will necessarily have widely varying organizational forms or education methods, but simply means that those decisions are not the subject of political regulation or higher review as they are in public schools.

Finally, and of critical importance, public and private schools differ considerably in terms of accountability — both to whom they are accountable and by what means. Public schools — created, regulated, and designed by democratically selected officials — are accountable to the public, which both uses the schools and pays for them. Political authorities outside the school establish the methods and measures of accountability. These may include minimal reporting of student progress to parents via report cards and achievement testing, or it may include elaborate measures of pupil success reported at the individual, school, district, or state level. In the last decade, public schools have certainly moved from the former to the latter in many states. Private schools may use many of the same accountability measures, but they differ in two crucial ways. First, they are primarily accountable to their clients and only their clients; and second, they develop and control the accountability systems internally.

What has developed in the last two decades are a host of alternative models. Schools are being devised that fall between the ultimate independence of private schools and the bureaucratic constraints of traditional public schools. Schools that emphasize specific cultural traditions, such Hispanic or African American schools, or single-race schools, are being created as alternatives to universal schools. Publicly created charter schools are being proposed that combine external accountability and school-based decisions. And, in some progressive districts, such as Milwaukee, public schools are allowing a wide range of diversified educational concepts, pedagogies, and curriculums that define specific schools.[2]

Although nontraditional alternatives remain the minority in K–12 education, alternatives have been introduced recently and at a rapid pace. It seems unlikely that the trend will reverse, because choice has a strong normative appeal. We are after all a country that proclaims and protects freedom to a degree many nations would consider extreme. Education theory and practice, however, also promote diversity and choice. We have a diverse population to educate, with varying ideas concerning what it means to be educated. We have little agreement on how to proceed in terms of substance, method, or measurement of result. We are unclear about the role of parents or their choices. And we have increasingly less consensus on how a school should be organized or run. This has produced decisive changes in public schools away from the traditional, assignment area school with a set mode of teaching and organization. Especially in large school districts, this has meant a range of alternative forms of schools and education and dramatically increasing choices for parents.

Private schools have probably changed less in terms of the form and the range of alternatives open to parents. That is because religious schools, the majority of which are Catholic, have remained the mainstay of the private market. While much has been written on Catholic schools in recent years, few writers if any have stressed their diversity (Hoffer and Coleman, 1987; Bryk, Lee, and Holland, 1994). What has changed in the private sector is the push for some form of public support. As chapter 7 describes, it is not coincidental that the push for vouchers and choice has been strongest in states with large Catholic populations. These states have higher percentages of private school enrollment and aging cities where the Catholic school systems are depressed and are serving ever-smaller percentages of Catholic students.

---

[2] For example, Milwaukee has had two large Montessori schools for over a decade. It also has several African American schools, which were initially set up to be boys' schools. It also has the only public Waldorf school in North America.

### Normative Conflicts

Our nation has long endured the tension between freedom of choice and equality. We cherish individual and family freedom on the one hand while trying to reconcile that freedom with a presumption of equality in terms of endowments, opportunities, and to a lesser extent, outcomes. Our educational system is a classic example of the difficulty in trying to balance these normative ideals. On the one hand we stress decentralized, local school control and student and family choices in educational patterns, while also resisting uniformity in standards, curriculum, and assessments. On the other hand we are consistently paying homage to equality of both inputs and achievement, and more or less refuse to discuss inequality of endowments.

The choice debate highlights and fuses these normative conflicts. But emphasis on norms varies and often dictates on which side protagonists fall. Those who favor choice always stress freedom, often positing freedom as an expression of equal opportunity. The most powerful of these arguments points to the simultaneous inability of the public education system to produce anything approaching equal outcomes, while at the same time restricting the choices of those families who suffer the most. Those families, in inner-city school systems, cannot buy private education, and they lack the resources and are the wrong color to move to higher performing suburban districts. Thus, the argument goes, they are trapped in school systems that are not serving their needs and within which their children are failing. This argument continues to provide the normative underpinning for programs like the MPCP. This book underscores how important it is to take this argument seriously.

Those who oppose choice stress the other dimensions of equality — equality of inputs and equality of results. They argue that voucher systems will accelerate the already significant differences between those who attend public and private schools. They believe that at best vouchers will cream off the best students remaining in public schools, and at worst will also subsidize those elite students already attending private schools. The result will be a more inequitable distribution of resources and an increasing achievement differential between schools and socioeconomic groups. This book stresses this result as a very real possibility of a universal voucher program.

### Money and Educational "Efficiency"

Education in America is a very expensive business. Annual national public expenditures on K–12 education were $339 billion in 1996–97.

This amounts to 4.5 percent of estimated Gross Domestic Product (*Digest of Education Statistics*, 1997, table 31). If the federal government paid for total expenditures, as in some countries, public education would have been 22.3 percent of 1996 federal outlays, and it would have been the largest federal program. It would have amounted to 112 percent of our spending on Social Security and 125 percent of all defense expenditures (*Budget of the United States, FY 1999*, historical tables).

Education expenditures are not, however, primarily federal. The federal contribution was only 6.8 percent in 1996–97, with states contributing 46.8 percent and localities 43.8 percent (*Digest of Education Statistics*, 1997, table 33). State and local K–12 education in 1992–93 was 24 percent of all state and local expenditures. That amounted to an average of $932 per capita (*Digest of Education Statistics*, 1997, tables 35, 36). State funds are distributed to local school districts through complex formulas based on student enrollment, with district wealth or income usually a factor as well.

Private school expenditures are impossible to document precisely. We know that private school enrollment, as a percentage of all students, has remained at approximately 10 percent over the last fifty years (see chapter 3). We also know that current average private school costs are less than public school costs, but also that there is considerable variance within the private sector market. Based on overall expenditures in 1993–94, private schools spent on average 75 percent of public school costs per student ($4,590 compared to $6,104 — *Digest of Education Statistics*, 1997, table 32). Salaries and benefits suggest an even wider disparity, however. For 1993–94, base teacher salaries in private schools were 64.3 percent of public school salaries, and at the highest step on the scale they were still only 67.4 percent of public school salaries. Administrative salaries were even less equal, with the average private school administrator making 58.2 percent of his or her public counterpart. For all employees, benefits were also considerably better in the public than the private sector (Choy, 1997).

There is also ample evidence that private school markets, excluding upper-income schools, are experiencing difficult times financially. This is most evident with Catholic schools, especially in inner-city environments. Between 1965 and 1989, 32 percent of Catholic elementary schools and 42 percent of the high schools were closed (*Catholic Schools in America*, 1995, p. 37). The changes in lay personnel were even more striking and had a direct effect of increasing costs. In 1950, only 7 percent of Catholic elementary teachers and 17 percent of Catholic high school teachers were lay people. By 1994, 88 percent of the faculties were lay people (*Catholic Schools in America*, 1995, pp. vi and 40).

How much would a voucher program cost? The answer is that it depends on the program. One recent estimate by Henry Levin and Cyrus Driver was that a full-cost, universal voucher program would add 27.2 percent to current expenditures on public education. Using 1992–93 data, that would have meant an additional $72.7 billion annually (Levin and Driver, 1997, table 6). That estimate must be considered a high bound because it assumes vouchers and costs based on full school costs at the public school level, complete service provision (exceptional education, food, health, etc.), and additional transportation, information, record keeping, and adjudication costs (Levin and Driver, 1997).

A very low bound can be estimated simply by assuming that the voucher amount would be set at the average amount states currently contribute to public education. For 1993–94, that would have meant a voucher of $2,756 (*Digest of Education Statistics*, 1997, tables 33, 40, 63). If those state dollars are multiplied by the total private (but not home-schooled) population, the increase in annual public expenditures would have amounted to an increase of $13.3 billion, or 5 percent over current total expenditures on public K–12 education. The increase to states would have been 11.3 percent.[3]

The actual costs would undoubtedly fall between these two bounds. These varying estimates demonstrate how sensitive cost estimates are to program details and assumptions concerning voucher prices. However, even with the very lowest estimates, we are talking about a considerable amount of money. And most of that money, at least initially, would flow to existing private schools, some of which are in dire financial straits. Thus for private schools the voucher stakes are very high.

### Constitutional Issues

The First Amendment to the Constitution reads

> Congress shall make no law respecting an establishment of religion, or pro-
> hibiting the free exercise thereof; or abridging the freedom of speech, or of the
> press, or the right of the people to peaceably assemble, or to petition the
> Government for redress of grievances.

In this century this amendment has been interpreted to have two impli-cations for public involvement in private religious education. One impli-

---

[3] A voucher of $2,756 is in line with many initial state voucher proposals in the 1990s, but as will be described below, it is approximately half the MPCP voucher amount after six years. It also was only 60 percent of private school per pupil costs in 1993 and 45 percent of public school per pupil expenditures. Finally, it would have been somewhat lower than the national average of $3,116 for private school tuition in the same year (*Public and Private School: How Do They Differ?*, 1997).

cation, based on the establishment clause, has been to bar many public subsidies for religious schools. The second, based on the free exercise clause, has prevented states from substantial regulation of private schools, because to do so would entangle government in the exercise of religion. These barriers between public and private education were extended to all private schools because the vast majority of private schools are religiously affiliated. In addition, state constitutions and statutes often promulgated even more explicit prohibitions on state support for or regulation of private schools (Kemerer, forthcoming).

Until recently, the Supreme Court ruling affecting government action pertaining to religion was *Lemon v. Kurtzman* (1971).[4] That decision set up a tripartite test as to when government actions affecting religious practice are constitutional. The tests were (1) the action must promote a secular legislative purpose; (2) its primary effect must neither advance nor inhibit religion; and (3) there must be no excessive entanglement between the state and religion. *Lemon* was used in what to date has been considered by most observers the closest case to a voucher program. In that case, *Committee for Public Education v. Nyquist*, which was a test of low-income tuition reimbursement and tax credit programs in New York in 1973, a 6 to 3 majority ruled that the provision of both grants and tax deductions violated the establishment clause.[5]

The effect of the *Lemon* and *Nyquist* rulings was to provide a fairly secure wall of separation between religious practices and state actions in education. This effect stayed in place for over a decade before a number of cracks appeared in the wall. The first and probably most important case was *Mueller v. Allen* (1983).[6] In that case, a 5 to 4 majority opinion upheld a Minnesota private school tuition tax credit law. The majority decision cited the secular purpose of the statute, the fact that the credit went to parents and not directly to schools, and the modest nature of the subsidy. Subsequent cases have relied on *Mueller*. In *Witters v. Washington Department of Services* (1986), Mr. Witters, a blind student receiving state rehabilitation funds, was allowed to enroll in a Christian seminary.[7] The ruling again stressed that the subsidy flowed

[4] *Lemon v. Kurtzman*, 403 U.S. 388, 103 S. Ct. 3062, 77 L. Ed. 2d 745 (1971).

[5] *Committee for Public Education v. Nyquist*, 413 U.S. 756, 93 S. Ct. 2955, 37 L. Ed. 948 (1973). Frank Kemerer, one of the leading constitutional experts on school choice, notes that a footnote in the majority opinion in Nyquist might allow subsidies if "monies were 'made available without regard to the sectarian–nonsectarian, or public–nonpublic nature of the institutions benefited.'" Kemerer interprets this as a program that was designed to provide vouchers to attend a wide range of both public and private schools. See Kemerer (1995), p. 21; Kemerer and King (1995), p. 308.

[6] *Mueller v. Allen*, 463 U.S. 388, 103 S. Ct. 3062, 77 L. Ed. 2d 721 [11 Ed. Law Rep.[763]] (1983).

[7] *Witters v. Washington Department of Services*, 474 U.S. 481, 106 S. Ct. 748, 88 L. Ed. 2d 846 (1986).

through an individual to a religious organization. In *Zorbrest v. Catalina Foothills School District* (1993), the court ruled that a sign interpreter could be used in a Catholic school because the service was religiously neutral and thus did not affect the establishment clause provision.[8] Finally, in the most recent case, *Agostini v. Felton* (1997), the Supreme Court held that federal funds (Title I of the Elementary and Secondary Education Act of 1965) providing remedial instruction on a neutral basis to disadvantaged students in sectarian schools did not violate the establishment clause.[9]

Vouchers may prove to be the ultimate test of the First Amendment barrier. Voucher proponents believe that the targeted voucher programs in Milwaukee and Cleveland provide an important extension of the precedents set in *Mueller, Witters, Zorbrest,* and *Agostini,* thus once and for all overturning the *Nyquist* ruling. The Milwaukee program originally did not include religious schools and therefore was only tested against the Wisconsin constitutional provision that state funds must be used for a public purpose. The Wisconsin Supreme Court upheld it in 1992 on a 4 to 3 decision. When the program was expanded in 1995 to include religious schools, another suit was filed, this time including the First Amendment objection. On June 10, 1998, the Wisconsin Supreme Court, on a 4 to 2 decision, upheld the program as not in violation of either the Wisconsin Constitution or the First Amendment. The ruling clearly stated that *Nyquist* should not dominate, and repeatedly cited the cases more favorable to public subsidy of families sending children to religious private schools.[10] On November 9, 1998, the U.S. Supreme Court, on an 8 to 1 vote, decided not to review the Wisconsin decision, thus letting the Wisconsin court decision stand. Similar suits were filed in 1996 against the Cleveland voucher program, which unlike Milwaukee included religious schools when it began in September 1996. As of this writing, those cases are before the Ohio Supreme Court.

Voucher programs will be contested against state constitutional provisions as well as the U.S. Constitution, and the hurdles in state courts may be tougher. For example, although the *Witters* case was ruled constitutional under the U.S. Constitution, the result was to remand it back to the Washington state courts. The Washington Supreme Court ruled that the subsidy violated the state's constitution, which quite explicitly prohibits the expenditure of public money on any religious instruction. A similar ruling barred a limited voucher program in Puerto Rico in 1994. In Wisconsin there is a provision against supporting any "reli-

[8] *Zorbrest v. Catalina Foothills School District,* 509 U.S. 1, 113 S. Ct. 2462, 125 L. Ed. 2d 1 [83 Ed. Law Rep. [930]] (1993).

[9] *Agostini v, Felton,* 117 S. Ct. 1997, 138 L. Ed. 2d 391 (1997).

[10] *Jackson v. Benson,* Wisc. S. Ct., No. 97–0270, June 10, 1998, fn. 9.

gious association" with public funds. In the past, that provision had been used to strike down a number of efforts to provide financial assistance to private schools.[11] However, a recent Wisconsin Supreme Court ruling overturned the appeals court invocation of that clause. Despite the U.S. Supreme Court ruling allowing the Wisconsin ruling to stand, subsequent state rulings (in Wisconsin and elsewhere) might still interfere with widespread expansion of vouchers (Kemerer, forthcoming).

Obviously, however, the constitutional stakes are high and go considerably beyond the two programs involved; in fact, they have been part of the politics of vouchers all along. As Clinton Bolick, the chief defense counsel for the private schools, said in reference to the MPCP in 1995: "We are very anxious to get a case up to the Supreme Court as quickly as possible to remove the constitutional cloud once and for all" (*Wall Street Journal*, 31 July 1995, p. 3B). Three years later, after a Wisconsin Supreme Court decision upholding vouchers for religious schools, Bolick was even more emphatic about the significance of the MPCP: "What is about to happen in Milwaukee is a huge story everywhere. . . . The Milwaukee program is the largest functioning school choice program, as a result, all eyes are on the court to see what they decide" (*Milwaukee Journal-Sentinel*, 10 June 1998, p. 1).

## Conclusion

Although the MPCP in many ways is both a modest program and a modest test of vouchers, it clearly touches on and can be characterized as a glaring symbol of all the tensions outlined above. It provides a frontal clash of opposing educational philosophies; it exemplifies the normative clash between fundamental American values of liberty and equality; it potentially involves a lot of money; and it is at the crux of a major constitutional struggle.

## Theoretical and Research Issues

The theoretical and research issues involved in educational choice extend from broad questions of how best to fund and organize our nation's education system to microissues concerning who might participate in different forms of choice programs, for what reasons, and with

[11] For example, the Wisconsin Supreme Court in 1963 ruled that a law providing transportation subsidies for private schools, most of which were religious, was unconstitutional. A subsequent constitutional amendment was passed excepting these aids from the general provision.

what effects. Educational choice involves general normative and theoretical issues that are basic to the structure of our society and how it is governed, and also invokes major questions concerning the fundamental organization of education in America. A daunting number of unanswered empirical research questions remain as well, the answers to which will have a major bearing on the more general policy and institutional issues.

### Theoretical Issues

At the most general level, educational choice represents one of the most fundamental normative conflicts in our society: the clash between individual freedom and equality of opportunity and result. One of the fundamental rationales for a "free" and public education is to provide equal access to this crucial social good. We fund this system of education primarily by amortizing its costs across our communities and over generations. In an attempt to ensure equal access, we do not charge individual families to send their children to school, and we do not allow schools to select students. Thus schools are, at least in theory, more or less equal. In practice, both inputs and outcomes are far from equal. When inequality between schools and districts emerges, protracted legal and policy battles take place over equalized funding and integration. Within schools there is great resistance to placing students in different tracks (such as in reading or math) and curriculums (such as vocational education tracks). Thus, while our schools are far from equal, equality remains a fundamental issue in all aspects of education in America.

On the other hand, as I argued above, the educational choice movement is driven by another fundamental value in our society — individual freedom. Just as we cherish our ability to select where we live, move, and work, and innumerable other freedoms associated with individual autonomy, so we cherish choosing where and how our children are educated. Most in this country exercise that choice by selecting where they live, but a consistent minority also opt out of public education, choosing to purchase private education. The MPCP was driven by a belief that when these options are foreclosed by race and poverty, the government should override the public education system and provide an alternative so families may choose to have their children attend a private school of their choice.

The role of race in educational choice suggests a second set of theoretical issues. The basic question is whether choice is a method of enhancing educational opportunities and achievement for racial minorities or for securing and protecting schools primarily benefiting whites. More specifically, is race used politically to initiate programs, which later expand and have quite different racial consequences?

Another major set of theoretical issues involves how we should best organize and govern our social and economic institutions, especially schools. Quite obviously, the dominant public education system provides a state-governed quasimonopoly. While this system varies widely in terms of precise organization of schools, grades, personnel, and the sizes of the respective units (both districts and schools), the system does resemble a monopoly in terms of the available product in most areas (Witte, 1990). In this sense it is quite distinct from the independent provision of education through a fully private market. That religious organizations and doctrine have significantly affected such a market in practice in the United States does not affect the purely theoretical distinction between free market and monopoly provision. Also, as indicated above, public education represents a very different system of governance and accountability from a private, market-driven system — the public system being politically and bureaucratically controlled, the private being consumer dominated.

The theoretical issues involved in choice also include direct policy issues concerning the nature of choice systems. The ranges of choice systems have been discussed above, but details are very important. For example, should voucher systems be targeted or wide open? What limitations, if any, should there be on selecting and expelling students? What requirements and regulations, if any, should be placed on choice schools in terms of teacher qualifications, curriculum, reporting results, or finances? What is the impact of court decisions and constitutional constraints on the design of choice programs?

As will become clear while the Milwaukee story unfolds, each of these determinations may have a major impact on the expected long- and short-term outcomes. One of the themes of this book is that one cannot expect to get the same results from a targeted and a universal voucher program. The implications of that may well lead to very different policy conclusions concerning the two programs.

### Empirical Issues

For any given choice program, these theoretical issues lead to direct empirical research questions. First, we need to know, under varying program conditions, who chooses to participate in choice schools and who remains in assigned public schools. Do choice systems extend opportunities to those who cannot exercise them or will they simply subsidize choices that would have been made anyway? Will increasing choice produce greater inequality by creaming off the best students into private or exclusive schools? What role does race play in these selection processes? To answer these questions, we need to compare choosing and non-choosing families. We are concerned with the demographic characteristics of students and families, their prior educational experiences, attitudes of parents toward education and the importance they place on it, and how they view their alternative school choices.

Choice systems affect not only students and families, but also schools. As a result, a number of research issues exist, to address such questions as: Do these programs keep schools open that would otherwise have closed? Do they benefit choice schools in terms of financial well-being, teacher quality and turnover, enhanced curriculums, improved pedagogy, and ability to add resources and technology? What are the effects on choice-school costs? If previously private, do their costs increase, as public money becomes available? Similarly, what is the commensurate impact on nonchoice schools? Will they decline if resources shifted to choice schools reduce the resources for those remaining? Will they become more segregated? For both sectors, will teacher morale or job security be affected? Will competition spur nonchoosing schools to improve and to innovate? What can be learned about school governance and organization from each sector? Finally, will former private schools lose their distinctiveness as they become amalgamated into the new public-private school system?

A third set of research issues concerns the results of the program both for students and for choice and nonchoice schools. Do students achieve more in choice or nonchoice schools? Does their attendance and retention increase once in private schools? Is mobility between schools reduced? Does their attitude toward school and motivation to learn improve? Do graduation rates and postsecondary enrollment increase? In short, does choice enhance or inhibit education, and for whom?

Finally, the politics of educational vouchers raises a number of research issues, many with broad implications. What political factors favor creation of an initial voucher program? What political and normative arguments are used? Who are the primary actors involved and what are their intentions? Although arguments for and against vouchers almost always point to educational effects and opportunities, a more crass political explanation may look to who will get what and who might lose what if vouchers are created. If the program is initially targeted, can it remain so, or is there an inevitable transition to a more universal program? What determines if the transition moves ahead or is restrained? Do initial coalitions give way to new ones? What are the roles of the media and the courts in this shift? Finally, who is likely to benefit from a more universal program, and how does that fit with the original intent of the legislature?

## Implications

The research results will have implications for both education policy and more general normative and institutional issues. As indicated above, an immediate policy issue will be whether targeted voucher programs more or less automatically lead to universal programs and if they do, what are the policy implications? Other implications have to do with changed regulatory systems and unionization that may emerge under voucher systems. Specifically, will private schools receiving vouchers face increased regulations and be more likely to be unionized? Another important set of implications concerns the general method used to fund education in America. Will vouchers significantly alter the current approach to public funding through which the costs of universal education are spread across communities and generations?

The broadest and most critical policy issue involves the basic structure of education in America. Should education be provided as a public community service, or should it be private? If private, what will result? Will it positively affect all schools, as the competitive market strategy suggests, or will it lead to greater inequalities between schools? In addition, will the court actions connected to vouchers alter the present separation of private and public schools in terms of their respective legal status in state statutes? Will the distinction between public and private schools effectively disappear? Should governance follow the democratic/ centralized model of current public schools or the market/decentralized model of private schools?

Each of these implications for education policy also affects our general approach to public policy and the values implicit in those choices. For some, vouchers are a key wedge in the battle to reduce state-centered approaches to public policy in favor of market incentive approaches. There is no doubt that if vouchers became widespread, and had the intended effect on the delivery of education in general, there would be spillover effects into other policy arenas. And in all these cases, the implications for the trade-off between equality and freedom will be a riveting point of tension.

## Summary

The continuing conflict over educational vouchers in America is energized by (1) the clash of institutional models inherent in the debate;

(2) normative conflicts, especially between freedom and equality; (3) the amount of money potentially involved; and (4) the constitutional importance of the issue. These conflicts raise a broad set of theoretical and research issues ranging from abstract and general questions to very concrete and specific issues. The results of the research, to the degree this study provides useful evidence and argument, have implications for education policy and broader public policy in the United States.

The program and research reported in the following chapters cannot definitively answer any of the questions raised. But they can offer evidence and perhaps research models that may be applied to future cases, in turn adding to our knowledge of these critical issues. The limitations of both the program and research design are discussed in the following chapter and continue to be expounded as research results are described in chapters 4 to 7. The last chapter discusses the broader implications of the MPCP for voucher policies and politics, and for the future direction of education in America.

# 3

## Educational Choice and the Milwaukee Voucher Program

IN RECENT YEARS a number of articles and books have been written on educational choice (Wells, 1993; Henig, 1994; Cookson, 1994; Lieberman, 1993; Witte and Rigdon, 1993; Clune and Witte, 1990). It is unnecessary to describe the programs treated in this literature in great detail because these previous works do a more than adequate job. What is more important is that the reader understand the progression of policies in the context of public and private education in the United States. This chapter begins with a description of the changing status of private schools. I then outline how choice policies have developed, beginning with public school choice, moving to private school choice programs, and culminating in proposals for vouchers. The initial Milwaukee voucher program is then described in historical context. The chapter concludes with a discussion of the research methods and data used in the study.

### Private Schooling in Historical Context

Religious schools throughout our history have dominated private primary and secondary education. Over the last hundred years, the history of Roman Catholic schools explains the major shifts in the private school market. The Ursuline Sisters founded the first Catholic school in New Orleans in 1727. The rise of common public schools, with their distinctive Protestant orientation and the use of the Protestant Bible as a primary text, accelerated the expansion of Catholic schools. That expansion was given formal and authoritative support by Catholic bishops at the Third Plenary Council of Baltimore in 1884. Edicts produced by that council called for the establishment of Catholic schools throughout the country and mandated attendance at these schools by Catholic children (Beutow, 1970; Gleason, 1985). The result was a dramatic expansion in Catholic schools from 1884, when there were approximately 2,500 schools and 500,000 students, to the peak of Catholic school enrollment in 1965, with 13,292 schools serving 5.5 million Catholic students (*Catholic Schools in America*, 1995, chap. 3).

The percentage of students in private schools has remained relatively constant over the last fifty years. In the post–World War II period, private schools have enrolled between 10 percent and 12 percent of those attending kindergarten through twelfth grade. Of those in private schools, Catholic schools have always enrolled the most students. At their peak in 1965–66 they accounted for almost 90 percent of the students in private schools. Since that point, Catholic schools have declined precipitously (to 2.4 million students in 1994) and currently account for just under half of the private school enrollment (*Digest of Education Statistics*, 1992, table 57; Rose, 1988; *Catholic Schools in America*, 1995, chap. 3).

The decline in Catholic school enrollment was a result of several trends. First, birth rate and school age populations declined throughout the United States. Second, Catholic schools began to close because fewer Catholics were in the parishes, fewer Catholics were attending Catholic schools, and costs were increasing due to the dramatic rise in the number of lay staff in the schools (*Catholic Schools in America*, 1995, chap. 3).[1] Although some increasing attendance by non-Catholics made a small difference, non-Catholics currently make up only 12.8 percent of Catholic school enrollment (*Catholic Schools in America*, 1995, p. vi). Increased mobility also reduced the number of Catholic schools. Finally, as Catholics moved from the cities to the suburbs, and from their traditional stronghold in the East and Midwest to the West and Southwest, they failed to build new schools where they moved (Greeley, 1977, 1989).

Although Catholic students no longer made up the majority of private school students by 1990, the percentage of religiously affiliated private school students remained very high. In one of the most recent definitive surveys (1987), 84.3 percent of all private school students were in religiously affiliated schools (*Digest of Education Statistics*, 1992, table 57). This was very close to the 84.8 percent figure estimated in a different study five years earlier (Rose, 1988, p. 36).

The denominational mix has changed since the 1960s. Numbers on non-Catholic denominations are not exact and vary somewhat by categorization (especially for "Christian" students). There is no question, however, that Christian schools have grown during the period of Catholic school decline. One source estimates a growth in Christian schools of 400 to 500 percent from 1960 to 1975 (Rose, 1988, p. 35). According to a study by the Council of American Private Education, Christian

---

[1] In terms of school closings, between 1965 and 1989, 32 percent of Catholic elementary schools and 42 percent of the high schools were closed (*Catholic Schools in America*, 1995, p. 37).

school enrollment rose 220 percent in the ten-year period from 1965 to 1975. The same study estimated that by 1982 between 600,000 and 700,000 students were enrolled in Christian schools, behind Catholics at 3.2 million, but much larger than the Lutherans with 220,000 students (cited in Rose, 1988, pp. 35–36).

Over the last three decades, as Catholic schools in large cities have lost students and closed, Christian schools have often replaced them. Thus the percentage of private school students in religious schools has remained more or less constant over the last century. Therefore, the religious character of private schools currently remains the defining characteristic of our private school sector.

## The Road to Vouchers

Where students attend school in the United States has primarily been determined by where they live. Our public school tradition, in which school assignment is based on residency, has been and continues to be the primary determinant of school choice or assignment. However, that tradition masks considerable variation based on socioeconomic status. Choice depends on the ability to select one's residence or the ability to pay for private schools.

A study in 1993 demonstrated the extent of that relationship. It divided families into four categories: (1) public school students assigned to their schools; (2) public school students from families who moved to their homes with schools in mind; (3) students in public choice schools (e.g., magnet schools); and (4) students in private schools. The results broken down by income class are depicted in table 3.1. As is readily apparent, the first two categories account for the vast majority of students, split almost evenly between "assigned" and "residential choice" families. The effect of income on all choice categories is apparent. Clearly, residential selection and private schooling are very much affected by increasing income. As has been confirmed by other studies (Gamoran, 1996; Plank et al., 1993), the prevalence of lower income students in public choice schools is a function of magnet schools in poor, urban districts. The most striking relationship is between income and private school enrollment, with only 3 percent of the families with incomes below $15,000 going to private schools, while 16 percent with incomes above $50,000 attend private schools.

Educational choice programs, which break the link between residence and school assignment, date back to the 1960s and can be broken roughly into two categories: public school choice and private school choice.

**TABLE 3.1**
School Choice in America, by Income, 1993 (percentages)

|  | Total | Less Than $15,000 | $15,000– $30,000 | $30,001– $50,000 | More than $50,000 |
|---|---|---|---|---|---|
| Assigned public school | 41 | 49 | 46 | 42 | 28 |
| Public school "chosen" by residence | 39 | 39 | 35 | 40 | 48 |
| Chosen public school | 11 | 14 | 12 | 9 | 8 |
| Private school | 9 | 3 | 7 | 9 | 16 |

*Source*: National Center for Education Statistics, National Household Education Survey, 1993.

Charter schools as they are expanding and developing in the 1990s are anomalous hybrids of the two categories.

### Public School Choice

Public school choice in the form of magnet or specialty schools began in the first half of the century with the creation of such famous schools as the Bronx School of Science and the University of Chicago Lab School (founded by John Dewey). Systematic efforts to expand school choice began in earnest in the 1960s and 1970s. The first significant efforts were magnet schools as a response to *Brown v. Board of Education* and the busing requirements that followed. Magnet schools, set up with a range of specialties from gifted and talented or college preparatory schools to language, science, or performing arts specializations, were created throughout the 1970s in most large school districts subject to or anticipating desegregation court orders. Most were initially districtwide schools that were quite selective and in most cases clearly designed to keep white students in the districts (Rossell, 1990). In the 1980s they not only expanded to many more districts, but also were expanded within districts to include many schools that had specialty "magnet" programs within individual schools (Blank, 1990; Henig, 1994; Wells, 1993).

Public school choice also expanded in several other forms in the 1980s, with the state of Minnesota leading the way. Minnesota pioneered statewide alternative learning centers for at-risk students, and then, in 1987, statewide open enrollment (Rubenstein, Hamar, and Adelman, 1992; Funkhouser and Colopy, 1994). The former gave at-risk students a choice of a number of different schools with a variety of learning approaches. The latter in theory allowed any student to apply to any school in any district in the state. In practice, districts were able to restrict the flow into their districts by limiting the number of available seats, but were not able to prevent students from leaving for other districts. Because state aid followed the students, the program was thought to create an incentive for schools to reform. Since its inception, the program has had limited impact, with approximately 1.5 percent of the public school students taking advantage of the option (Funkhouser and Colopy, 1994; Rubenstein, Hamar, and Adelman, 1992). Over half of the states have now adopted open-enrollment programs, and the policy continues to be proposed in other states (including Wisconsin).

The expansion of public school choice was in part facilitated by the changing political climate in the states. During the 1980s, state houses and legislatures became more Republican, and thus the sponsors of choice programs, usually Republicans (see chapter 7), were in a better position to enact legislation. Similarly, the attitudes of education establishment groups including state departments of education, teachers, administrator associations, and parent–teacher groups, gradually began to accept all forms of public school choice. For example, the most recent choice phenomenon is charter schools, which come in myriad forms, usually require approval, oversight, and charter renewal by local school boards, and thus have also been supported by many education organizations and interest groups (Vergari and Mintrom, 1995; Wells, Grutzik, and Carnochan 1996). Even the National Education Association (NEA), considered the most entrenched opponent of choice, has followed the lead of the American Federation of Teachers (AFT) in endorsing almost all public school choice options. They have even touted their own model charter schools (National Education Association, 1997).

## Private School Choice

Inclusion of private schools in the choice movement has been another matter, and this issue defines the current battle. Private school choice options began with tuition tax credit programs, programs that provide state tax credits to individuals to reimburse private school costs. The first use of such credits was in the South following *Brown v. Board of Education* (1954). As those programs were found to be overt efforts to escape integration, they were ruled unconstitutional. The first program without such intent began in Minnesota in 1967 and was finally ruled constitutional in 1983. That case, *Mueller v. Allen*, remains a crucial precedent in the constitutional battle over private school choice.[2] Subsequent to the *Mueller* decision, a number of states enacted varying versions of tuition tax credits, but as the court surmised, they have had a limited impact on families and state treasuries (Witte, 1990).

Programs have also been enacted, again initiated in Minnesota, to provide subsidies for high school students attending postsecondary schools, including private (and religious) schools. This program is very popular in that it allows a student, among other options, to earn college and high school credit simultaneously, with the state paying the college tuition. It has not been challenged in court, either because of its popularity among the middle class or because of U.S. Supreme Court rulings affirming the constitutionality of state support for private, religious colleges.

### Voucher Proposals

The modern idea of educational vouchers is attributed to Milton Friedman (1955), and appeared in a paper that became widely read when it was included as a chapter in *Capitalism and Freedom* (1962). As a policy, it attracted fleeting attention in the 1970s when an experiment was proposed by the then U.S. Department of Health, Education, and Welfare to set up a voucher experiment. There were no volunteers among school districts until a failing district in serious financial trouble in Alum Rock, California, came forward. After initially turning the district down, the government began negotiating with the relevant parties. What emerged was a modest proposal that allowed students to transfer among public schools, but the planned inclusion of private schools never came to pass. The experiment was dropped completely after several years (Bridge, 1978; Witte, 1990; Witte and Rigdon, 1993).

The voucher idea was dormant for a decade after the conclusion of the Alum Rock experiment. Vouchers were revived with the election of Ronald Reagan and were linked to the growing interest in all types of privatization. The rationale for and political agenda of the voucher movement were stated clearly and unambiguously several years ago by its founding father, Milton Friedman. He wrote:

> A radical reconstruction of the educational system . . . can be achieved only by privatizing a major segment of the educational system — i.e., by enabling a private, for-profit industry to develop that will provide a wide variety of learning opportunities and offer effective competition to the public schools.

[2] *Mueller v. Allen*, 463 U.S. 388, 103 S. Ct. 3062, 77 L. Ed. 721 (1983).

Such a reconstruction cannot come about overnight. It inevitably must be gradual.

The most feasible way to bring about a gradual yet substantial transfer from government to private enterprise is to enact in each state a voucher system that enables parents to choose freely the schools their children attend. I proposed such a voucher system 40 years ago. . . . For this condition to be realized, it is essential that no conditions be attached to the acceptance of vouchers that interfere with the freedom of private enterprises to experiment, to explore and to innovate. . .

I sense that we are on the verge of a breakthrough in one state or another, which will then sweep like wildfire through the rest of the country as it demonstrates its effectiveness. (Friedman, 1995)

The potential for this wildfire was present in 1980, but the first spark has not yet come. Numerous voucher proposals were made in the last decade. National legislation was proposed several times, beginning with proposals in the Reagan administration spearheaded by Secretary of Education William Bennett. Those proposals died quickly, never reaching a floor vote. Until recently, the most prominent proposal was probably President Bush's call for a GI Bill for Children in 1992. That bill, announced at the White House as the president was surrounded by participants and supporters of the MPCP, would have provided funds for a number of voucher experiments. It was defeated in the Senate in 1992 by a 56 to 38 vote (*Education Week*, 29 January 1992, p. 1). In 1996 an attempt to add voucher programs to the Religious Restoration and Freedom Act and an all-out attempt by Republicans to include such a program as part of the 1996 tax reduction package were defeated.

Three major voucher bills were proposed in the 105th Congress. There was a $1 billion proposal for education vouchers imbedded in the America Community Renewal Act of 1997 and a voucher demonstration proposal for thirty cities in Senate Bill 1 introduced by Senator Trent Lott (R–Miss.), the Safe and Affordable Schools Act. In addition, a voucher proposal for Washington, D.C., passed the House, but was defeated in the Senate through a filibuster. While all of these plans targeted low-income families, they also included religious schools, and none of them placed restrictions on school selection of students other than barring discrimination based on race or ethnicity and, in some cases, religion. Thus the issue remains very much alive at the national level.

Major statewide referendums on vouchers in various forms have occurred four times, and these were generally not limited to low-income students. They were defeated by more than two to one margins in

Oregon (1990), Colorado (1992), California (1993), and Washington (1996). Numerous state legislative proposals have been introduced that would have created statewide vouchers, but most never came up for floor votes. As of 1997, proposals were defeated in floor votes in Pennsylvania, Ohio, Connecticut, Michigan, Florida, Minnesota, and Texas.

Some of these states and others have fallen back on targeted voucher programs for low-income families, often in specific cities. These have been considered in New Jersey, Pennsylvania, Ohio, Wisconsin, and the District of Columbia. To date, only two such proposals have been enacted. The Milwaukee program has been operating since 1990, but did not involve religious schools until it was expanded a second time in June 1995. A similar program in Cleveland, which included religious schools from the beginning, was enacted in 1995 and began in 1996–97.

## Education in Milwaukee

Milwaukee, located on the shores of Lake Michigan about 75 miles north of Chicago, is the largest city in Wisconsin, with a metropolitan population of over one million people. Historically the city was primarily white, composed largely of people of European extraction. The largest group initially were Germans, thus its early reputation as the beer capital of America. Poles, Norwegians, and Italians were also well represented. The south side of the city, demarcated as the area south of a large east–west industrial rail corridor, was heavily Polish. The north side was mostly German.

White politicians, usually Democrats, have dominated city and county politics. In keeping with the quasi-social democratic German population, Milwaukee boasted the most prominent Socialist mayor in the United States, Frank Zeidler, and the mayor with the longest tenure of large city mayors—Henry Maier. The current mayor, John Norquist, also a nominal Democrat, has endorsed a number of conservative, market-oriented reforms, including unrestricted vouchers for private schools.

The mass exodus of blacks from the South beginning between the wars affected Milwaukee. After World War II, the racial and socioeconomic composition of the city began to change. Between 1940 and 1990, whites in the city declined from 98.4 percent to 63.4 percent, while blacks increased from 1.5 percent to 30.5 percent (U.S. Bureau of the Census, 1990, SEWPRC).

The economic structure and conditions of the city were also transformed. The city was originally a prosperous blue-collar, middle-class city with large numbers of skilled and unionized craftsmen in machine tool, heavy industries, and brewing. Between the late 1960s and the late

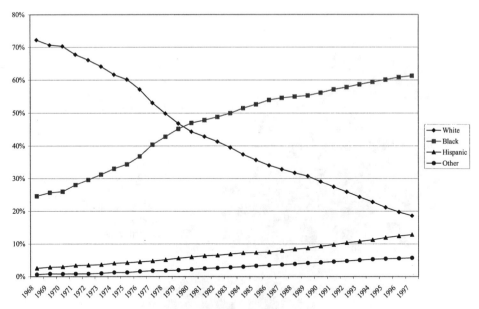

**Figure 3.1** MPS Student Enrollment, Percent by Race, 1968–1997

1980s, a general decline occurred in the prosperity of the city and its people. This deterioration resulted from population shifts in which poorer minority families replaced more prosperous white families and from the economic recessions during those periods. During the period from 1970 to 1990, the percentage of Milwaukee households with incomes below the poverty line increased from 11.4 percent to 22.2 percent (U.S. Bureau of the Census, 1990, SEWPRC). Milwaukee was a classic Rust Belt city where the industrial base and its associated high-paying union jobs had become outmoded and inefficient relative to newer industrial plants with younger, lower-wage employees.

The history of public education in Milwaukee has undergone even more dramatic changes than the city. These changes are linked to the demographic and economic shifts in the general population, but are even more extreme. I will focus first on changes in public schools, and then on the private-public school enrollments over time. Figure 3.1 portrays the changing racial composition of Milwaukee Public Schools (MPS) from 1968 to 1997. As with many other northern cities, the percentage of racial minority children in the schools increased dramatically, from 28 percent in 1970 to over 80 percent in 1997. Initially almost all the racial minority students were black, but in more recent years, almost 20 percent of the student population is neither white nor black.

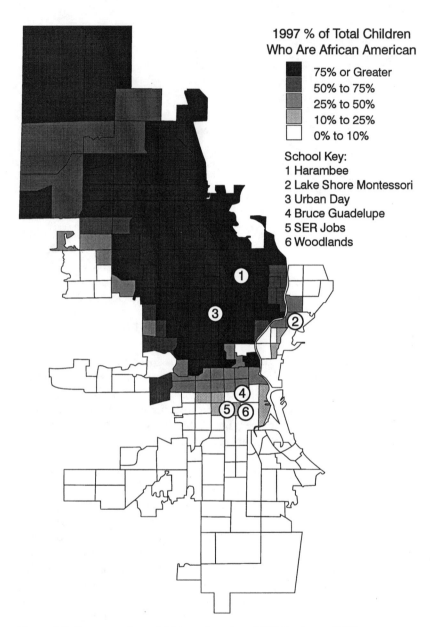

**Figure 3.2** Concentration of African American MPS Students, 1997

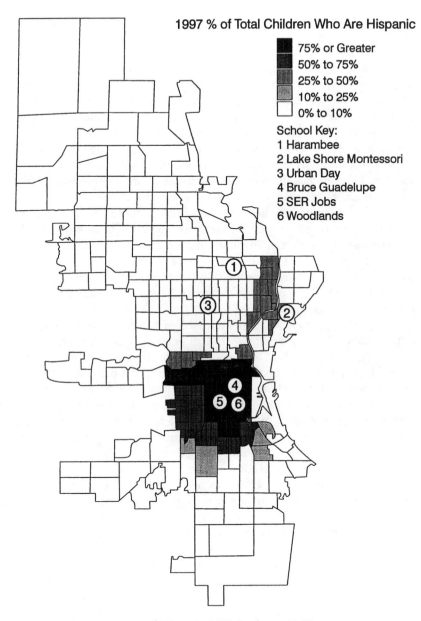

**1997 % of Total Children Who Are Hispanic**

- 75% or Greater
- 50% to 75%
- 25% to 50%
- 10% to 25%
- 0% to 10%

School Key:
1 Harambee
2 Lake Shore Montessori
3 Urban Day
4 Bruce Guadelupe
5 SER Jobs
6 Woodlands

**Figure 3.3** Concentration of Hispanic MPS Students, 1997

As populations changed, racial concentrations in neighborhoods became more extreme. Blacks tended to settle on the north side of the city, with the second largest ethnic group, Hispanics, first living in the central city and more recently moving to the near south side (as the white ethnic groups moved to the suburbs). Figures 3.2 and 3.3 portray the 1997 concentration of blacks and Hispanic students in MPS. The concentration is obvious and extreme, indicating the residential locations on the north and south sides of the city. Asian and white students live primarily in the outlying areas of the city. The figures also indicate the major choice schools for most of the period of this study. As will be noted in chapter 5, with one exception, the racial composition of the schools matches the student residency patterns of MPS.

What is not shown on the maps are the Milwaukee suburban school districts. Their maps would be almost exclusively white. With one or two exceptions, the ring of 24 suburban districts are 95 percent or more white, and this remains even after a major public school transfer program that brings approximately 6,000 minority students into these districts from MPS. Thus on a city-suburban basis, Milwaukee is a highly segregated metropolitan area.

The number of poor students increased in lockstep with the changes in race. In 1970, 15 percent of MPS students qualified for free- or reduced-free lunch. In 1997, 68.8 percent were eligible. Exceptional education students also increased dramatically, from 9.8 percent in 1983 to 14.0 percent in 1997 (*Milwaukee Public Schools*, 1998, pp. 7, 10).

As with the general pattern in the country, enrollment changes in MPS reflect in-migration of minority families, higher birthrates among minority families, and white flight to the suburbs. Ironically, that white flight initially affected both public and private schools. As indicated in figure 3.4, in 1960 over 50,000 students (mostly Catholics) attended private schools in the city. That was more than one out of every three students. The decline in private school enrollment began before the overall decline in public school enrollment, with the latter beginning about 1970. Once begun, both were the result of white flight. The result was the closing or conversion to "community school" of a number of Catholic schools in the late 1960s. Twenty years later, three of those schools became the main schools in the Milwaukee voucher program.

The changing racial composition and the segregated character of individual schools in MPS led to an NAACP lawsuit filed in 1967, finally leading to a desegregation order in 1976. That order required desegregation based on black enrollment in nearly all of the 120 schools in the system. The district, under the eye of a court-appointed magistrate, chose a combination of school closings, forced busing, and an extensive program of magnet schools to accomplish the task. The school closings led to several public protests and lawsuits. The forced busing clearly led to white flight to the suburbs. It also produced a short-term increase in private school enrollment beginning in 1978 (see figure 3.4). The magnet program initially was a national model, but later led to some public and teacher protest as schools tended to fall into either elite or remedial categories (Witte and Archbald, 1985; Archbald, 1988). Both the magnet program and forced busing remain in place. There is also a broad and, for some, very popular metropolitanwide transfer program to take minority students to the suburban districts and to bring white suburban students to MPS. That program is described in detail in the next chapter.

The historical decline of MPS is a prior assumption of those in the media as well as of both voucher supporters and opponents. The truth is that the decline, which undoubtedly has occurred to a degree, is very difficult to document or measure with any accuracy. This is so simply because there are no continuous, reliable outcome measures that extend over a number of years. Standardized tests were given since the late 1950s, but the raw data no longer exist and the existing reports used varying methods of reporting that were geared to simple findings for public consumption. An analysis of available data for selected years beginning in 1959 is contained in the appendix at the end of this chapter. Although caution must be used in interpreting these data, it appears that test scores began to decline somewhat before racial and economic shifts radically changed the student population. Indeed, a considerable decline occurred in the mid-1960s, which has accelerated over time. Before 1966, in all grades tested, district averages appeared to be at or above expected grade equivalents. Following 1966, that norm was never again reached.

There are similar problems in using attendance and discipline measures (expulsions, suspensions), because they are not comparable over time or even between schools due to changes in definitions, variances in reporting, and differences in enforcement practices from one school to the next (Witte and Walsh, 1985, 1990). Dropout rates were defined differently in three periods from 1960 onward. Dropout data prior to 1981 are not comparable to later numbers. From the period 1981–82 to 1987–88, dropout figures did not include students in alternative education programs, and thus the annual rates for grades 9 to 12 were from 10.1 percent to 12.4 percent. When that was changed to count alternative school students as dropouts, and when mandatory compulsory attendance was changed from age sixteen to age eighteen, the rates immediately went up to 14.4 percent and averaged 14.2 percent from 1988 to 1997 (data provided by MPS, 1998).

The lack of accurate data does not provide a defense of the quality of

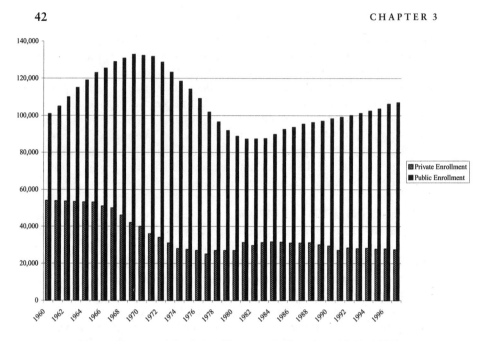

**Figure 3.4** Public and Private School Enrollment in Milwaukee, 1960–1997

public education in Milwaukee or a denial that quality has declined—it probably has, and precipitously. Both test score and dropout data indicate the seriousness of the problems. Further, there is considerable evidence that in comparison with neighboring suburban school districts, which are overwhelmingly white and nonpoor, MPS does very badly on average. In a report I coauthored, based on extensive research of educational quality in the Milwaukee metropolitan area in 1984–85, we described this comparison as two worlds of education separated by a few miles. Test score averages differed by over a standard deviation, and dropout rates were under 2 percent in the suburbs and over 12 percent in MPS (Governor's Study Commission, 1985).

The one caveat to these conclusions is that average measures mask variation, and variation among students and schools in MPS is enormous. A relatively small number of schools, usually citywide magnet schools, have numbers equal to their best suburban counterparts. Others, and they are more numerous, are worse than any school in the suburban districts (Witte and Walsh, 1990). This wide range, which is probably similar to most other cities of Milwaukee's size, is very important because I will ultimately argue that the private schools in the voucher program more or less match this range in quality—as do their achievement test score average and ranges. Further, I will try to persuade the reader that this is exactly the result one should expect as long as schools must accept all students who live in the city.

## The Milwaukee Voucher Program

*Enactment of the Milwaukee Parental Choice Program*

The media has given credit for the founding of the voucher program in Milwaukee to black state Representative Annette "Polly" Williams, an overtly liberal Democrat who twice was manager of Jesse Jackson's state campaign. Williams had given up on educating her own children in public schools in the 1980s; they attended an independent private school called Urban Day. Representative Williams and one of her daughters were on the board of directors of the school when the choice legislation was passed in the summer of 1990. That school, originally St. Michael's Catholic School, was the largest recipient of vouchers in the MPCP. Eventually, Williams found an unlikely ally in white conservative Republican Governor Tommy Thompson.

The first voucher bill, however, was introduced by Thompson in 1988, and was not supported by Polly Williams, who at the time was on an impossible quest to carve out an all-black school district in the heart of Milwaukee. The Thompson bill is important because it clearly revealed his intial intentions and heralded later expansion and subsequent divisions with Representative Williams and a number of other black leaders.

The governor's bill, 1987 Assembly Bill 816, was to be added to the 1988–89 state budget, which is the dominant political and policy document in Wisconsin. It contained few of the restrictions that would be included in the program finally enacted in 1990. For example, it would have included all private schools (not just nonsectarian ones), allowed current private school students (up to sixth grade) to receive vouchers, and it would have applied to all of Milwaukee County. The Thompson bill also did not limit the number of students who could get vouchers; niether did it require random selection of students by schools, specify any standards for schools, or require any study or reporting on results of the program.

After it was easily removed from the budget by then controlling Democrats, Thompson modified the bill in 1989 to exclude religious private schools. Democrats also removed that bill (Senate Bill 31) from the omnibus budget package. On October 11, 1989, Williams introduced an alternative, which Thompson supported (Assembly Bill 601). It was cosponsored by thirty-six Republicans and eleven Democrats in the Assembly and nine Republicans and three Democrats in the Senate. Passage of the bill was not insured, however, until (1) it was considerably modified, making it a limited and experimental voucher program; and (2) it was supported by Democratic Senator Gary George, the only black senator and then cochair of the Joint Finance Committee (JFC).

The JFC controls the budget bill and thus most public policy in the state (Rom and Witte, 1988).

Modifications of the original draft bill reduced its scope and added restraints. Although the original draft was limited to nonsectarian schools and to students from families with incomes equal to 175 percent of the poverty line or lower, the JFC added limits on the maximum number of students and the size of the voucher. They also disallowed current private school students from being eligible (a move opposed by Williams); required random selection of students; added minimal school performance standards; and stipulated an annual study of the effects of the program. Foreshadowing later efforts to expand the program, a Democratic assemblywoman, Shirley Krug, who represented mostly white working class constituents, attempted to include the nonpoor by requiring only that 50 percent of the vouchers go to students of families with incomes equal to 175 percent of the poverty line or less. Her effort lost in committee (Wisconsin Legislative Reference Bureau, 1990b). The program was then deemed experimental, with a sunset provision ending it in 1994–95. The governor subsequently used his veto power to eliminate that provision (Wisconsin Legislative Reference Bureau, 1990a).

These modifications were enough to induce two other black representatives from Milwaukee (Spencer Coggs and Gwendolyn Moore) to support the bill. They subsequently have both changed their minds. Senator George insured passage by adding the bill to the Budget Adjustment Bill. Although no direct votes on the bill were taken, a key procedural vote to kill a third reading of the bill lost by one vote in the Assembly on a 48 to 48 tie.

### The Initial Program

The provisions of the original program are outlined in the first column (1990) of table 3.2. The program at that stage could be characterized as a targeted and limited voucher program. Families were required to live in Milwaukee and have incomes equal to 175 percent of the poverty line or less (approximately $20,000 for a family of three in 1990). Students in private schools or other public school districts in the prior year were not eligible.

Program limitations were also placed on schools, the most important of which stated that the private schools could not be religiously affiliated or have a religious component in their instruction. They had to be registered private schools (an easy matter in Wisconsin), which meant they had to meet applicable health and safety codes, have a sequential curriculum, and instruct students for a minimum number of minutes per

**TABLE 3.2**
The Milwaukee and Cleveland Voucher Program Requirements

| | Milwaukee | | | Cleveland |
|---|---|---|---|---|
| | 1990 | 1993 | 1995 | 1995 |
| *Student Eligibility* | | | | |
| Low income | Yes | Yes | Yes | No |
| Prior private school students | No | No | Yes, K–3 | Yes, K–3 plus 1 grade each year, 50% limit |
| Disabled students | No | No | No | No |
| *School Eligibility* | | | | |
| Sectarian | No | No | Yes | Yes |
| Geographic area | City of Milwaukee | City of Milwaukee | City of Milwaukee | City of Cleveland |
| *Program Limits* | | | | |
| Choice students per school | 49% | 65% | 100% | 100% |
| Students in the program | approx. 1,000 | approx. 1,500 | 15,000 | Limited by $ maximum |
| *Program Requirements* | | | | |
| Selection of students | Random, siblings in | Random, siblings in | Random | Up to state superintendent of education |
| Standards for schools | Yes | Yes | Yes | No |
| Research reports Required | Yes | Yes | No | Yes |
| *Maximum Voucher Amount* | $2,446 | $2,985 | $4,600 | $2,250 |

year. Admission could not be based on race, religion, gender, or prior school records. However, the courts later exempted schools from having to accept disabled students, including the learning disabled. If there were more choice applicants than seats available in any grade, the schools had to select students at random. After the first year, the Wisconsin Department of Public Instruction accepted an informal rule that allowed siblings of already accepted choice students to be exempt from random selection. That rule was formally included as part of the 1993 changes in the law. Prior to the time of enrollment, schools had to declare the maximum number of choice students they would admit. However, the total enrolled was limited initially to 49 percent of the students in the school (that was raised to 65 percent in 1993).

The private schools had to meet at least one of four standards. The measures were extremely modest, and none of the schools ever failed to meet the requirement in the first five years of the program. The four standards were

**1.** At least 70 percent of the pupils in the program advance one grade level each year.

2. The private school's average attendance rate for the pupils in the program is at least 90 percent.

3. At least 80 percent of the pupils in the program demonstrate significant academic progress.

4. At least 70 percent of the families of pupils in the program meet parental involvement criteria established by the schools (Wisconsin Statutes, Section 228.119.23, 1990).

If all else failed, the schools were free to specify any criteria for parental involvement, thus ensuring recertification.[3]

The program was capped initially at 1 percent of the MPS enrollment, which at the time was about 90,000 students. That limit was raised to 1.5 percent in 1993. Private schools received the MPS student state-aid payment in lieu of tuition and fees ($2,446 in 1990; $4,894 in 1998). Despite being an outspoken opponent of the program, the Department of Public Instruction was given the responsibility for administering the program and annually evaluating its consequences.

The initial voucher program in Milwaukee was intended to provide educational opportunities for poor families, who would have had considerable difficulty placing their children in private schools on their own. Most of the students would either transfer from the public schools in the city or would attend those schools as kindergartners. Religious schools were excluded in an effort to avoid a First Amendment lawsuit. Many called the program experimental, although the governor had used his veto authority to eliminate a terminal date of 1995.

## Research Methods and Data

The study on which this book is based employed a number of methodological approaches. Surveys were used to assess prior educational experiences and attitudes in MPS, and, for MPCP participants, their attitudes and behavior within their private schools. We also employed case studies of private schools, and extensive analysis of outcome measures, including achievement test data, parental involvement, and attrition from the program.

Surveys were mailed in the fall of each year from 1990 to 1994 to all parents who applied for enrollment in one of the choice schools. Similar surveys were sent in May and June of 1991 to a random sample of

[3] Very little was made of these standards. Although the Department of Public Instruction did keep records, our evaluations never even recorded the standards met by individual schools. The most common standard selected by the schools was the simplest to document—attendance. The theory from the beginning was that such standards ran counter to the general philosophy surrounding choice—that students and parents hold schools accountable by their selection of and exit from schools.

5,474 parents of students in MPS.[4] Among other purposes, the first surveys were intended to assess parent knowledge of and evaluation of the choice program, educational experiences in prior public schools, the extent of prior parental involvement in MPS, and the importance of education and the expectations parents hold for their children. We also obtained demographic information on family members. The follow-up survey of choice parents was mailed in June of each year. These surveys were designed to measure the same behaviors and attitudes while their children were in private schools. Thus we were able to measure shifts in parental involvement, expectations, and satisfaction with school environment and quality.

In addition to surveys, detailed case studies were completed in April 1991 in the four private schools that enrolled the majority of the choice students. An additional study was completed in 1992, and six more case studies were completed in the spring of 1993. Case studies of the K–8 schools involved approximately 30 person-days in the schools, including 56 hours of classroom observation and interviews with nearly all of the teachers and administrators in the schools. Smaller schools required less time. Researchers also attended and observed parent and community group meetings and board of director meetings for several schools.

The research also includes analysis of four or five years of outcome measures including data on achievement test scores, attendance, parental attitudes, parental involvement, and attrition from the program. Descriptions and limitations of those data will be provided in chapter 6.

---

[4] Although the response rates (given in table A3.3) on some of our surveys are low relative to face-to-face interviews with national samples, they are higher than the approximately 20 percent response rates that MPS reports for its usual surveys. We have independent measures of race and qualification for free lunch from the Milwaukee Student Record Data Base for both the random sample and the choice students. Thus we were able to assess sampling bias and construct weights to offset that bias. For MPS the only statistically significant sampling bias was for race, where we had a less-than-expected response for African Americans, an oversample of Asians and whites, and a slight undersample of low-income families. Table A3.4 provides race and income data on survey respondents. For choice students, there was a disproportionately high response from African Americans and a low response from Hispanics. The results presented in this report are for unweighted samples.

We have also analyzed scales and demographic variables using three weights: a weight based on expected race; a weight based on expected low/nonlow income; and a weight combining both race and income. The combined race and income weight is the most accurate. Because for the MPS respondents the sampling bias for race was considerably larger than for income, the income-weighted analysis produced no significant differences except on the income variable itself. The race/income analysis produced only one marginally significant difference on attitude scale means. It also produced significantly different effects for household income, for percentage of female parents on AFDC, and for percentage of single-parent families.

Finally, beginning in the fall of 1992, brief mail and phone surveys were completed with as many parents as we could find who chose not to have their children continue in the program. These surveys of "attritees" consisted of only two questions: Where is your child attending school now? Why did you leave the choice program?

In accordance with normal research protocols, and with agreement of the private schools, to maintain student confidentiality, reported results are aggregated and schools are not individually identified. Some of the characteristics or histories of individual schools may identify them in the narrative of chapter 5. However, every effort has been made to insure the confidentiality of interview statements by employees and specific outcome results of individual schools. Schools that were not the subject of case study research, withdrew from the program, or went bankrupt are identified through the use of media accounts or official state reports.

# Appendix to Chapter 3 _____

## Historical MPS Achievement Test Data

HISTORICAL achievement test data in MPS "basement" archives came in a variety of forms as reporting formats changed over time. The Iowa Test of Basic Skills (ITBS) was first given in 1959. From 1959 to 1973, reports were limited to grade equivalents, which are a transformation of raw or standard scores into years and months. An expected grade equivalent is nothing more than the median of the national population for the respective grade and month. Thus a district population will be above the national median if their grade equivalent is higher than expected and below if the grade equivalent falls below the norm.

Test scores for selected early years are presented in Table A3.1. For both reading and math, MPS students appeared to be at or above the national averages until 1970. The scores from 1966 to 1973 all show this same decline. Thus, these data indicate that the decline in MPS test scores occurred quite early.

From 1973 to 1988, the district reported both the Metropolitan Achievement (MAT) and Iowa Test of Basic Skills scores in a variety of ways. For some years it was possible to determine median scores and for other years it was not. Since 1988, the district has relied not on

TABLE A3.1
Iowa Test of Basic Skills, Grade Equivalents, 1959, 1965, and 1970

| Year | Grade | Expected Grade Equivalent | Actual Reading Grade Equivalent | Actual Math Grade Equivalent |
|------|-------|--------------------------|--------------------------------|------------------------------|
| 1959 | 4 | 4.2 | 4.1 | 4.1 |
|      | 6 | 6.1 | 6.4 | 6.2 |
|      | 8 | 8.1 | 8.3 | 8.2 |
| 1965 | 4 | 4.2 | 4.2 | 4.2 |
|      | 6 | 6.1 | 6.3 | 6.1 |
|      | 8 | 8.1 | 8.0 | 7.9 |
| 1970 | 4 | 4.2 | 3.55 | 3.86 |
|      | 6 | 6.1 | 5.35 | 5.33 |
|      | 8 | 8.1 | 6.93 | 7.00 |

Sources: MPS Citywide Reference Data, September 1960, 1966, 1971.

medians but rather on the percentage of students at or above the fiftieth national percentile. Thus, scores presented by our research in chapters 4 and 6 provide better recent estimates of test means from 1990 to 1995. Table A3.2 provides earlier data for 1975, 1981, and 1985, which clearly indicate that the students scored better on the ITBS than the MAT. For 1981 and 1985, median math scores were actually above the national norm, while for all three years, reading scores were mostly below.

TABLE A3.2
MPS Metropolitan Achievement (1975) and Iowa Test of Basic Skills (1981, 1985), Median National Percentiles

| Year | Grade | Median Percentile Reading | Median Percentile Math |
|------|-------|---------------------------|------------------------|
| 1975 (MAT) | Middle Elementary | 37.2 | 36.6 |
| | 5 | 35.6 | 39.1 |
| | 7 | 32.9 | 33.3 |
| 1981 (ITBS) | Middle Elementary | 40.0 | 53.0 |
| | 5 | 38.0 | 52.0 |
| | 7 | 36.0 | 45.0 |
| 1985 (ITBS) | 2 | 51.0 | 60.0 |
| | 5 | 40.0 | 52.0 |
| | 7 | 42.0 | 51.0 |

*Sources:* MPS Citywide Statistical Profiles, 1976, 1982, 1986.

TABLE A3.3
Survey Sample Sizes and Response Rates

| | Surveys Mailed | Surveys Not Delivered | Surveys Returned | Response Rate (%) |
|---|----------------|-----------------------|------------------|-------------------|
| MPS parents 5/91 | 5475 | 224 | 1598 | 30.4 |
| Choice parents wave 1, 10/90 | 349 | 31 | 149 | 46.9 |
| Choice parents wave 2, 6/91 | 360 | 33 | 166 | 50.8 |
| Choice parents wave 1, 10/91 | 453 | 29 | 207 | 48.8 |
| Choice parents wave 2, 6/92 | 531 | 38 | 219 | 44.4 |
| Choice parents wave 1, 10/92 | 318 | 17 | 132 | 43.9 |
| Choice parents wave 2, 6/93 | 656 | 35 | 238 | 38.3 |
| Choice parents wave 1, 10/93 | 349 | 17 | 154 | 46.4 |
| Choice parents wave 2, 6/94 | 732 | 63 | 273 | 40.8 |

So, although the image of MPS as an abysmal school district is prevalent, historical achievement test score data, such as they are, appear to be more mixed. The apparent decline occurred earlier than might have been anticipated based on changing race and poverty characteristics of the student body, and the patterns of change are not as conclusive as would be expected. Survey sample characteristics are provided in tables A3.3 and A3.4.

TABLE A3.4
Race and Income Response Rates (percentages)

| | Actual Accepted in Choice (1990–93) | Choice Responded to Survey (Oct. 1990–93) | Actual MPS Control Group (1991) | MPS Responded to Survey (May 1991) |
|---|---|---|---|---|
| *Race* | | | | |
| African American | 71.5 | 75.5 | 55.3 | 42.5 |
| Asian American | 0.4 | 0.3 | 3.8 | 6.0 |
| Hispanic | 20.6 | 16.3 | 4.7 | 10.1 |
| Native American | 0.8 | 1.1 | 0.9 | 0.5 |
| White | 5.9 | 6.2 | 29.3 | 40.3 |
| Other | 0.9 | 0.6 | 1.0 | 0.8 |
| (N) | (1517) | (611) | (5365) | (1541) |
| *Income* | | | | |
| Low income | NA | NA | 63.9 | 59.5 |
| Non-low income | NA | NA | 36.1 | 40.5 |
| | | | (5438) | (1541) |

# 4

## Who Participates in Choice Programs?

IN THIS CHAPTER I address issues that affect experiments with educational vouchers, as well as debates that are central to the structure of American education. The basic issues involve the composition of our schools and the appropriateness of allowing and supporting schools that range widely in terms of educational expectations, goals, and results for children. Put in oversimplified terms, should we allow or encourage a wide variety of schools, catering to specialized student skills, abilities, and desires, or should we attempt to create schools with similar approaches and with similar mixes of student abilities? Further, should we allow parents with different means the ability to create and purchase different levels and quality of education for their children? Or, should we redirect this investment either through equalization of conditions and resources in public schools and/or by limiting spending from private sources in either public or private schools?[1]

Deeply imbedded in these issues are basic normative judgments over which Americans have differed for generations. To what degree should our education system be geared to producing equal opportunity and equal results rather than maximizing the amount of education across the system and thus allowing each student to achieve his or her maximum level of knowledge? The issues also invoke varying assumptions concerning power over public policies. Should parents be free to control where their children attend school and to provide whatever resources they wish to a chosen school, or should those choices be subject to democratic and community choice and control?

The answers have shifted in American education over time and currently represent a somewhat unique compromise created by a well-regulated public school system and a more or less unrestrained private school system. Within the public system, there is a perceived emphasis on equality, with difficult, often unsuccessful battles waged when there are major breaches of either equality of opportunity or result. Thus, when

---

[1] Some of the most often referred to examples of extreme educational choice in other countries, for example the Netherlands or Belgium where all schools are supported by the state, provide the latter forms of restrictions. Total spending is strictly controlled and equalized across the various public and private school sectors. All schools in these systems are also regulated in terms of curriculum, examination systems, etc.

magnet schools were extended in the 1970s and 1980s, after initially creating elite magnets in an attempt to hold middle-class families, there was a reaction in many large districts aimed at reducing the exclusive admission requirements of these schools. The fear was the movement toward dual systems within a district (Blank, 1990). Similarly, when wide disparities in spending between districts in states were revealed, suits were brought in federal court, and when states lost, they often revamped state education finance in an attempt (not always successful) to create further equality (Knickerman and Reschovsky, 1980).

As noted earlier, the private sector in this century has provided an alternative arrangement, quite untouched by government efforts to equalize or regulate. And the results are well known — private school students come from more elite families and on average achieve at higher levels (Hoffer, Kilgore, and Coleman, 1982; Hoffer and Coleman, 1987; Chubb and Moe, 1990). Spending within the sector is on average lower, but varies considerably from very poor parish church schools to opulent boarding schools that cater to the wealthiest families.

Voucher programs bring all of these issues to the surface. The fears of opponents of vouchers are simple: Vouchers will (1) further reduce equal access and equal results in terms of achievement by increasing the elite selection of students by schools; and (2) accelerate the current problem of segregation of students by race, class, and educational achievement.

Proponents of vouchers either argue that parents should have the right to send their children to any school they want (and the state should facilitate that choice) or that programs can be designed that will prevent the type of student creaming assumed by opponents. The first argument invokes a normative position, placing the value of freedom above the value of equality; the second invokes an empirical argument concerning the design of voucher programs. This chapter has something to say about the second of these arguments. The normative aspects of the debate will not be resolved in this book, but will be discussed in the final chapter.

The relevant questions relating to participation can be broken down into a series of more detailed questions. To answer the question of creaming we must know the characteristics of student applicants and those enrolled in terms of student ability, prior educational experiences, gender, and race. We also need to understand the families from which they come in terms of family structure, attitudes, and economic circumstances. Finally, we want to know how families learned of the program, which schools attracted which students, and why families turned to the voucher program.

Data used to answer these questions for the MPCP come from program administration records and parent surveys. Most of the findings are not broken down by year, but rather consolidated over the years. The reason is that findings are very consistent from year to year, and thus consolidated data provide a more adequate summary of findings.

In addition, a number of tables contain data broken down by groups: applicants, selected and nonselected Choice students, attrition Choice students, and two MPS control groups — the full random sample and the low-income sample. Data on several of these groups are included here for comparative purposes; some of the other data will be discussed in subsequent chapters. The most appropriate comparison group to the Choice families, on most measures, is the low-income MPS sample. That group, which included about two-thirds of Milwaukee students, is defined as qualifying for free or reduced-priced lunch. The income level for reduced-priced lunch is 1.85 times the poverty line; free lunch is 1.35 times the poverty line. Almost all low-income students qualified for full free lunch and also would have qualified for the MPCP.

To try to understand if these findings are a unique result of MPCP requirements and implementation, I will compare these results to findings on other choice programs, both in Milwaukee and in other cities. The conclusion from that analysis will be that, as the saying goes, "The devil is in the details." Participation and selection requirements and implementation procedures are critical in determining who enrolls in various choice programs.

## Enrollment in and Knowledge of the Milwaukee Parental Choice Program

### The Application and Selection Process

The enrollment process in the MPCP varied little over the five-year period of this study. Nonsectarian private schools applied for entrance to the program to the State Department of Public Instruction. All these schools had to do was complete a one-page application form verifying that they were a certified private school without religious affiliation or instruction and that they would abide by the conditions of the Choice program (random selection, an obligation to meet one of four program standards, nondiscrimination, and reporting requirements).

Once parents heard of the program, they approached a participating private school (or schools). The school then ascertained their eligibility by having them fill out a form that requested where the student had attended school in the previous year, family size, and family income. Family size was required because the poverty line varies by family size.

The family income section of the form was a modified free-lunch eligibility form used in the public schools. If the student had not been in a private school or another district in the prior year, and if the appropriate maximum income box or lower had been checked (depending on family size), the student was deemed eligible. Statutes or administrative rules required no fact checking, and no instructions were provided which stated how much help could be given in filling out the application.

By agreement between participating private schools, random selection was done by drawing numbers of applicants out of a box. This occurred by grade (when grades were oversubscribed) and all students were placed in rank order, thus also providing a randomly selected waiting list for those students who did not make the cut. Applications were taken through July 31, at which time random selection could take place.

A sibling rule began informally in the first year and was formally approved in the second and subsequent years. This meant that if a sibling was already enrolled in the private school, as a Choice or tuition-paying student, the Choice applicant was automatically admitted (i.e., excluded from random selection). No records were kept on how many students were admitted under this rule.

Because the schools were not required to accept students who qualified as disabled under Wisconsin disability statutes, accepted students could be rejected if the school categorized them as handicapped. Records were not required or kept on how many students were rejected as disabled, or in what manner that was determined.

### Enrollment in the Choice Program

Enrollment statistics for the Choice program are provided in table 4.1. Enrollment in the program increased steadily but slowly, never reaching the maximum number of students allowed by the law. September enrollments were 341, 521, 620, 742, and 830 from the 1990–91 school year to the 1994–95 school year. The number of schools participating were 7 in 1990–91, 6 in 1991–92, 11 in 1992–93, and 12 from fall 1993 to 1995. The number of applications also increased, again with the largest increase in 1992–93. In the last two years, however, applications leveled off at a little over 1,000 per year. Applications exceeded the number of available seats (as determined by the private schools) by 171, 143, 307, 238, and 64 from 1990–91 through 1994–95. Some of these students eventually filled seats of students who were accepted but did not actually enroll.

The number of potential schools in the program was an obvious limitation. Only twenty-three secular private schools existed in Milwaukee

**TABLE 4.1**
Participation and Attrition from the Choice Program, 1990–95

|  | 1990–91 | 1991–92 | 1992–93 | 1993–94 | 1994–95 |
|---|---|---|---|---|---|
| Number of students allowed in the Choice Program (limited to 1% of MPS enrollment) / 1.5% 1994–95 | 931 | 946 | 950 | 968 | 1,450 |
| Number of private nonsectarian schools in Milwaukee | 22 | 22 | 23 | 23 | 23 |
| Number of schools participating | 7 | 6 | 11 | 12 | 12 |
| Number of applications | 577 | 689 | 998 | 1,049 | 1,046 |
| Number of available seats | 406 | 546 | 691 | 811 | 982 |
| Number of students participating |  |  |  |  |  |
| September count | 341 | 521 | 620 | 742 | 830 |
| January count | 259 | 526 | 586 | 701 | — |
| June count | 249 | 477 | 570 | 671 | — |
| Graduating students | 8 | 28 | 32 | 42 | 45 |
| Number of returning Choice students | NA | 178 | 323 | 405 | 491 |
| Attrition rate[a] | 0.46 | 0.35 | 0.31 | 0.27 | 0.28 |
| Attrition rate without alternative schools | 0.44[b] | 0.32 | 0.28 | 0.23 | 0.24 |

[a] The attrition rate for year $t$ is defined as: $1.0 -$ [the number of returning students in year $t + 1$ / (the September count in year $t -$ graduating students in year $t$)].
[b] If Juanita Virgil Academy is excluded, the attrition rate is 0.29.

during this period, compared with approximately 100 religious private schools. Of the secular schools, about half chose not to participate in the MPCP during the first five years. We contacted those schools in the third year of the program. The reasons for nonparticipation varied: Several schools concluded it was too costly for the school (the voucher would not match tuition); others were devoted contract schools with MPS;[2] and others were wary that this program was established by African Americans, primarily for African Americans.

However, the limited supply was not much of a constraining factor,

[2] Wisconsin allows school districts to contract with secular private schools to educate preschool and at-risk students. The contracts are yearly and average about 80 percent of the per-member cost in the public school district. A number of independent private schools that had a history of contracting unsuccessfully fought the voucher program — advocating instead expansion of contracting options. Most of those schools later refused to enter the MPCP.

because applications were far from the avalanche that choice supporters often tout. Although total applications exceeded the total seats available, the available seats were usually not filled because not enough seats were offered in the most desirable schools. It is difficult to determine how many more applications would have been made if more schools participated and more seats were available. In 1992–93, when the number of participating schools increased from six to eleven, applications rose by 45 percent. From fall 1993 to 1995, however, available seats increased by 22 percent and 21 percent, but applications increased by only 5 percent in 1993–94 and declined in the last year. As described below, these results differ considerably from the concurrent privately funded voucher program in Milwaukee.

## Learning about Choice and the Adequacy of Information on Choice

The issue of information on school choices has become a major side issue in the debate over vouchers. Those generally opposed see information on schools as costly to create and obtain and unevenly available to families, as well as being skewed in favor of those with greater economic and social resources (see Levin, 1992; Levin and Driver, 1997). In Milwaukee, partly due to the small size of the program, information on schools did not appear to be a great problem. Families were accustomed to extensive school choice in the public schools as a result of efforts to desegregate the schools. This created discussion and informal networks, often within racial groups, as well as a formal system of information about schools and the selection and assignment process. The MPCP fit within this system with little difficulty.[3]

Our annual surveys asked Choice applicants how they learned about the program. The results were very consistent over the years. The most prevalent source of information on choice was friends and relatives (50.9 percent), which essentially means word-of-mouth information. That informal communication was almost double the frequency of other sources (newspapers — 24.2 percent; television and radio — 21.4 percent; private schools — 17.7 percent). This could be interpreted as a

---

[3] The information system in MPS was quite elaborate with a department in the district office devoted to information and school selection and assignment. There was an official book with four or five pages of data on each school, plus school-initiated literature advertising the special features of the schools. This system facilitated the extensive magnet school system that developed during the 1980s. One of the recommendations of my reports on the program was that the choice schools should have been formally included in this system. It was not enacted, but MPS did answer questions on the program and directed interested families to the State Department of Public Instruction or participating private schools.

negative finding, indicating that parents were not seriously researching schools and learning about options like the MPCP. Although reliable evidence does not exist on how parents in general choose schools — most often by selecting their residence — it is likely that word-of-mouth and using trusted parents of other children as guides is a common source of information for most families. There are undoubtedly parents who analyze test-score data and other measures of student achievement, but they must be a small minority. At least in the MPCP, parents were forced to select and visit schools, if only to fill out application forms. That is probably not the case for most inner-city parents in public schools.

We also asked parents how satisfied they were with the amount and accuracy of information available on the MPCP and schools and with the assistance they received. Satisfaction with the amount of information on the program in general was high in all years and was highest in the last two years as the program procedures became well established. For the full five years of the study, those satisfied or very satisfied with the amount and accuracy of the information on the program and schools ranged from 66 percent to 76 percent. Seventy-seven percent were satisfied with the assistance they received from the private schools, and 65 percent were satisfied with assistance from the Department of Public Instruction.

There was, however, a difference in satisfaction of parents selected and not selected into the Choice schools. Looking ahead to table 4.4, which portrays additive scales for these questions measuring satisfaction with administration of the MPCP, there is a large difference between those applicants who enrolled in the program and those not selected.[4] As indicated in the rows for Scale T3 (see top panel, table 4.4), Choice enrollees for 1990–94 have a mean dissatisfaction with administration of the program of 11.6, while nonselected parents have a much higher average dissatisfaction score of 14.4.

## Characteristics of Applicants and Selected Choice Students

### Demographic Characteristics of Choice Families and Students

The MPCP was established and the statute written explicitly to provide an opportunity for relatively poor families to attend private schools.

[4] Table 4.4 contains information on scales composed of sets of questions measuring an underlying concept. The exact questions for the scales appeared in program reports (Witte et al. 1994, tables A1–A6). We created simple scale scores by adding together responses to each item. Table 4.4 contains statistics on the scales, defines the scale direction, and reports the Cronbach Alpha statistic for the scale. Cronbach Alpha is a measure of how well the items form a scale. It has a maximum value of 1.0 when all items are perfectly correlated with each other.

The program clearly accomplished that goal. Relevant demographic statistics are presented in table 4.2 which, unless otherwise noted, are based on our surveys. For comparison purposes six groups are identified, including the combined year samples for Choice applicants, Choice students actually enrolled, students not selected, students who left the program (and did not graduate), and the MPS control group.

In terms of reported family income (see table 4.2a), the average income was $11,630 over the first five years. Although not included in the table, for the first four years, the average income of each cohort was very similar. However, for some unknown reason, incomes of 1994 Choice families increased considerably to an average of $14,210. Low-income MPS parents reported a slightly higher family income, which averaged $12,100 in 1991. The average in the full MPS control group was $22,000.

In terms of race, the program had the greatest impact on African American students, who comprised 74 percent of those applying to MPCP schools and 73 percent of those enrolled in the first five years (see Table 4.2b). Hispanics accounted for 19 percent of Choice applicants and 21 percent of those enrolled. Both of these groups were disproportionately higher than the MPS sample. Compared with the low-income MPS sample, however, Hispanics were the most overrepresented, with Asians and white students the most underrepresented. The overrepresentation of Hispanics was due to a new building and considerable expansion in capacity of Bruce-Guadalupe Bilingual School, which has an emphasis on Spanish culture and is located in a neighborhood with a heavily Hispanic population (see figure 3.3).

In terms of marital status (see table 4.2c), Choice families were much more likely to be headed by a nonmarried parent (75 percent) than the average MPS family (49 percent), and somewhat more likely than the low-income MPS parent (65 percent). The percentage was almost identical for the five separate years.

One important difference between MPS and Choice applicants was family size (see table 4.2d). For the combined years, only 42 percent of the Choice families reported having more than two children. The average number of children in families applying to the MPCP was 2.54. This compared with 54 percent of the MPS families having more than two children (2.95 children per family) and 65 percent of the low-income MPS families (3.24 on average).

A unique characteristic of Choice parents was that despite their economic status, they reported higher education levels than either low-income or average MPS parents (see Table 4.2e). Over half of the Choice mothers reported some college education (56 percent), compared with 40 percent for the entire MPS sample and 30 percent of the low-income MPS respondents. That number was even higher in 1994, with 64 per-

**TABLE 4.2**
Household Demographics, 1990–94

**Table 4.2a**
Household Income (percentages)

| | 1 | 2 | 3 | 4 | 5 | 6 |
|---|---|---|---|---|---|---|
| *Income* *($ thousands)* | *Choice* *Applied* *(1990–94)* | *Choice* *Enrolled* *(1990–94)* | *Choice* *Nonselect* *(1990–94)* | *Attrition* *(1990–93)* | *Low-* *Income* *MPS (1991)* | *MPS* *Control* *(1991)* |
| 0–$5 | 18 | 16 | 19 | 18 | 19 | 13 |
| 5–$10 | 37 | 40 | 33 | 40 | 34 | 23 |
| 10–$20 | 29 | 30 | 29 | 27 | 29 | 21 |
| 20–$35 | 16 | 15 | 17 | 15 | 14 | 24 |
| 35–$50 | 1 | 0 | 1 | 1 | 3 | 13 |
| 50 and over | 0 | 0 | 0 | 0 | 0 | 8 |
| Mean Income | 11.63 | 11.34 | 12.24 | 11.77 | 12.13 | 22.00 |
| (N) | (1,020) | (627) | (325) | (293) | (880) | (1,513) |

**Table 4.2b**
Race[a] (percentages)

| | 1 | 2 | 3 | 4 | 5 | 6 |
|---|---|---|---|---|---|---|
| *Race* | *Choice* *Applied* *(1990–94)* | *Choice* *Enrolled* *(1990–94)* | *Choice* *Nonselect* *(1990–94)* | *Attrition* *(1990–93)* | *Low-* *Income* *MPS (1991)* | *MPS* *Control* *(1991)* |
| African American | 75 | 73 | 78 | 75 | 67 | 55 |
| Asian | 0 | 0 | 0 | 0 | 5 | 4 |
| Hispanic | 19 | 21 | 14 | 16 | 11 | 10 |
| Native American | 0 | 0 | 1 | 1 | 1 | 1 |
| White | 5 | 5 | 4 | 7 | 15 | 29 |
| Other | 1 | 0 | 3 | 1 | 1 | 1 |
| (N) | (2,673) | (1,490) | (886) | (676) | (3,179) | (5,365) |

**Table 4.2c**
Parent Marital Status (percentages)

| | 1 | 2 | 3 | 4 | 5 | 6 |
|---|---|---|---|---|---|---|
| *Marital Status* | *Choice* *Applied* *(1990–94)* | *Choice* *Enrolled* *(1990–94)* | *Choice* *Nonselect* *(1990–94)* | *Attrition* *(1990–93)* | *Low-* *Income* *MPS (1991)* | *MPS* *Control* *(1991)* |
| Married | 25 | 23 | 30 | 24 | 35 | 51 |
| Single | 39 | 40 | 35 | 42 | 32 | 22 |
| Separated | 12 | 13 | 11 | 9 | 11 | 8 |
| Divorced | 15 | 16 | 14 | 15 | 14 | 13 |
| Widowed | 3 | 3 | 3 | 5 | 2 | 2 |
| Living together | 5 | 5 | 7 | 5 | 6 | 4 |
| (N) | (1,032) | (633) | (331) | (294) | (924) | (1,637) |

**TABLE 4.2** (*cont.*)

Table 4.2d
Family Size (percentages)

| Children per Family | 1 Choice Applied (1990–94) | 2 Choice Enrolled (1990–94) | 3 Choice Nonselect (1990–94) | 4 Attrition (1990–93) | 5 Low-Income MPS (1991) | 6 MPS Control (1991) |
|---|---|---|---|---|---|---|
| 1 | 28 | 26 | 30 | 19 | 9 | 13 |
| 2 | 30 | 32 | 28 | 31 | 26 | 33 |
| 3 | 19 | 22 | 14 | 24 | 27 | 26 |
| 4 | 13 | 11 | 13 | 16 | 18 | 15 |
| 5 or more | 10 | 8 | 15 | 10 | 20 | 15 |
| Mean number of children/family | 2.54 | 2.5 | 2.66 | 2.72 | 3.24 | 2.95 |
| (N) | (1,060) | (645) | (343) | (287) | (908) | (1,611) |

Table 4.2e
Parents' Education (percentages)

| | 8th Grade | Some High School | GED | High School | Some College | College Grad | Some Post-graduate | (N) |
|---|---|---|---|---|---|---|---|---|
| *Choice applied* | | | | | | | | |
| Mother | 4 | 12 | 9 | 20 | 46 | 7 | 2 | (1,027) |
| Father | 10 | 20 | 7 | 26 | 29 | 5 | 3 | (624) |
| *Choice enrolled* | | | | | | | | |
| Mother | 3 | 12 | 9 | 21 | 46 | 7 | 1 | (626) |
| Father | 7 | 19 | 7 | 28 | 29 | 6 | 3 | (383) |
| *Choice nonselect* | | | | | | | | |
| Mother | 7 | 11 | 9 | 19 | 46 | 6 | 2 | (333) |
| Father | 16 | 22 | 7 | 21 | 30 | 3 | 1 | (199) |
| *Attrition 1990–93* | | | | | | | | |
| Mother | 4 | 9 | 11 | 19 | 48 | 8 | 1 | (292) |
| Father | 6 | 18 | 8 | 32 | 30 | 4 | 2 | (175) |
| *Low-Income MPS 1991* | | | | | | | | |
| Mother | 12 | 25 | 9 | 25 | 26 | 3 | 1 | (881) |
| Father | 15 | 22 | 9 | 25 | 21 | 6 | 2 | (535) |
| *MPS Control 1991* | | | | | | | | |
| Mother | 8 | 18 | 7 | 28 | 29 | 6 | 5 | (1,525) |
| Father | 9 | 16 | 8 | 26 | 27 | 9 | 6 | (1,127) |

[a]Based on MPS Student Record Data Base (SRDB). In cases where Choice students could not be found in the SRDB, race data were taken from the school enrollment sheets.

cent of the mothers new to the program reporting some college education. Higher education was consistent with the higher incomes reported
for the last year. The biggest difference in education appears in the category titled "some college." Although fathers more closely match the
MPS control groups, they were also somewhat more educated. As we
shall see below, the association between higher parental education and
choice is also characteristic of other choice programs.

### Why Parents Participated in the Choice Program

Table 4.3 provides the responses to survey questions rating the importance of various factors in parents' decisions to participate in the MPCP.
The results were consistent across the years. The leading reasons given
for participating in the program were the perceived *educational quality*
and the *teaching approach and style* in private schools. The disciplinary
environment and the general atmosphere that parents associated with
those schools were the next most important factors. Frustration
with prior public schools, although not unimportant, was not as important a reason for applying to the MPCP as the attributes of the private
schools. At the bottom of the list were siblings in the school and its
location.

These results again can be interpreted quite positively. Critics of educational choice have often argued that if parents are given choices, they
are likely to pick their neighborhood school out of sheer convenience.
That could mean that they might choose a school that does not fit the
needs of their child or have the best track record. It could also mean,
given residential segregation in many large school districts, that the
choice of neighborhood schools could lead to resegregation of schools.
The evidence from this program is that this does not happen. We will
also see below that distance to the private school is not a significant
variable in explaining who applies to the Choice program. That location and distance to school are not overriding factors in applying to the
program are even more important given that Choice applicants were
much more likely to be in the lower grades (with over 60 percent in
grades K–2).

### The Importance of Education and Educational Expectations

Based on our measures, Choice and MPS parents were similar in terms
of the importance they place on education. We measured the importance of education relative to other important family values. Scale descriptive statistics are given in table 4.4.

...ce Levels of Differences in Scale Means for Comparative Groups and (N)

| Scale | 1 Choice Applied to Low-Income MPS | 2 Choice Enrolled to Low-Income MPS | 3 Nonselected Choice to Choice Enrolled | 4 Choice Prior Public to Choice Private |
|---|---|---|---|---|
| Adm | NA | NA | .000 (230) | NA |
| ort | .063 (1640) | .436 (1352) | .007 (392) | .000 (494) |
| l | .000 (1386) | .000 (845) | .711 (425) | .000 (392) |
| f | .000 (1445) | .000 (895) | .107 (433) | .001 (421) |
| g | .000 (1424) | .000 (892) | .478 (396) | .000 (410) |
| | .000 (1598) | .000 (1406) | .699 (390) | .409 (491) |
| | .000 (1074) | .000 (648) | .181 (342) | .000 (284) |

he low-income comparison group (see table 4.4, Scales A3–A5). ncluded parental involvement based on school contacts, initiated by the school or the parents (e.g., regarding behavioral problems, conferences, and report cards); parental involvement in school zational activities (e.g., membership and attendance at PTA and aising); and parental involvement at home (e.g., reading with stu- and helping with homework). There were no significant differ- n parental involvement between Choice applicants and those who d in MPCP schools. The mean differences between either of these and the full MPS sample or the low-income MPS control group nificant at the .001 level for all measures. See table 4.5 for these ilities.

## l Satisfaction

els of satisfaction with their prior public schools were also sig- y different between Choice and MPS parents (see table 4.4, ). Satisfaction was measured by asking parents to rate, on a nt scale, their level of satisfaction with educational quality, ip of the principal, quality of teachers, disciplinary environ- d so on. The scale was coded so that a higher score represented *dissatisfaction*. Both Choice applicants and enrollees were ap-

**TABLE 4.3**
Factors Affecting Decisions to Participate in the Choice Program, Applicants, 1990–94 (percentages)

| | Very Important | Important | Somewhat Important | Not Important |
|---|---|---|---|---|
| Educational quality in chosen school | 88.6 | 10.5 | .7 | .3 |
| Teaching approach or style | 85.7 | 13.2 | .7 | .4 |
| Discipline in chosen school | 74.6 | 22.1 | 2.9 | .4 |
| General atmosphere in chosen school | 74.3 | 22.5 | 2.7 | .5 |
| Class size[a] | 72 | 22.4 | 4.9 | .7 |
| Financial considerations | 69.8 | 23.3 | 4.8 | 2.1 |
| Special programs in chosen school | 68.4 | 25.7 | 3.6 | 2.3 |
| Location of chosen school | 60.5 | 22.2 | 11.7 | 5.6 |
| Frustration with public schools | 59.5 | 23.9 | 10.7 | 5.9 |
| Other children in chosen school | 36.6 | 29.2 | 14.8 | 19.4 |
| (N) | | (964) | | |

Question: "Please rate all of the following issues and their importance in your decision to participate in the Choice program."

[a]This question was not asked in the first two years of the study. The N for these responses is 581 in the 1990–94 responses.

Educational expectations were probably unrealistically high for all groups. However, Choice parents were higher than MPS and low-income MPS parents. Eighty-six percent of Choice parents in the first four years indicated that they expected their child to go to college or do postgraduate work. This compared with 76 percent of the MPS parents and 72 percent of the low-income MPS parents. Because sample sizes were large, the differences in these proportions were close to being statistically significantly different by the conventional .05 one-tailed test. The probabilities of differences of means on scales being zero between various groups are reported in table 4.5.

## Experience of Choice Parents in Prior Public Schools

A more complete picture of Choice parents includes the level of parental involvement in their child's prior public school as well as attitudes to-

**TABLE 4.4**
Scale Data—Means, Standard Deviations, Reliability, and Sample Sizes

| Source of Scale, Range, and Direction by Group | Mean | Standard Deviation | Alpha | (N) |
|---|---|---|---|---|
| **Dissatisfaction with the administration of the choice application process** | | | | |
| **T3-DisChAdm - Range = 6–24 (High = More Dissatisfied)** | | | | |
| Choice applied, 1990–94 (fall) | 12.6 | 4.4 | .91 | (609) |
| Choice enrolled, 1990–94 (fall) | 11.6 | 3.6 | .88 | (364) |
| Nonselected choice, 1990–94 (fall) | 14.4 | 5.0 | .92 | (206) |
| | | | | |
| **Importance of education compared to other goals** | | | | |
| **A1 - EdImport- Range = 7–15 (High = More Important)** | | | | |
| Choice applied, 1990–94 (fall) | 11.6 | 1.9 | .72 | (996) |
| Choice enrolled, 1990–94 (fall) | 11.7 | 1.8 | .70 | (627) |
| Nonselected choice, 1990–94 (fall) | 11.4 | 1.9 | .73 | (301) |
| Choice private school, 1991–95 (spring) | 11.5 | 1.9 | .77 | (732) |
| Nonselected choice, 1991–95 (spring) | 11.3 | 1.9 | .76 | (210) |
| Low-income MPS, 1991 | 11.8 | 2.0 | .74 | (811) |
| MPS control, 1991 | 11.7 | 2.0 | .71 | (1,554) |
| | | | | |
| **Frequency of parent contacting school** | | | | |
| **A2 - PiParScl - Range = 0–21 (High = More)** | | | | |
| Choice applied, 1990–94 (fall) | 8.8 | 4.9 | .79 | (775) |
| Choice enrolled, 1990–94 (fall) | 8.6 | 5.1 | .81 | (466) |
| Nonselected choice, 1990–94 (fall) | 9.0 | 4.6 | .74 | (269) |
| Choice private school, 1991–95 (spring) | 9.4 | 4.8 | .78 | (722) |
| Nonselected choice, 1991–95 (spring) | 8.0 | 5.0 | .83 | (212) |
| Low income MPS, 1991 | 5.8 | 4.4 | .79 | (807) |
| MPS contril, 1991 | 6.0 | 4.3 | .78 | (1,529) |
| | | | | |
| **Frequency of school contacting parent** | | | | |
| **A3 - PiSclPar- Range = 0–12 (High = More)** | | | | |
| Choice applied, 1990–94 (fall) | 3.6 | 2.9 | .67 | (811) |
| Choice enrolled, 1990–94 (fall) | 3.7 | 2.9 | .67 | (495) |
| Nonselected choice, 1990–94 (fall) | 3.5 | 2.7 | .63 | (276) |
| Choice private school, 1991–95 (spring) | 4.4 | 2.9 | .70 | (740) |
| Nonselected choice, 1991–95 (spring) | 3.8 | 3.0 | .71 | (223) |
| Low-income MPS, 1991 | 2.7 | 2.5 | .67 | (834) |
| MPS control, 1991 | 2.7 | 2.5 | .65 | (1,594) |

**TABLE 4.4.** (*cont.*)

| Source of Scale, Range, and Direction by Group | Mean | Stand Devi |
|---|---|---|
| **Parental involvement in school organizations** | | |
| **A4 - PiSclOrg - Range = 0–5 (High = More)** | | |
| Choice applied, 1990–94 (Fall) | 2.4 | |
| Choice enrolled, 1990–94 (Fall) | 2.4 | |
| Nonselected choice, 1990–94 (fall) | 2.4 | |
| Choice private school, 1991–95 (spring) | 3.0 | |
| Nonselected choice, 1991–95 (spring) | 2.3 | |
| Low-income, MPS 1991 | 1.7 | |
| MPS control, 1991 | 1.9 | |
| | | |
| **Parental involvement in educational activities with** | | |
| **A5 - PiChild - Range = 0–15 (High = More)** | | |
| Choice applied, 1990–94 (Fall) | 8.7 | |
| Choice enrolled, 1990–94 (Fall) | 8.8 | |
| Nonselected choice, 1990–94 (fall) | 8.7 | |
| Choice private school, 1991–95 (spring) | 8.9 | |
| Nonselected choice, 1991–95 (spring) | 8.8 | |
| Low-income MPS, 1991 | 7.5 | |
| MPS control, 1991 | 6.9 | |
| | | |
| **Dissatisfaction with prior school** | | |
| **A6 - DisPrScl - Range = 8–32 (High = More** | | |
| Choice applied, 1990–94 (Fall) | 16.5 | |
| Choice enrolled, 1990–94 (Fall) | 16.4 | |
| Nonselected choice, 1990–94 (fall) | 16.7 | |
| Choice private school, 1991–95 (spring) | 13.6 | |
| Nonselected choice, 1991–95 (spring) | 15.4 | |
| Low-income MPS, 1991 | 14.4 | |
| MPS control, 1991 | 14.5 | |

ward the school and student success th[e]
degree of parental involvement in the s[...]
help for children at home, and parent [...]
Those results are also presented in tabl[e]
sults are provided in table 4.6.

### Parental Involvement

It is apparent that Choice parents we[...]
the prior education of their children

**TABLE 4.6**
Prior Test Scores

| | Applied Choice | | Low Income MPS | | MPS Control | |
|---|---|---|---|---|---|---|
| | R | M | R | M | R | M |
| *1990* | | | | | | |
| % at or above 50% of NPR | 23.3 | 31.1 | 27.2 | 36.2 | 34.8 | 42.8 |
| Median NPR | 29 | 31 | 32 | 37 | 37 | 42 |
| Mean NCE | 39.1 | 39.7 | 40.1 | 42 | 43.6 | 45.8 |
| Standard deviation of NCE | 15.9 | 18.9 | 17 | 19.2 | 18.5 | 20.2 |
| (N) | (262) | (257) | (2,136) | (117) | (3,157) | (3,130) |
| *1991* | | | | | | |
| % at or above 50% of NPR | 27.1 | 22.6 | 28.2 | 36.2 | 36.1 | 43.4 |
| Median NPR | 26 | 30 | 32 | 38 | 38 | 43 |
| Mean NCE | 37.5 | 37.9 | 40.2 | 42.9 | 43.7 | 46.3 |
| Standard deviation of NCE | 16.8 | 17.7 | 17 | 19 | 18.6 | 20.2 |
| (N) | (199) | (204) | (2,470) | (2,447) | (3,668) | (3,643) |
| *1992* | | | | | | |
| % at or above 50% of NPR | 28.2 | 31.4 | 28.2 | 35.3 | 36.6 | 43.2 |
| Median NPR | 29 | 33 | 32 | 38 | 38 | 43 |
| Mean NCE | 40.0 | 40.3 | 40.2 | 42.4 | 43.9 | 46.0 |
| Standard deviation of NCE | 17.6 | 19.5 | 17.7 | 19.5 | 19.0 | 20.7 |
| (N) | (234) | (226) | (2,839) | (2,801) | (4,024) | (3,991) |
| *1993* | | | | | | |
| % at or above 50% of NPR | 25.7 | 26.7 | 28.2 | 34.7 | 37.5 | 42.1 |
| Median NPR | 29 | 28 | 32 | 37 | 37 | 37 |
| Mean NCE | 38.0 | 40.0 | 40.2 | 42.0 | 43.3 | 45.2 |
| Standard deviation of NCE | 19.1 | 18.6 | 17.7 | 19.3 | 19.0 | 20.6 |
| (N) | (179) | (175) | (3,069) | (3,049) | (3,980) | (3,962) |
| *1994* | | | | | | |
| % at or above 50% of NPR | 27.4 | 23.3 | 25.9 | 34.4 | 35.3 | 43.8 |
| Median NPR | 26 | 25.5 | 32 | 36 | 40 | 44 |
| Mean NCE | 37.3 | 35.8 | 38.7 | 41.4 | 42.9 | 46.0 |
| Standard deviation of NCE | 17.4 | 19.0 | 17.5 | 20.0 | 19.0 | 20.9 |
| (N) | (146) | (86) | (1,940) | (1,208) | (4,127) | (3,204) |

R = Reading Scores; NPR = National Percentile Ranking; M = Math Scores; NCE = Normal Curve Equivalent proximately two points less satisfied with their prior schools, than were nonchoosing MPS parents. This was over one-third of a standard deviation difference and was statistically significant at the .001 level (see table 4.5).

In terms of individual items on the scale, on every dimension Choice parents were less satisfied than the average or low-income MPS parents. What is distinctive is that the factors with which Choice parents were most satisfied had little to do with the operation or outcomes of the school (textbooks and school location). On the other hand, the greatest dissatisfaction among Choice parents was with the amount the child learned and the discipline policy of the school. Further, in comparing the magnitude of differences between Choice and MPS parents, the differences between the groups were greatest for those items on which Choice parents were least satisfied.

Another indication of parental dissatisfaction with their prior MPS school was measured by a simple question that asked parents what grade they would give their prior school (on an A to F scale). Consistent with other expressions of satisfaction, Choice parents graded their prior schools considerably lower than MPS parents. That was especially true for the first-year Choice parents, who on a 0 (for F) to 4-point (for A) scale, rated their prior schools as a C (2.0). The second- and third-year averages for Choice parents were 2.5 in both years, but the last year average grade for prior public schools rose to 2.7. In comparison, the MPS low-income and total control group rated their schools at a 2.8 average.

### Prior Student Test Scores

The attitudes of parents toward their children's prior public school within MPS may be a reflection of the fact that their children were not doing well in those schools. In general, Choice students had prior test scores at or, in some years, below the low-income MPS students.[5] The test scores in table 4.6 are for the Iowa Test of Basic Skills (ITBS), which is given in grades 1–8. The tests used are the Reading Comprehension Test and the Math Total Test. The latter consists of three sub-

---

[5] Test scores were not available for all students in either group because tests were not given every year in MPS. Therefore, there were no tests for four- and five-year-old kindergarten students, and few for first-grade students. Lateral entry into higher grades could also have missed some students because primary testing was done in grades 2, 5, 7, and 10. For the few high school students in the MPCP, the tenth-grade test was excluded because very few of these students were tested and because students were entering alternative schools (schools for students contemplating dropping out of school or pregnant teenage students).

tests: Math Concepts, Math Problem Solving, and Math Computations.[6] The results reported are for the last test taken while the student was in MPS. The reason for using any prior test (rather than just the prior year test) is that I am trying to provide as complete a picture as possible of a relatively small number of Choice applicants with prior tests. The majority of those tests, however, were taken in the spring of the year of application (56 percent in 1990, 58 percent in 1991, 52 percent in 1992, and 54 percent in 1993).

In all five years, ITBS scores taken in prior public schools by students applying to the MPCP were significantly below the average MPS student taking the same test.[7] The scores were also below the low-income MPS cohort in each year. In terms of differences of means for the Normal Curve Equivalents (NCE), the differences between Choice and low-income MPS groups were significant at the .05 level for both tests in all years except the first year of the program. The differences were largest in the second year. The prior test scores for the last year, 1994, were the lowest of any cohort, especially in math. The absolute level of the scores indicates the difficulty these students were having prior to entering the program. The median national percentile for Choice students ranged from 25.5 to 31, compared with the national median of 50. The mean NCE, which are standardized to a national mean of 50, ranged from 35.5 to 39.8, which was about two-thirds of a standard deviation below the national average. *In short, the academic achievement of the Choice students was very low when they entered this program.*

## Combining Factors in a Multivariate Model

A more complete picture of those who applied to the MPCP can be ascertained by combining the variables we have discussed into a multivariable choice model. Such a model will capture the combined effects

[6] A number of the tests taken in MPS were dictated by rules for the federal Chapter I Program, which required testing in every grade in reading and math using a standardized achievement test. In 1993 the federal regulations changed from requiring total math testing, consisting of three subtests, to requiring just problem solving testing. With that change, MPS dropped Chapter I testing using all three subtests for some students. Fortunately, the correlation between the Problem Solving component and the Total Math score is .88. We were able to use an estimated regression model with Problem Solving estimating Total Math for students taking just the Problem Solving portion. The details of this procedure were described in Technical Appendix F of the *Fourth Year Report* (Witte et al. 1994).

[7] Because sample sizes were relatively small for choice students, the most reliable statistic in these tables is the mean Normal Curve Equivalent (NCE). Median and percentage at or above 50 percent National Percentile Rankings are included because these statistics are routinely reported by MPS. Because a number of students may be bunched together with small samples, both of these numbers are volatile.

of demographic characteristics, prior school experiences, and parental attitudes toward education. With some statistical assumptions and limitations, we will also be able to weigh the relative importance of various variables in the individual choice process.

A number of statistical models can be used for this purpose. One of the most straightforward is the log-linear (Logit) model, which allows one to convert the estimated effects of each variable into relative odds of having applied to the MPCP. The model is based on a comparison of Choice applicants and MPS families eligible for the MPCP, but who did not apply. The Logit model is the most commonly used technique for estimating this type of binary choice. The results of that model are provided in Table 4.7.

The results generally confirm the conclusions based on descriptive statistics described above. The final column of the table (Exp(B)) indicates the log-odds of having applied for Choice, after having controlled statistically for the other variables in the model. Thus, African Americans were 2.7 times more likely to have applied to the MPCP than the white reference group, after taking into consideration gender, distance to prior school, and so on. Hispanics were even more likely to be overrepresented, while Asians essentially did not apply, which also made the estimate very unreliable as indicated by the significance of the estimated coefficient. Girls, on the other hand, were slightly more likely than boys to have applied. All these conform to the data presented in table 4.2. The fact that distance was not significant also confirms the low priority of that factor when parents were asked what motivated them to apply (see table 4.3). Similarly, low grade levels, family income, mother's education, marital status, parental involvement, expectation, and satisfaction with prior public schools all confirm the findings described above.

The only contradictory result was the positive reading prior-test score, which was not quite significant by conventional .05 two-tailed tests of probability, but was close. Math was significant and indicated lower scores for Choice students. Thus the most conservative conclusion is that there was no difference in prior test scores between the Choice applicants and the MPS low-income control group.

### Nonselected Choice Students

To this point I have emphasized the characteristics of those who applied to Choice, not of those who ultimately enrolled; hence I have focused on the student/parent choice issue, not the selection by schools. I did

**TABLE 4.7**
Choice v. MPS Logit (Low-Income MPS Students Only)

| Variables | B | S.E. | Sig. | Exp(B) |
|---|---|---|---|---|
| African American | 1.003 | .234 | .000 | 2.726 |
| Hispanic | 1.323 | .267 | .000 | 3.755 |
| Asian | −1.297 | 4.975 | .794 | .273 |
| Other minority | 1.543 | .490 | .002 | 4.679 |
| Gender (Female = 1) | .20 | .109 | .067 | 1.221 |
| Distance from present school | −.032 | .028 | .259 | .969 |
| Prior math | −.018 | .007 | .01 | .982 |
| Prior reading | .015 | .008 | .06 | 1.015 |
| Grade level | −.268 | .053 | .000 | .765 |
| Income | −.033 | .012 | .007 | .968 |
| Mother's education | .254 | .083 | .002 | 1.289 |
| Marital status (Married = 1) | −.112 | .135 | .405 | .894 |
| Parental participation (High = More) | .079 | .024 | .001 | 1.082 |
| Educational expectations (High = More) | .251 | .119 | .035 | 1.285 |
| Satisfaction with prior school | | | | |
| (High = More) | −.163 | .023 | .000 | .85 |
| Constant | 1.621 | 5.064 | .749 | |

| | Chi-Square | Df | Significance |
|---|---|---|---|
| −2 log likelihood | 552.8 | 624 | .981 |
| Model chi-square | 202.0 | 15 | .000 |
| Goodness of fit | 600.1 | 624 | .747 |
| | | Percent correctly assigned: 79.53% | |

*Source*: Witte and Thorn, 1996, table 7, p. 206.

this because the issues must be separated. However, the second issue is also critically important, and, as we shall see, is apparently quite dependent on the structure of the program.

The MPCP specified random selection by schools in cases where grades were oversubscribed. Two possible exceptions for this were the exemption of siblings of students already in the school, and exclusion of disabled students. The crucial question is whether this procedure and these conditions produced significant differences in those who applied and those who were enrolled in the private schools.

The answer is generally no. A number of the tables already discussed include data on nonselected Choice students (referred to as Reject students).[8] I analyzed the success of the randomization process by analyzing differences of means on demographic and attitude and behav-

[8] These are defined as students not selected in the random selection who never enrolled in choice schools. They do not include students who enrolled in the MPCP from waiting lists.

ioral scale variables. Several of the demographic variables, while not significantly different between the groups, actually ran counter to a creaming selection process. For example, Reject students came from families with more income and a higher proportion of married parents than enrolled students. More African Americans were rejected than other students, but that is clearly because one of the all-black schools was very oversubscribed and nearly 100 percent of the applicants were black. Hispanics were more likely to be selected because in the last two years a large number of new seats opened up when Bruce Guadalupe opened a new school. There were no appreciable differences in the groups in the parent education and family size variables.

In terms of attitude and behavioral survey scales, there were only two substantive differences between nonselected and enrolled choice students: (1) on the higher importance placed on education for enrolled students (see table 4.4, scale A1); and (2) on the greater dissatisfaction with administration of the choice process for nonselected students (see table 4.4, scale T3). Both of these differences were statistically significant at the .01 level. The latter, which was a very large difference, was probably a natural reaction to not being picked. The former might indicate that if interviews were conducted with families during the process, those families placing less importance on education could have been discouraged from completing the application process. Once the application was filed, they were included in the data even if they withdrew before selection. Schools were also permitted to interview or make known to parents the requirements and expectations of the schools before or after selection. No data or systematic information exist on the extent or content of those practices, although as described in the next chapter, all schools did conduct some form of interviews. Regardless of why the difference in the importance parents placed on education existed, it may well be a factor in explaining achievement differences between Choice and Reject students in chapter 6.

*Summary and Interpretation*

Both descriptive and multivariate statistics reveal an interesting set of conclusions concerning Choice applicants. The overall portrait of Choice students and families was complex but very consistent over the years. The data clearly indicated that choice programs can be targeted toward poor families attempting to find an alternative to what they view as a poor educational environment for their children. The Choice students came from poor, mostly single-parent households. Similar to MPS parents, approximately 60 percent were receiving AFDC or public assistance. The parents also expressed considerable dissatisfaction with prior public schools, and, based on prior test scores, there was some evidence that their children were not doing well in those schools (both in relative and absolute terms).

Despite being poor, however, the Choice families were smaller than those in the comparison groups, thus providing an opportunity for parents to focus more on each individual child. In addition, the parents (especially mothers) were more educated, appeared to have somewhat higher educational expectations for their children, and were more likely to work at home with their children on education problems. Finally, these parents participated in their children's prior schools at higher rates than the average parent.

This portrait presents something of a paradox. The MPCP was specifically designed to provide an opportunity for poor parents to send their children to schools of their choosing, which they could not otherwise afford. Five years of very consistent data indicate that in this it succeeded. In addition, there were numerous indications that these parents were dissatisfied with the public schools their children had been attending and that their children were not learning as much as the average child in MPS. Thus one could argue these were exactly the types of families that should have access to an alternative source of education. One could also reasonably argue, however, that if these students and families remained in their prior schools, they could exercise considerable influence in attempting to improve those schools. Parents were educated, angry, involved, and had high expectations for their children. If engaged and given the opportunity, they could push the public system rather than leave it.

In terms of Albert O. Hirschman's famous concepts, the MPCP was a classic trade-off between "exit" and "voice" (Hirschman, 1970). Exit offered families an opportunity to move their children to what they believed would be a more favorable environment. But this prevented those same parents from staying in their public schools and trying to improve them through their insistence, their opposition, and their protests. As Hirschman cleverly observed, both exit and voice were designed to send signals to underlying organizations—signals that choice proponents believe can only be effectively transmitted by the exit option.

## How Do These Results Compare to Other Choice Programs?

In nearly all respects, evidence from the Milwaukee voucher program leads to the conclusion that the creaming of students in limited and targeted voucher programs can be avoided. This is an important finding, but we must be very careful to place it in the context of this program. One way to do that is to compare this result with evidence from other choice programs. The most appropriate comparison would be to other voucher programs—of which there is only one—and there is limited information on that program. However, studies of other types of choice programs, involving either public or private schools, are also quite useful.

### The Cleveland Voucher Program

Unfortunately, in America there is only one other publicly funded voucher program—in Cleveland, Ohio. The parameters of that program are included in the last column of table 3.2. Ohio used the Milwaukee legislation as a model. However, since it was enacted in 1995, the Ohio program followed Milwaukee's expanded program and included religious schools and prior private school students from the beginning. It also allowed families with any income to receive vouchers, although families below the poverty line received 90 percent of their tuition (up to about $2,500) while nonpoor families received only 75 percent. The first year of the program (1996) it was limited to kindergarten to grade 3 and to 2,000 students, with both limits to be expanded annually. The state Superintendent of Education was allowed to design the selection process based on income and prior private school status. Thus, the second voucher program in America was nowhere near as targeted or limited as the first.

The enrollment process in 1996 was extremely complicated, and students were still being enrolled in December of the first year. However, the results, with one twist, underscored the importance parochial schools and students already in private schools will play in a more or less universal voucher system. By December 1996, 1,994 students were officially enrolled in fifty-five private schools in the Cleveland voucher program. Of those schools, forty-six were parochial and thirty-five Catholic. Seventy-seven percent of the students attended parochial schools. The twist was that of the 454 who did not attend parochial schools, 352 attended two new nonsectarian schools started by the chair of the Commission that had recommended the program. The state Superintendent of Education had used his statutory authority to limit "prior private school students" to 25 percent (494).[9] Those slots were filled almost immediately, and, 80 percent of the prior private school students simply

[9] 42 percent of the enrollees were kindergarteners with no prior school. The state superintendent ruled that all of these students were to be considered public school students and thus did not count in the 25 percent limit (Ohio Department of Education, 1997).

continued on in their same schools — now with vouchers. Although suburban public schools were eligible to receive voucher students, none applied (Ohio Department of Education, 1997).

Subsequent data for the next two years confirmed these patterns. For the first three years (1996–98), fully 80–88 percent of the voucher students attended parochial schools under the Cleveland program (data supplied by Ohio Department of Education, October 1998).

Thus the majority of voucher aid in Cleveland was going to religious private schools. Without the two new schools that began as independent private schools, it appears that almost all the vouchers would have been used in parochial schools. There is also considerable support for the proposition that unrestricted vouchers would simply provide subsidy for students continuing in the same private school they had been attending.

A number of other programs are relevant for comparative purposes — two are also in the Milwaukee area and several others are in San Antonio, Texas. Both Milwaukee and Texas are home to privately funded voucher programs that include and primarily serve parochial schools.

## Privately Funded Voucher Programs

In a number of cities, private groups or foundations have established scholarship programs to aid students attending private schools. One of the first such programs was created by Patrick Rooney, CEO of the Golden Rule Life Insurance Company in Indianapolis in 1991.[10] That program was used as a model for numerous others, including the Partners for Advancing Values in Education Program (PAVE) in Milwaukee and the Community Education Opportunity Program (CEO) in San Antonio, Texas. These programs have low-income qualifications similar to the MPCP. To varying degrees, data exist on the applicants in each of these three programs.

The Golden Rule Scholarship Program began in Indianapolis in 1991. It is limited to reduced-free lunch qualified students who receive tuition grants up to $800 for half of their tuition expenses for private schools. The families must pay for with the other half. Applications are accepted

[10] A prior program in New York City was a personalized scholarship program funded by wealthy New Yorkers. It began in 1986, but as Paul Hill reported, the program "expressly seeks students who are minority, low income, threatened by family and neighborhood problems and struggling in school." There is very little quantitative data on this program, and it is clear that selection into the program was not based on an open application process as used in the other private voucher programs described below (see Hill, 1995).

on a first-come, first-served basis, but once students are in the program, they continue to be funded if they meet the income limit. Half of the grants each year are reserved for first-time private school students (including preschoolers). Nothing systematic is written about how schools select students or on what basis they may reject or expel students.

A study by Michael Heise, Kenneth Colburn, Jr., and Joseph Lamberti reported limited data on the participating schools and characteristics of voucher families. They reported that 80 percent of the private, choice schools responding to their survey were religiously affiliated and that 65 percent of the students in the program were Catholic. Most of the schools were located in Indianapolis core neighborhoods (Heise et al., 1995, pp. 116–117).

In terms of families, there appear to be a number of similarities with the MPCP. Although average incomes were not computed, in comparison to 1990 census data on households in Indianapolis and children in public schools, the grants were clearly going to poorer families. In addition, as in the MPCP, choosing families were less likely to be from families with married parents than public school nonchoosers. However, these differences were modest and the prevalence of single-parent families much lower than for families in either Choice or public schools in Milwaukee. Finally, and again anomalous with income and marital status, as in Milwaukee, parental education was considerably higher in choosing families (Heise et al., 1995, tables 1 and 2). Parental attitudes, parental involvement, and prior test score results were either not available in this study or there were no comparable data on nonchoosing families.

The PAVE program has existed in Milwaukee since 1992. It grew out of an alliance between the business community, private foundations, and the Catholic church (see chapter 7). It was designed to provide tuition scholarships, which were to be matched by parents, for low-income (185 percent of the poverty line) students to attend any private school in Milwaukee. Because parochial schools were the main recipients of scholarship students, the program has funded many more students than the MPCP. In its first year of operation, 1992–93, it received 4,094 applications to over 102 schools (compared to 998 applications for the MPCP). It awarded 2,089 scholarships. In 1993–94, an additional 2,200 applications were received (continuing students not included), and 2,370 students received scholarships (Beales and Wahl, 1995a, p. 6). Of these, only 31 percent were transfer students, while 69 percent continued in their prior school (Beale and Wahl, 1995a, table 2, p. 8). The matching scholarships averaged $542 for primary school and $1,321 for high school. Over 91 percent of the students attended religiously affiliated schools, with Catholic schools enrolling 60 percent of them (Beales and Wahl, 1995a, table 4, p. 10). In addition and as expected, many more PAVE than MPCP parents had heard of the program through their church (Beales and Wahl, 1995b, p. 55).

In comparison to the MPCP, both requiring matching tuition and providing access to religious schools obviously made major differences in selection into the PAVE program. However, in addition, the selection process was neither random nor was it on a first-come, first-served basis. The Reason Foundation report was very candid in describing this process.

> PAVE differs somewhat from other privately funded choice programs in the way it distributes scholarships. Rather than granting scholarships directly to students on a first-come, first-served basis, PAVE coordinates with a private-school administrator at each of the participating schools. . . . After selecting the private school for which they hope to receive a PAVE scholarship, applicants meet with the school's PAVE administrator. Assuming space allows, and the applicant meets school admission standards, if any, the applicant and school jointly fill out the remainder of the application and send it to PAVE. . . . The purpose of this arrangement is to give more discretion to local administrators who better know the circumstances of the families and students they serve. (Beales and Wahl, 1995a, p. 7)

Thus it is clear that schools were allowed to screen students carefully and select from within the low-income applicants. And since there was an oversupply of applicants in the program, unlike the MPCP, selection in PAVE must have been extensive.

Because evaluation of the PAVE program used many of the survey instruments we developed for the MPCP evaluation, comparisons can be made. Although reliable prior achievement data were not available for PAVE students, there were some interesting and revealing demographic differences between Choice and PAVE families. For some inexplicable reason, the researchers appointed by PAVE report that their survey did not ask for family income. While parental education was almost identical in the two programs (and considerably higher than the average MPS parent), the percentage of students from families with married parents was 43 percent in PAVE compared to 23 percent in MPCP (Beales and Wahl, 1995a, table 4). In terms of race, 46 percent of PAVE students were white, 37 percent black (Beales and Wahl, 1995a, table 3). This compared to 5 percent white and 73 percent black in the MPCP. The authors, were positive about this racial breakdown because it compared so favorably with the Catholic schools in Milwaukee, which they reported for 1993–94 as 92 percent white (Beales and Wahl, 1995a, Table 6, p. 14). Finally, PAVE parents had even fewer children than families in the MPCP. The average for PAVE was 2.3 compared to 2.54

in the MPCP and 3.24 in MPS low-income families (Beales and Wahl, 1995b, p. 56).

On other measures, there were a number of similarities between the MPCP and PAVE program. For example, both elicited much lower evaluations of prior public schools than nonchoosing MPS parents. Similarly, when asked why they applied to the programs, both sets of parents ranked educational quality and discipline in private schools as primary reasons.

A number of these results carried over to the San Antonio Children's Educational Opportunity (CEO) program. That program is also limited to free-lunch qualified students. It differed from PAVE in two ways: As in Indianapolis, selection was on a first-come, first-served basis, and only half the vouchers could go to existing private school students. As with both other programs, it provided only half of the student's tuition and included religious schools.

The profile of CEO program applicants is consistent with some of the characteristics of students in the other programs. The similarities were that parents in all programs were significantly more educated and were very dissatisfied with prior public schools (Martinez et al. 1995, tables 3, 6, 7, 10). In line with the PAVE profile, CEO families were more religious than nonchoosing families (Martinez et al. 1995, tables 8 and 10).

On two critical dimensions, CEO families were considerably different from MPCP families. On both measures of family income and the prospect of being on public assistance, CEO families were better off than nonchoosing San Antonio public school student families (Martinez et al. 1995, tables 2 and 10). Finally, in terms of prior test scores, the CEO students were much better students than their public school counterparts. For CEO students, Martinez, Goodwin, and Kemerer report average Normal Curve Equivalents of 47 and 46 on reading for CEO enrollees as compared to 27 NCEs for both scores for nonchoosing San Antonio public school students (Martinez et al. 1995, p. 86).

Thus the CEO results seem to imply considerable creaming off of the best families and students. Families had higher incomes, parental education, and parental involvement, and their children were doing considerably better in school before enrolling in the CEO program. There were indications of similar differences in the PAVE program, but PAVE evaluators reported no income information and they did not have access to prior test information.[11]

---

[11] Some evidence of prior achievement can be inferred from test results in private schools after one year in PAVE. The authors of the PAVE study report as evidence of success that for 106 seventh-graders, the average Iowa Test in Math was 54.1 NCEs and 55.5 NCEs in Reading. They compare this with MPS scores from my reports of 42.7 and 40.9 respectively. Although the authors use this as evidence of superiority of private

In summary, while there is mixed or missing evidence on family income, privately funded voucher programs clearly attracted religiously oriented families who wished to attend religious schools and were alienated from their prior public schools. These families had higher levels of parental education, involvement, and expectations for their children. The only available direct evidence on prior achievement (CEO) also indicated their children were superior students when going into these programs.

These differences existed *despite the fact that these programs were limited to low-income families*. What this means, of course, is that one must be very cognizant of the selection process. The number of applicants and their distribution in private religious schools further indicates the draw of religious schools in the private school market. Thus, based on evidence from these programs, we have to anticipate that if the income limitations and random selection criteria were removed from voucher programs, current private school users might well take most vouchers.

### The Milwaukee Metropolitan Public School Choice Program

In addition to the MPCP, there also exists in Milwaukee a more extensive and much more expensive program to allow public school students to transfer between public schools in the city and suburbs. This program, known by its legislative title number as the Chapter 220 Program, began in 1978 and was substantially expanded in 1987. With the goal of aiding metropolitan integration, it allows minority students from MPS to attend public schools in the twenty-four suburban districts, while white students from the suburbs may enroll in MPS. At present nearly 7,000 students annually take part in the program, with approximately 6,000 students going to the suburbs and 1,000 students coming into MPS.

A study comparing the selection processes in the voucher program with that in the Chapter 220 Program has already been published (Witte and Thorn, 1996). A key table from that study is reproduced as table 4.8. The logit model estimates the probability of nonwhite MPS students going to the suburbs under the Chapter 220 Program in 1991, relative to our random control group of low-income MPS students.

---

schools, given reasonable growth rates of 1 to 2 percent per year, the test scores actually suggest that most of these differences were due to prior achievement. Thus they strongly suggest, as did the description of the PAVE selection procedure (see p. 77 above), that better prior students were selected into the PAVE program (Beales and Wahl, 1995b, pp. 60–63 and table 10).

TABLE 4.8
Chapter 220 v. MPS Logit

| Variables | B | S.E. | Sig. | Exp(B) |
|---|---|---|---|---|
| African American | 1.463 | .161 | .000 | 4.317 |
| Hispanic | 1.771 | .212 | .000 | 5.874 |
| Asian | 1.939 | .249 | .000 | 6.955 |
| Gender (Female = 1) | .048 | .095 | .616 | 1.049 |
| Distance from present school | .355 | .026 | .000 | 1.427 |
| Prior math | −.005 | .006 | .471 | 1.996 |
| Prior reading | .021 | .007 | .003 | 1.022 |
| Grade level | −.013 | .044 | .772 | .987 |
| Income | −.001 | .008 | .866 | .999 |
| Mother's education | .102 | .078 | .188 | 1.108 |
| Marital status (Married = 1) | .347 | .117 | .003 | 1.415 |
| Parental participation (High = More) | −.066 | .026 | .01 | .936 |
| Educational expectations (High = More) | .18 | .105 | .087 | 1.197 |
| Satisfaction with prior school | | | | |
| (High = More) | −.089 | .021 | .000 | .915 |
| Constant | .178 | .647 | .783 | |

| | Chi-Square | Df | Significance |
|---|---|---|---|
| −2 log likelihood | 733.4 | 992 | 1.000 |
| Model chi-square | 626.9 | 14 | .000 |
| Goodness of fit | 807.1 | 992 | 1.000 |
| | Percent correctly assigned: 83.22% | | |

*Source*: Witte and Thorn, 1996, table 9, p. 208.

Hence the table is directly comparable to table 4.7 for MPCP students (which comes from the same study).

The conclusions are almost the exact opposite of the Milwaukee voucher program results and indicate that the suburban districts, when given the chance to select students, clearly creamed off higher achieving students from higher socioeconomic status families. Student applications for the program going to the receiving schools included extensive information on achievement and behavioral records of the student applicant — and it is clear the selecting schools made use of the information.

Being nonwhite is a condition of the program, and all minority groups are therefore overrepresented. However, the interesting result is that Asian students, who were nonexistent in the MPCP, are extremely well represented in the suburban choice program. Over 11 percent of the participants were Asians, compared to 2 percent of MPS students. The logit estimates are that they are almost seven times as likely to be selected than their numbers in the population would predict.

In contrast to the MPCP, but as we would expect, distance from the present school for Chapter 220 students was greater than for the average MPS student. Those in the program were simply farther away from their home — which was not the case in the MPCP. Prior achievement appeared to work in the reverse of the MPCP, but was consistent with private voucher programs. Math scores were not different, but those in Chapter 220 clearly had better reading scores. Higher mother's education, coming from a household where parents were married, and greater parental expectations for children all were associated with being in the transfer program. As with the MPCP, parents were very dissatisfied with their prior (MPS) public school. The only anomalous finding not consistent with the creaming hypothesis is that prior parental involvement among Chapter 220 parents seemed to be lower than for MPS parents who did not choose. It is unclear what this finding indicates, but perhaps Chapter 220 parents had simply decided against working with the prior public schools because of their very high levels of dissatisfaction with those schools.

What is important to note is that in the same city, with the same student and family populations, two choice programs produced very different results in terms of who participated. The smaller but randomly selected voucher program resulted in a nonelite student group; a similar choice program in terms of students,[12] but with no restrictions on school selection, resulted in a much more select student group. At a minimum this comparison suggests that the details matter. More likely, it provides evidence for the conclusion that, absent explicit restrictions, schools will be as selective as permitted.

## Conclusions and Implications

The first conclusion from this chapter is that a targeted voucher program can be constructed that prevents creaming off of the best students. However, in comparison to other programs reviewed, it is also apparent that that result is very dependent on the program context. Both the Cleveland voucher program and the evidence from privately funded voucher programs indicate the draw of private religious schools in utilizing vouchers. Whether this persists over a long period of time is not known. The expanded Milwaukee or Cleveland programs provide the possibility of determining which schools will be the ultimate beneficiaries. Some of the data already indicate most students in Cleveland go

---

[12] Both programs enrolled mostly minority students. The Chapter 220 Program was not open to white students, but on the other hand it did not contain an income restriction as did the MPCP. Thus the socioeconomic pool was probably similar except for race. Over 78 percent of the nonwhite students in 1991 qualified as low-income students.

to parochial schools. Milwaukee data from 1998 demonstrate the same pattern (see chapter 7).

Perhaps even more troubling were data from privately funded voucher programs and the Milwaukee Chapter 220 Program. Selection processes varied in the privately funded programs, but suburban public schools in the Chapter 220 Program had an opportunity to screen students before admitting them. The results were a fairly classic case of creaming off the best students and families. Although prior test scores were not available in the PAVE program, indirect evidence on test scores (see fn. 11 above) and a number of other indicators suggest private schools were quite selective in that program.

The point is that the random requirements of the MPCP seemed to produce a unique result. That result served the interests of poor families and students with educational problems. However, a close examination of other choice programs also indicates how fragile and even unlikely that result may be. This suggests that there is an enormous temptation for all schools to admit the best students they can, which conforms with common experience throughout the education system. It occurs beginning in day care and carries through to the top postgraduate universities. Why should inner-city schools be different? Why should schools in the inner cities, be they public schools with many poor students or private schools with few, not be expected to pick students with greater achievement potential and less likelihood of causing trouble?

# 5

## The Milwaukee Choice Schools

THE PRIVATE SCHOOLS participating in the MPCP were not a representative sample of private schools in Milwaukee or elsewhere in the nation.[1] However, the case studies and contacts I maintained with these schools over five years are still extremely valuable in understanding the character and diversity of private schools and their advantages and disadvantages when compared to public schools. They are also useful in describing the difficulties and successes that are possible in a difficult educational environment.

In describing these schools, I will stress three themes. First, these MPCP schools were extremely diverse in terms of fundamental mission, approach to education, governance structure, and quality. Second, independence was a hallmark of these schools, both in terms of external controls and internal day-to-day behavior—teachers were allowed to teach and administrators to administer. Third, I argue that it is a tragic mistake to romanticize these schools, expecting them to produce some sort of magic that will overcome the disadvantages their students bring with them to school. Because of the theater that surrounded the Milwaukee program, with literally hundreds of media stories focused on three or four schools, that is exactly what may have happened. At the end of the chapter, the reality of school life in the innercity will be highlighted again, as it was in chapter 1. I will document the school failures as well as the success stories; they are about evenly matched. Those failures serve not as general condemnation of the MPCP schools, but as a reminder that simply waving a wand over a school and calling

---

[1] The private schools that enrolled choice students in the MPCP from 1990 to 1995 cannot be taken as an adequate sample of all private schools in Milwaukee. First, there were only a few of them. Four schools enrolled most of the students on whom this study is based, and the maximum number of schools at any given time was twelve. Second, there were no traditional high schools in the program. For several years, there were two schools that enrolled high school students, but they were alternative schools that specialized in at-risk students or teen parents. Finally, the schools were all nonsectarian—they were not connected to a religious organization and did not have religious instruction. The latter point may seem to be the most important distinction, but it may not be. That is in part because all of the major schools in the program were religious schools at one point, and they continued to have religious personnel in the schools. While they did not have religious education, in the words of one of the sisters in a school, "We are not afraid to use the word 'God' in this school."

it private will not somehow solve educational problems that run much deeper.

## Participating Schools

In the summer of 1990, ten private schools expressed interest in and notified the Department of Public Instruction of their intent to participate in the MPCP. Seven schools enrolled students. The majority of students (317 of 341) were in five prekindergarten-to-eighth-grade schools: Bruce Guadalupe Community School, Harambee Community School, Juanita Virgil Academy, Urban Day School, and Woodlands School. The other two schools (Lakeshore Montessori and SER Jobs For Progress) had fewer students and served different educational purposes.

In the first year of the program, one school, Juanita Virgil Academy, went bankrupt and disbanded. When it ceased operations in February 1991, it had 71 Choice students remaining, most of whom ended up in MPS. In the second year of the MPCP, no additional schools admitted students. Beginning in the fall of 1992, five additional schools admitted a total of forty-seven students. Three of those schools were Montessori schools and one was a Waldorf school. All served elementary students, with the Montessori schools primarily serving students aged three to six. The Waldorf School of Milwaukee was four-year-old kindergarten through grade six. The other school, Learning Enterprises, provided alternative education for at-risk-high-school age students, much like SER Jobs. Another school, Messmer High School, applied to participate but was denied by the Department of Public Instruction because it was considered to be a sectarian school. That denial of certification was appealed and subsequently upheld by a hearing examiner. In 1993–94 an additional alternative high school, Exito, joined the program. Those twelve schools continued in 1994–95. But Exito, Milwaukee Preparatory (which began in the fall of 1995), and the Waldorf School all went out of existence in 1996 under acrimonious circumstances.

### History of the Choice Schools

For the five years of this study, four schools enrolled over 80 percent of the students and over 95 percent of those students on which we have detailed data—especially test data. Those four schools exemplify many of the themes of this chapter. Not coincidentally, they also share a common history. At one point, all were prominent Catholic private schools that for one reason or another gave up religious training well before the

MPCP began. Three of the four had been converted into community schools in the late 1960s when the church decided to discontinue subsidizing the schools and their dwindling Catholic enrollment. During the transition the Archdiocese was generous in allowing staff from religious orders who wished to remain to continue in the schools. A number did, but by 1991 only a handful remained.

The largest school, Urban Day, which enrolls close to 500 African American students, is located in the center of Milwaukee's inner city and is housed in what used to be St. Michael's Catholic School.[2] Two nuns, who have been with the school a total of almost sixty years, still work in and are mainstays of the school staff. Although the school had some modest cash flow problems in 1991, it has always been quite well funded with considerable extramural support and funding from the corporate community. The building is in excellent condition but lacks a playground. Representative Polly Williams' children attended the school, and Polly and one of her daughters were on the Board of Directors when the MPCP began.

Harambee Community School, also with an almost all-black student body, was also a prior Catholic school—St. Elizabeth's. It is located on the edge of the central city in the original building. The building was in modest disrepair in 1991, but was remodeled and repaired over the years of the program. When we conducted a study of the school in 1991, the principal was a nun who had been with the school for a number of years. She left several years later, but has since returned. Unlike Urban Day, however, when the MPCP began, Harambee had declared it was not going to open in the 1990–91 school year because of lack of resources. The creation of the program reversed that decision, and today it is financially on solid footing, with over 400 students.

Bruce Guadalupe was also dropped by the Catholic Archdiocese in the late 1960s, but remained as an independent Catholic school, first as Trinity School and then as St. John's. For most of those years, a very dynamic nun who was fluent in Spanish was principal. She retired at about the same time the school lost its lease and connection to St. John's. The school had specialized in Hispanic students since the 1970s and had a long history of bilingual education. When we first studied the school in 1991, it had moved to its third location in three years. It was housed in an ancient and decrepit building, St. Patrick's, on the near south side in the old Polish area of the city. That neighborhood, centering on Walker's Point, was a newly emerging Hispanic area, with a residual of older ethnic whites in the neighborhood and in St. Patrick's parish. When we began our study, the school was close to bankruptcy,

---

[2] See the maps in chapter 3, figures 3.2 and 3.3, for school locations.

with an academic year budget deficit as late as March of 30 percent of its operating expenses. It was also in a close to chaotic state. It had essentially been taken over by the emerging Hispanic United Community Center (UCC), which was located a block away. The resurrection and subsequent progress of that school, described in the next chapter, is one of the true success stories of this study.

The final school of the four main schools in the program, Woodlands School, also had a long-standing Catholic connection but of a much different sort. Until 1988, it had been associated for over 30 years with Alverno College — a Catholic teaching college. It had been a laboratory school in which Alverno student practice taught and Alverno faculty did research. In a very emotional and heated move, the college decided in 1988 that it could no longer afford the school. The school to that point had served a middle- and upper-middle-class white population on the west side of the city. With a considerably reduced enrollment, the school was taken over by parents and moved to a south side facility in the vacant St. Stanislas elementary school, approximately five blocks from Bruce Guadalupe. When we studied the school in 1991, it had stabilized, but there were still major concerns among its almost all-white parents and faculty.

The other schools had widely varying histories and clientele. The four Montessori schools that eventually participated and the Waldorf School were mostly white, middle-class schools. They charged substantial tuition and all stated that they joined the MPCP in part to try to integrate their schools. Some had been in existence for a long time, and others, such as the Waldorf School, for a relatively short period. None had significant religious histories. One school, Highland Community School, had been started in the heady 1960s as a true community school, meaning it was to mirror its neighborhood in terms of race, class, and gender. That meant that students were admitted proportionally to match the demographics of children in its boundary area. One of the original founders was still in the school as a teacher after having been principal and director for a number of years. It initially served as a contract school with MPS; however, as voucher payments increased, it also joined the MPCP.

The three alternative schools, SER Jobs for Progress, Exito, and Learning Enterprises, varied considerably from each other. SER Jobs emerged out of an Hispanic-run adult learning and training center, which had declared bankruptcy the year before the MPCP began. It started a middle school and high school program for students who were essentially being offered a last chance alternative before dropping out. Most of the students and administrators were Hispanic. The school was in a converted department store on the near south side, several blocks from Woodlands and Bruce Guadalupe.

Learning Enterprises was run by a black woman and had been in existence several years before the MPCP began. The basic idea for the school was that it provided day care for babies in the same building as high school instruction for their parents (mostly mothers). There were also other at-risk students in the program.

Finally, Exito School was started in 1992 as an at-risk middle school by a man who had been principal of Bruce Guadalupe in September of 1990, but who had left the school under adverse circumstances in November 1990. He had also had some experience with at-risk students in MPS prior to working in private schools. The tragic story of that school and that man, as well as another original school, Juanita Virgil Academy, will be described below.

### Student Enrollment, Admission, and Expulsion

Students in the MPCP ranged in age from four to nineteen years old. Of the 620 students enrolled in September 1992, 531 (86 percent) were in four schools. In 1993, the number rose to 612 of 742, but the percentage declined to 82 percent. For 1994–95, 697 of 830 (84 percent) were in the largest schools; 69 students (8 percent) were in two alternative programs; and the remaining 64 students (8 percent) were in one middle school at-risk program, four Montessori schools, and the one Waldorf school.

The racial composition of Choice students by school was mixed. In 1994–95, the student body of four of the schools was almost all African American. Four others were predominantly African American (above 70 percent). One school was 93 percent Hispanic and the remaining three schools were mostly white. This pattern was partly the result of conscious specialization on the part of schools (for example, African American cultural schools and a Spanish bilingual school) and partly the result of location. The implications of this segregated pattern of enrollment will be discussed below.

The admission process varied considerably in most schools between students admitted as Choice students and those admitted as tuition-paying students. In general, following staff interviews, Choice parents were given the MPCP application and the selection procedures were explained to the parents. They were also given information on the school, including written and verbal information on expectations for parents and students, and were often asked about learning or other disabilities. However, the formal admission procedures imposed on other students were often, although not always, foregone. Because several of the main MPCP schools were in very dire financial straits, in the first several years they admitted every MPCP applicant who qualified.

Admission procedures for nonchoice tuition-paying students were usually much more extensive and may be more indicative of what might happen under an unrestricted voucher program. In traditional (as opposed to alternative) schools, these procedures included an interview of parents and students by the principal. For transfer students, submission of prior records (usually last year's report card) was required. Many of the schools also stressed with prospective families the obligations of parents to be involved—both in school activities and in fund-raising. Because of the constant need for funds, most schools had formal fund-raising goals for families and they were often required to sign contracts to contribute either hours or money in addition to tuition. Whether or not Choice families were exempt from such agreements became a point of contention in several schools.

In some schools, there was also an interview and other observation of the student by their future teacher. In one school, this process was termed "living-in" for a day and included informal and formal testing as well as three separate parent interviews. In another of the major schools, admission decisions were the joint responsibility of the principal and a parent-dominated admissions committee. The same committee reviewed each student at the end of the year for re-admission.

Unfortunately, the MPCP statutes and rules did not require schools to report expulsions or non-readmission of students. Thus we could compute attrition, but not why that attrition occurred—or specifically whether it was voluntary or not. However, there is no evidence that formal expulsion of MPCP students or others—was high in any of the major MPCP schools. These schools were accustomed to working with difficult children and often saw it as their mission. On the other hand, when we asked the directors or principals whether they would be willing to give up their independent powers to expel students if it became a requirement of the MPCP, they all said no. As one principal put it when asked to describe the procedures for expelling students:

> We work with children and (parent) conferences—but after so many chances we ask them to take the child out. Also, if parents don't cooperate. Why would we take their money if we can't help them? We are a private school and they aren't abiding (by) that. We have leverage and we would not give that up. We rely on parents. We have an orientation session so that they know what we expect of them. We would not give that up.

Other principals described a similar process, also focusing on the parents. One told me very concisely: "We really expel the parents. If they won't work with us, won't come in, won't respond, won't cooperate, then we ask them to take their child elsewhere." Expulsion procedures for Choice students were no different than for non-Choice students. And, as noted above, it was clear that principals would not give up the possible leverage over parents that it provided — even though it was seldom used.

## School Organization and Governance

With one exception, all the schools in the MPCP were independent of any higher authority, political or religious, and thus they were all self-governing units. Beyond that, however, the patterns of governance varied considerably across schools. Some schools represented wonderful models of governance, empowering various combinations of stakeholders, while others were run by their owners or directors without any formal documents or any external oversight. The one nonindependent school was Bruce Guadalupe, which by 1991 had been taken over by the United Community Center (UCC). The UCC Board and governing structure were very instrumental to the running and ultimate success and prosperity of that school.

Most of the schools had formal boards of directors, including parents, community members, and often patrons or their representatives. They also usually had formal by-laws, ranging from detailed constitutional handbooks to smaller sets of procedures and lists of responsibilities. In most schools, parents were well represented on boards and key committees. In all of the schools except two alternative programs, there were also formal parent organizations (often several due to fund-raising obligations). In several schools, elaborate and well-functioning committees were also utilized. The most common were finance, fund-raising, and personnel. But some schools also had committees for student admission and expulsion, curriculum, buildings, and even marketing.

Finally, the schools varied considerably in terms of their financial accountability procedures. The majority employed some variant of accounting and outside auditing procedures legislated for nonprofit organizations. Because of separation of church and state, private schools did not have to abide by such procedures, but most did. Unfortunately, as we will see below, those schools that went bankrupt had little in terms of accounting and no external audits. They also had the weakest, if any, governance structures.

## Finances

Neither the legislation nor subsequent administrative rules governing the evaluations on which the primary data for this book are based specified detailed financial analysis or accounting of private school finances. However, during case studies, we gathered financial data and asked about school costs and income. While the evidence is not as systematic as it might have been if financial reporting had been part of the formal evaluation, several conclusions were quite obvious. First, as in other characteristics of the private schools in this program, financial conditions, tuition levels, and accounting and audit procedures varied enormously between private schools. Second, for most private schools enrolling significant numbers of students in the program, the initial voucher amount ($2,446) was very attractive relative to tuition charged to non-Choice students. Third, the 1995–96 voucher price ($4,600) was not only attractive relative to tuition, but also compared very favorably to school expenditures per pupil. In short, by 1995–96, most Choice students represented a profit for the private schools in which they were enrolled.

When the MPCP began in 1990, four of the original seven schools were in serious financial difficulty. One had declared bankruptcy the year before and had reorganized. Another, Juanita Virgil Academy, went bankrupt during the first year of the program. Two others were rumored to be on the verge of closing in the spring of 1990. With the exception of Juanita Virgil Academy, all of these schools are in much better financial condition today.

The eleven private schools in the program in 1992–93 received their funding from a range of sources. Nine of the schools had tuition-paying students in addition to MPCP students. Five schools also had contracts with MPS to serve the needs of preschool or at-risk children. All the schools but one also engaged in fund-raising of one form or another. Parental involvement was required in most schools, connected to fund-raising and other activities such as chaperoning trips, helping with materials, and working on facilities projects.

Tuition and fees varied widely. Most schools based their charges on a ten-month year. In 1990, in the three largest schools tuition for the first child was between $650 and $930, and all had significant reductions for the second and third children. The one middle-class white school (with twenty-five Choice students) and several of the Montessori schools charged considerably more (up to $4,000). Our interviews clearly indicated that tuition for the large black and Hispanic schools was set relative to the Catholic school network in the city. Analysis of that market revealed that in 1991, the average cost of a Catholic elementary school in Milwaukee was just below $1,000 for the first child, again with significant reductions for more than one student (Witte et al., 1993).

The range for Choice schools studied in 1992–93 was from a low of $680 dollars to a high of $4,000. Two schools charged under $1,000 for the first child, three were in the $2,500 to $3,000 range, and four were over $3,000. One school had a sliding scale based on ability to pay that ranged from $50 to $4,000. Most schools had some scholarship money to defray tuition costs for poor families and all but one continued to have sibling reductions. Increases in 1993–94 ranged from 0 percent to 66 percent. The highest increase was in the lowest tuition school in 1992–93. Tuition and fees ranged from $1,080 to $4,000 in 1993–94, the last year for which we have financial data.

These estimates fit within the averages for private schools in the country. A study of tuition payments in 1993–94 found that the private elementary school average was $2,138, with Catholic schools averaging $1,628 and nonsectarian schools averaging $4,693 (Choy, 1997, table 60).

Estimates of operating expenses were available for the main schools in the program. The 1990–91 estimates based on interviews and analyses of available balance sheets were between $2,500 to $3,300 per child for the kindergarten to eighth-grade schools. The revenue side of the balance sheets included money raised through voluntary contributions and fund-raising resulting in cash (bingo, pizza sales, etc.). However, the costs of parent or volunteer time for school activities (classroom help, chaperons, etc.) were not included as expenses. It was not possible to get an accurate estimate of Montessori schools because students as young as three were often there only for part of a day. Some students also stayed for afterschool care. Similarly, at-risk schools had a range of students in varying situations, and it was not possible to compute the exact costs.

The voucher amount can be compared either to tuition, as an indicator of the attraction of Choice students for the school, or to operating costs to determine the effect of vouchers on balance sheets. For five of the tuition-charging schools in 1993–94, the MPCP voucher of $2,985 was at least a break-even amount relative to tuition charges. For three schools (only one K–8) the voucher represented a net loss compared to tuition. For the two schools with only MPS contract and Choice students, the Choice students generated several thousand dollars less than the contract students. For the school with variable tuition, it was not clear where the voucher fit. Since the vast majority of students applied to the lowest-tuition schools, the voucher price from the beginning of the program made most applicants financially attractive for the schools.

In terms of operating costs, the 1993–94 voucher came close to covering costs for three of the four main schools. However, in the last two years of the program, because vouchers were set to MPS per pupil state aid, the voucher price increased considerably due to a steep increase in state aid for all Wisconsin schools. Although we have no detailed cost per student information after 1993–94, unless there was a startling increase in expenditures by the schools, the $4,373 voucher in 1994–95 and the $4,600 voucher in 1995–96 would have covered the costs of all the schools. For the largest three schools, there would have been considerable profit.

*Staffing*

Information on MPCP school staffs was obtained from case studies of the original schools in 1991 and of new MPCP schools in 1993. In addition, each year we tracked staff turnover rates, new personnel rates, the demographic composition, and the types of certificates teachers held for each of the five years.

A senior teacher in one of the original schools, when summarizing the staff in the school, highlighted a number of the problems and advantages of the personnel in the set of private schools. She said (and I paraphrase because the interview was conducted with notes):

> There are essentially three types of teachers here: those who are here from a commitment to the school and the mission — either as religious teachers, or past students or parents; another group who can afford to work for these wages because they have other family income (implying a spouse); and a third group of young teachers, right out of college, who could not find jobs elsewhere.

That description was appropriate for all the original schools and most others, and clearly applied initially to all the schools with substantial numbers of Choice students.

That description also indicates both the advantages and problems these schools faced in terms of personnel. Obviously there was a cadre of very dedicated people at the center of most of these schools. They endured low wages, low benefits, and other problems because they believed in the school and its mission of educating low-income minority students. There was also another group of teachers, almost all white and from the suburbs or well-off sections of town, who were either very effective teachers (if they remained) or were looking elsewhere. In several schools, administrators talked of the shock effect on white suburban teachers, and either "establishing a match or not." If not, they were either let go or quit.

Finally, there was a group of young, very energetic teachers who were flush with the enthusiasm of their first teaching job, but who could not live decently on the salary. In one school, three such young women told our interviewers that they had been forced to move back in with their parents because they not could not afford an apartment on their own.

That group, while often very effective with the children, also contributed to the very high turnover rates. Thus, while staff turnover was not always a bad thing, and new teachers could be a boon to a school, those advantages were offset by the constant loss of those teachers and the continuing acclimation of new personnel to the school.

These scenarios highlight the turnover problem — for both teachers and administrators. Partly as a result of turnover, the schools often had new teachers in the schools each year, some even joining in the middle of the year. Teacher turnover in 1991–92, the first year we could track it, was an extraordinary 36 percent. In that second year of the program, 56 percent of the personnel were new hires, up from 36 percent in 1990–91. A third of the new personnel, however, were filling expansion positions, due in part to the MPCP. Both turnover and new personnel rates in subsequent years decreased considerably. From 1992 to 1995, the staff turnover rate in all schools averaged 20 percent and the new personnel rate declined to an average of 22.6 percent.

The initially high turnover and new personnel rates obviously affected staff seniority. Seniority of teachers at the time of our case studies was extremely low, as indicated in table 5.1. In the first year of the program, only 22 percent of the teachers had been in their schools over three years. In one of the schools, which was completely in flux during the 1990–91 year, twelve of twenty-four total personnel in the school were added between January and June of 1991. This meant that not only were teachers hired on a crash basis at the beginning of the year, but also during the year. Seniority of teachers in the schools added since 1991, as well as reduced turnover in the original schools, produced more stable staffing in subsequent years. The average teacher seniority from 1992 to 1994 was 6.5 years, compared with 4.2 years in the original five schools studied in 1991. Twenty-six percent of the teachers had ten or more years of experience in their current schools. Seniority data were not collected in 1994–95. Obviously, this still differs considerably from the seniority levels in most public school systems.

Certification data are also presented in table 5.1. In 1990–91, in the original five schools studied, 62 percent of the teachers had state certification. In the additional six schools we studied later, only 54 percent were state-certified. Of those 54 percent, 21 percent had both state and specialty certification. Forty-three percent had just specialty certification. The high percentage of specialty certification was due to the addition of four Montessori programs and a Waldorf school. These schools have national and/or internationally recognized certification programs for their relevant pedagogical specialties. For the combined nine schools reporting in 1994–95, 64 percent of the teachers were Wisconsin certified, with 20 percent having other certifications.

**TABLE 5.1**
Teacher Seniority and Certification in Choice Schools, 1990–95

| | Less Than 1 | 1 | 2 | 3 | 4 | 5–9 | 10 or More | Mean Years | (N) |
|---|---|---|---|---|---|---|---|---|---|
| Seniority, 4 schools, 1990–91 | 14% | 22% | 18% | 20% | 4% | 8% | 12% | 4.2 | (50) |
| Seniority, 6 schools, 1992–94 | 0% | 19% | 15% | 15% | 19% | 7% | 26% | 6.5 | (28) |

| | Wisconsin | Other States | Just Specialty | Added Specialty | None | (N) |
|---|---|---|---|---|---|---|
| Certification, 4 schools, 1990–91 | 62% | 8% | 6% | 0% | 24% | (50) |
| Certification, 6 schools, 1992–94 | 54% | 0% | 43% | 21% | 4% | (28) |
| Certification, 9 schools, 1994–95 | 64% | 0% | 20% | 3% | 13% | (66) |

Turnover of administrators was also high in the earlier period, but also stabilized somewhat in later years. In 1990–91, in two of the schools, the principals or executive directors had been in their positions for only two years. In one school, the principal had been with the school for sixteen years and had been principal for thirteen. In another, a new principal came in 1990 and resigned part way through the year. For 1991–92, for the six participating schools, there were new principals or directors in three of the schools (one of the appointed principals had been a teacher the previous year). For the continuing schools in 1992–93, there were two new directors or principals, although one of the previous principals remained with the school as executive director. For the twelve schools participating in 1993–94, the average seniority of fifteen school administrators was 3.7 years as the year began. Two were beginning their first year, three were beginning their second year, and three more their third. The longest tenures were eight, fourteen, and fifteen years. Again in 1994–95, there were four new principals or administrators in the twelve schools.

With a few exceptions, staff turnover was not connected with dissatisfaction, but with pay and benefits. As one principal put it, concurring with the teacher cited above: "The teachers who stay here for a long time are either very dedicated or can afford to stay on what we pay." During our case studies in 1991 and 1993, teachers and administrators went out of their way to describe how they enjoyed the small class sizes

they taught, the autonomy they had in the classroom, the usually conge-
nial atmosphere in the schools, and the administrative support they received in disciplinary matters.

These attitudes conform well with national studies comparing public
and private schools. Teacher classroom autonomy, disciplinary support,
and involvement in school governance, as in national surveys reported,
are much higher for private school teachers than for teachers in public
schools (Choy, 1997).

In 1990–91, several of the schools were suffering from recent changes
in affiliation and location. One had moved into its existing building in
September 1990 (as had Juanita Virgil Academy). Another had moved
two years earlier, but many of the parents were not happy with the
location of the building. An unsuccessful effort to acquire adequate
funds to build a new building was abandoned during the 1990–91 year.
Both of these schools were historically affiliated with religious organizations, and being on their own created financial hardships. Moving
meant a loss of students, teachers, and administrators, as well as the
normal difficulties associated with changing facilities.

These problems stabilized in 1991–92. One school was able to open
a new facility in addition to its existing school. The other schools remained in their same locations. The new schools that joined the MPCP
in 1992–93 were generally more affluent schools, with higher tuition.
Although small in size, they have had very little turnover.

The racial composition of teachers fluctuated as schools replaced
teachers and expanded, and as new schools entered the program. In the
first year, the staff in these schools was predominantly white (75 percent) and female (89 percent). In subsequent years, the teaching faculties became more diverse. For the four years from 1991 to 1995, the
percentage of white teachers declined to 66 percent. Conversely, the
number of male teachers increased from 11 percent to 24 percent. Both
of these trends were probably due to the increasing financial security of
the MPCP schools.

## Curriculum, Pedagogy, and Classes

The MPCP attracted an eclectic set of schools. In addition to the type
and grade differences already noted, there was also considerable curriculum and pedagogical diversity. The four K–8 schools were all distinct, but in many respects the curriculum of these schools was similar
to the curriculums in most public elementary and middle schools.
With one exception, where two grade levels were combined in classes,
grade structures and teacher assignment were standard. One of the
schools offered Headstart classes and two others had pre-five-year old

kindergarten. The curriculum was relatively rich; music and/or dance classes were offered in each school, usually twice per week. Two of the schools had daily Spanish classes for most students (grades three to eight in one school), and French was offered in another school. Three of the schools also had computer labs and classes that utilized computers. Computer training occurred on average twice per week and in the higher grades students also used computers on their own for individual projects. One of the schools had health classes for all students once per week. All of the schools had physical education, usually twice per week.[3]

Two of the schools stressed African American culture, and one of the schools stressed Hispanic culture and bilingualism. Although this type of cultural emphasis has created intense debate around the country, in these schools the approach was positive. We never saw evidence of teaching cultural superiority or separatism. The emphasis was on understanding differences and understanding the history and accomplishments of various racial groups. In addition, although classrooms and hallways were decorated with multicultural themes, and historical and cultural examples were more prevalent than in schools without a specific cultural emphasis, instructional patterns, exercises books, and materials were not that dissimilar from other schools. For example, in one first-grade class, a male black teacher on two successive days taught lessons using the books*The Little Engine That Could*, and *The Red Hen*. Reforms and revolutions may come and go in education, but teaching children how to read is still done with materials and texts that survive these upheavals.

The schools seemed also to have adopted some of the aspects of their prior subcultures as Catholic schools. Students often wore uniforms (with students routinely complaining and everyone else approving); classroom discipline was clear; corridor and communal conduct was closely monitored.

The final school was primarily white, but had an increasing percentage of minority students, partly as a result of the MPCP. The school was modeled on an English day school with a focus on individual learning and responsibility, and on common values.

All four of these schools operated with standard classroom organization. The majority of the instruction was group instruction, with teacher-led learning and discussion. Each of the schools allowed considerable

---

[3] Recess and physical education facilities were relatively poor in the schools. One school had easy access to a city park for recess, one relied on a blocked off street, and two others used asphalt playgrounds, with some wood chips and playground equipment. All the schools had some indoor space for physical education, but it often served multiple purposes (cafeterias, detention areas, etc.).

variation among classrooms based on what the teacher believed worked best for his or her students. Although teachers met regularly and the schools were small enough that informal contact was continuous, only two of the schools had formally established curriculum plans in 1991.[4] Teachers expressed consistent satisfaction with their independence and with the administration that was there to aid, not control them. In short, the schools allowed teachers to teach. The only problems we noted were some new teachers who were left on their own because the schools lacked the curriculum resources of public school districts.

Our research teams conducted classroom observations in almost every classroom in the main MPCP private schools (fifty-six classrooms). Classroom observation was both ethnographic and quantitative. As researchers observed the rooms, they also coded activities based on five-minute time intervals. The average class was forty-five minutes, including nine observational periods. Researchers recorded information on what was going on, what materials and tools were being used, the discipline in the classroom, the active-passive nature of interchanges, and how learning was organized.

Our observations indicated that classes generally were conducted in the ordinary fashion. Children spent most of their time listening to the teacher, doing seat work, and engaging in nonacademic activities (in transit, bathroom, moving from one activity to the other, getting materials, fooling around, etc.). Teachers spent most of their time lecturing or instructing, and monitoring or reviewing students' work. Lessons were focused mostly on skills (e.g., reading and math problem solving) with considerable time spent on understanding. In general, texts and materials were not the focus of instruction — the teacher was. Most of the instruction was in whole class settings (83 percent of the classes were whole class for at least half the period). Approximately half the time was spent on instruction as opposed to monitoring, reviewing student work, or other activities. Whether students comprehended the material was somewhat difficult to judge. Our observers estimated a lack of comprehension for 26 percent of the classroom periods. This was offset by 44 percent of the periods in which students comprehended the material for more than half the class.

Time-on-task, meaning that students were doing what the teacher and instructional environment dictated, was very high. Thirty-seven percent of the students were on task the entire period, 40 percent for more than

---

[4] One of the schools without a curriculum plan initially in the fourth year hired as principal a past and retired MPS administrator who had also been a curriculum specialist. He agreed to stay for several years specifically to build the curriculum at the school. As of this writing, he is still there, has completely revised the curriculum, and has remained past his initial agreement.

half the period. Discipline in the classroom was modest, with disciplining students occurring less than half the time period in 82 percent of the periods observed. No disciplinary activity was observed in 14 percent of the classes. The vast majority of classes were either fairly clean or clean (61 percent). Physical and social order was also high. Eighty-eight percent of the classes were physically on the ordered as opposed to the chaotic side, and 81 percent were orderly in terms of the social setting. Most of the classes were quiet (62 percent); the rest perhaps appropriately noisy.

In our interviews, teachers repeatedly stressed that they enjoyed the small class sizes and the autonomy they had in the classroom. As expected, classes were more orderly in the lower grades. Also the numbers of students in each classroom declined in higher grades. It was not unlikely to find thirty or forty students in the kindergarten and grades 1 to 2 (but split into multiple classes), but only fifteen in grades 7 and 8.

Teachers complained about the lack of resources and the pay. In one school, teachers also consistently complained about the influx of new students and the shifts in administrative leadership. During the period in which we did our case study, the same school had a problem with discipline in part due to the arrival of a substantial number of contract students. MPS contracts with private schools to work with students with special problems, including behavioral problems. One of the schools had accepted thirty-eight contract students (approximately 20 percent of the school enrollment) four weeks before we arrived in April. These students were creating a great deal of difficulty in the school. Parents went to the extreme of having a parent on duty in the office to monitor the disciplinary conditions in the school. Four of these students were returned to MPS just prior to our visit.

We also felt that in one school the instructional time was very short. This was due to a late start, early finish, and a relatively long lunch break. The late starting and early ending times were directly the result of busing arrangements. Students not from the neighborhood rode yellow buses. Given the long, divergent routes, some of the most distant students were on buses for over three hours each day. To accommodate this, the instructional time was shortened.

What we observed in the classroom covered the range of teaching and learning. I personally observed a gifted teacher who had been instinctively teaching mathematics for fifteen years in almost the exact manner now being recommended by the National Council of Teachers of Mathematics. She was deservedly featured on the *Sixty Minutes* news show that covered the MPCP. I also witnessed classes taught by tired teachers who could barely hold the class together. In some classrooms there was regimented, strict discipline that required hands on desks and complete silence. In others there was joking and exchange, students split into nonsilent groups, working in organized chaos. In others, when there were problems of discipline or arguments, time-outs were often called. In one school, these sessions, as well as a systematic program that stressed individual and communal values, was called "time for living."

The four Montessori schools were all relatively small, and all of them followed the basic Montessori pattern of student responsibility for setting up activities, cleaning up, and replacing learning aids. There was an emphasis on individually selected and paced activity. All of the schools used many of the traditional Montessori learning devices and aids. The atmosphere was generally quiet and restrained with an emphasis on the child, not the teacher.

There were variations, however. Some of the schools emphasized stricter discipline and more rigor in terms of timing of activities (characteristic of the European Montessori movement). Schools also varied in terms of the amount of group activity that took place. In one school, for example, activity was essentially split between individual student activities and group activities such as story telling and singing. One school used the traditional Montessori bell ceremony to end class; others did not.

Montessori education, structured around diverse learning areas and individual student actions, was not always implemented effectively, however. One of the schools was quite chaotic when we observed it, and time on task was judged to be very low. In most Montessori classes we observed, individual activities (such as number games, painting, and working on word notebooks) were approximately fifteen minutes in length, including meticulous cleanup and returning objects to their proper place. In this school, attention spans were five to ten minutes, and teachers often were doing the replacement and cleanup. Rather than facilitating, encouraging, and asking students about activities, the teacher and aide were often trying to keep order.

Waldorf schools are based on the philosophy of Rudolph Steiner. It is unclear how authentic the Milwaukee Waldorf School was to Steiner's teachings, although several principles did seem operative in the school. The first was to stress a holistic conception of education that did not separate children's traditional educational activities (e.g., readings, math tables, writing) from other learning and skill development (e.g., music, art, working with one's hands, cooking, and eating). Second, teaching combined intellectual, physical, and spiritual activities to assist learning and was individual and child-centered, with teachers guiding students. Steiner preached that children should not be made to enter the adult world prematurely; thus, play and childhood activities played a major role in child development. Finally, teachers were to remain with their students throughout their years in the school.

The Waldorf School structured its learning around traditional classrooms. Classroom activity was varied between group practices and individual work. Art and music were pervasive in each classroom. Artwork often matched stories and other more traditional educational activities throughout the year. Exercises were often combinations of the physical and intellectual, such as the teacher calling on a student to provide an answer to a multiplication table by throwing the student a ball.

Food was also part of the educational experience, with some types of foods (such as red meats) frowned upon or forbidden, and others (such as cooked carrots) exalted. The meals served at the school followed traditional Steiner teachings and were seen as another extension of the holistic education process. Families were encouraged to follow such practices at home, although the staff understood there would be diversity in this.

Although the Waldorf philosophy places considerable importance on individual development, the theories also are quite precise in the evolution of children's skills across the full range of experiences. Teachers told me that by the end of this year, children should have mastered certain educational skills as well as progressed to an ability to use different types of art forms and materials, and physically to have achieved proficient levels of motor skills. The evolutionary development also included social relationships and changes in play habits.

Staff organization and interaction was an essential ingredient of the Waldorf School. The school was "teacher run." The administrator responded to teacher decisions and primarily handled administrative issues (enrollment, advertising, finances, supplies). The staff met once each week from 1:00 P.M. to 7:00 P.M., during which the teachers shared a common meal and covered whatever topics were necessary. Because the school had only been reorganized in its present form several years before, it had not yet had to face the traditional Waldorf practice of granting teachers a one-year sabbatical when their class graduated.

The Waldorf staff readily admitted that Waldorf education was not for everyone. The most common complaint was that the holistic approach did not permit enough concentration on basic educational skills. Because students (including Choice students) were admitted only after group meetings to explain the philosophy, tours of the school, and discussions with teachers and staff, parents generally understood the methods and practices before they enrolled their child. Thus attrition from the school was mostly due to moving or inability to pay the relatively high tuition and fees, and not to pedagogical disagreements.

The two alternative high schools participating in the MPCP differed considerably from each other. One of the schools initially ran one large high school class for students on the verge of dropping out of public school. In 1991–92, they also added a middle-school classroom for at-risk students. In 1993–94, they decided to focus on the middle school, and some of the high school Choice students transferred to the other alternative MPCP high school. In both schools, grades were given in courses, but the emphasis was on obtaining high school equivalent credits, not grades.

The second alternative school had a range of students, but focused on teenage mothers. There was a large, well-equipped day-care facility connected to the school and located on the premises. Mothers were able to drop off their children and attend classes, but never be far away if needed.

The first school essentially ran a single class, with the teacher covering a range of topics. There had been a new teacher each year, and each time I visited, attendance was very low (five to eight students with fall enrollments of twenty-five to thirty). Instruction focused on basics. There was considerable use of individually guided computer and non-computer instruction. The latter may have been a carryover from the adult literacy training that had been done for years in the school.

The second school was much larger (six teachers in 1992–93) and was organized more as a traditional high school with specialized-subject teachers and classrooms. In a number of classes we observed, there was a conscious effort to relate the materials to the lives of the students. For example, in one science classroom we observed a hands-on lecture/discussion focusing on toxicity, with continuous reference to problems faced by and hazards to the children of the student mothers.

The school had a friendly, laid-back atmosphere. Teacher–student relationships seemed as important as what was being learned in terms of education skills. Everyone was involved in counseling that included sex education, problems of future pregnancies, and discussion of sometimes very difficult home relationships. The staff seemed to have high morale, and there clearly was considerable communication among them. There was no staff turnover between 1992 and 1993, and four new positions were added to the school in 1993.

Both of these alternative schools had, by some standards, obvious deficiencies. Instruction was considerably below grade level; overall attendance was not nearly as high as normal MPS high school attendance; and there was major attrition from the MPCP. These schools, however, were working with specialized student populations. In one sense, for one of the schools at least, any attendance and any accumulation of credits could be considered an advance over students being out of school completely. In the other, external home and family responsibilities meant that the students needed a unique high school environment, which this school provided.

The most important conclusion to be drawn about the schools in the MPCP was that they were diverse. They served different student populations; their approach to education varied considerably; their classroom and staff organization was not uniform; and their systems of governance were unique in form and quality. In other words, these independent schools represented a range of different choices for parents and students.

From our classroom observations, what we came away with more than anything else was a feeling that there was no single formula for teaching, but rather a diversity of styles that fit the class and the teacher. What we know with confidence is that the teachers appreciated the opportunity to select their own style.

## Relationships between Private Schools and MPS

One interesting feature of these schools was their relationship with the Milwaukee Public School System. The degree of cooperation and coordination that exists between public and private schools is often overlooked in the heated controversy over choice. There are a number of formal and informal connections between public and private schools in Milwaukee. For example, private schools may enroll a student who has undiagnosed special needs or learning disabilities. The schools often coordinate with MPS to determine the best educational course for the student. That might mean enrolling in an MPS school, enrolling in a specialized private school, or simply acquiring extra services from MPS while continuing to be enrolled in the private school.

In addition to these instances of informal cooperation, MPS has for many years contracted with private, nonsectarian schools to provide services for specific student populations. In accordance with state law, these contracts are limited to services for either preschoolers or at-risk students. In 1991–92, three of the MPCP schools had contract arrangements with MPS; in 1992–93, four of the eleven schools also had contract students; and in 1993–94, the number increased to five out of twelve schools. These yearly contracts seem to be beneficial to both parties. Although MPS offers as wide a range of choices of different forms of schools as any district in the country, and is constantly touted as an example of public school choice, specific students in individual schools may need programs and attention that are not available in that school. Contract arrangements provide an added alternative to serve the needs of those students.

There are several potentially negative aspects of the contracting arrangements from the perspective of the private schools. First, MPS controls the yearly contracts, and schools could become financially dependent on them. Second, following an agreement with the Milwaukee Teachers Association, at least one MPS union teacher must be on site. Several schools cited instances where the MPS teacher did not fit in with the style or work arrangements in the schools. This created animosity and conflict because the schools had no real authority over the teacher.

The effect of contract arrangements on the MPCP was not inconsequential. The contract with MPS was based on a per-student charge and was contingent on curricular approval and performance criteria. It also provided private schools with approximately $2,000 more revenue per student than the MPCP payments in the first three years of the program. This difference may have led MPCP schools to limit the number of Choice students in favor of contract students. The price differential was also cited as one of the reasons some qualifying schools chose not to participate in the MPCP. In the last two years of the program, with vouchers above $4,000 per year, the differences between contract reimbursement and vouchers was negligible. That may have led to the increase to eighteen schools enrolled in the MPCP in 1995–96.

## The Effects of Economic Scarcity

The scarcity of economic resources ironically produced a number of positive effects for Choice schools. Schools of all varieties constantly argue that they are underfunded, but at least initially, the largest MPCP schools were in fact underfunded. Certainly in the first few years of the MPCP, most of these schools were operating with underpaid staff relative to public schools and modest curricular or other support help. They were using cast-off materials and equipment and in general enjoyed almost none of the frills of public schools. Their playgrounds were public parks, or in two cases, barricaded-off asphalt streets adjacent to the schools—hardly an ideal arrangement and obvious enough to warn off most middle-class parents.

But there was also hidden value in this economic scarcity. Parental involvement, for example, was not something parents were merely encouraged to do; rather they were required to do it as a condition of school membership. In addition, many of the extras in the schools, such as field trips, special programs, and summer-school activities, required parental participation or they did not occur. That involvement led to a constant parental presence, and consequently parents often became a real part of daily school activities. Numerous teachers and one principal started as parent volunteers. Not surprisingly, the parents also played a major role in governing the schools.

Another positive aspect of economic scarcity was that these schools were more or less forced to stick to basics because they did not have the luxury to indulge in nonessential learning activities. The obvious downside was that the students may have missed enrichment activities or had them delivered in a nonprofessional manner. On the other hand, when they did occur, they were extremely important to the school and even the community. For example, one school held elaborate graduation ceremonies for their eighth-grade class. Even when this school was in the depths of financial and organizational chaos in the first year of the program, an elaborate ceremony was put on by members of the community and parents, with younger children giving remarkable dancing and singing performances accompanied by local community musicians.

Finally, for those who support business–school and other community-linked partnerships, the economic travails of these schools necessitated those links—and often they were impressive. This included organized fund-raising and solicitation, of course, but it also gave businesses a role in the school if they so desired—and many did. Several of the schools appointed a business representative to their boards, and, as I outlined above, those boards had real decision-making powers.

In the next chapter I will outline the positive effects of the MPCP, and I will highlight how the program financially aided many of these schools. Although I did not have the opportunity to observe the subsequent effects of that improvement, one of the ironic drawbacks may be that the economics of scarcity will be lost.

## Issues

The MPCP led to a number of positive outcomes for the Choice schools, as described in the next chapter. However, several issues flow directly from or are related to the findings described above. Three issues need to be addressed: segregation in the schools; cost comparisons between public and private schools; and the failure of several MPCP schools.

### Segregation

The schools in this program were often racially segregated, more so than the average MPS school. Two of the largest schools were essentially all black and one almost all Hispanic. The alternative schools also tended to be predominantly black or Hispanic. The small and most prosperous schools were almost all white, and there were very few Asian students in any of the schools.

There were several mitigating factors, however. First, the schools had these characteristics before the MPCP and, if anything, in the white schools at least, the program facilitated racial diversity that was explicitly sought by the schools. Second, as I noted, there were no obvious negative consequences of racial and ethnic cultural emphasis. The programs were meant to provide a positive portrait of blacks or Hispanics without negative connotations for other races.

Finally, in these schools and in Milwaukee in general, there are substantial numbers of minority parents and educators who honestly are not concerned that their children attend integrated schools. Representative Williams not only holds this view, but consistently lambastes the public schools and state policy for wasting resources on busing that could be used for schools (public or private) in her almost-all-minority district. She routinely begins presentations with drawings in which circles represent schools and lines represent where students are bused. These spider web diagrams effectively introduce her arguments for discontinuing busing.

I personally disagree with this position, still clinging to the very rich and positive advantages to be gained from an integrated, multicultural learning environment. However, sensible people may differ with this position, and it is impossible to ignore the negative consequences of implementing integration policy. Given the racial imbalance that has developed in some of our largest school districts, it does seem questionable to focus so much on integration when as a result the overall education of minority students suffers.

## Cost Comparisons

In the relevant sections above, I described school costs in a general way, relying on quite broad cost-per-student ranges. I emphasized that we did not have access to detailed and systematic cost information. I also noted the presumably wide variation in costs per pupil across participating schools and perhaps over time as the voucher subsidy increased. The usual assumption by voucher advocates, citing the MPCP, is that private schools operate at considerably lower costs than public schools (Peterson and Noyes, 1996; Greene, Peterson, and Du, 1996; Peterson, 1997). However, for Milwaukee, no independent cost data, comparative or otherwise, were presented in their research.

A recent study of costs by Henry Levin, who is not a voucher advocate, compared the voucher payments to costs in the MPS (Levin, 1998).

Levin's study acknowledged the considerable cost differences between school levels and used the appropriate comparison — MPS K–8 schools. In the comparison, he factored out a number of other costs, including exceptional education and transportation, on the assumption that the private schools do not educate disabled students and are reimbursed for transportation costs in addition to the voucher payments. To a degree the assumption may be overstated in that the private schools do educate some very slow learners who might well be labeled "learning disabled" in the public schools.

However, even if Levin's figures are adjusted somewhat, his conclusion that the attributed cost of MPS K-8 schools was $3,469 while the voucher payment to private schools was $4,373 would not vary that much (Levin, 1998, p. 384). Thus even if we scale back Levin's estimates, the claims of voucher advocates that private schools in Milwaukee are half the cost of public schools are an obvious distortion of the comparative costs (Peterson and Noyes, 1996; Greene, Peterson, and Du, 1996; Peterson, 1997).

Perhaps more important to this debate are the dynamics of the voucher environment. The private schools are able to hold costs down for two primary reasons: (1) they pay their staff below public school levels; and (2) they can do this because they are not unionized. The first of these was clearly a constant irritant in the schools and was a major factor in the high staff turnover rate. Thus, if funds were available, there would be both internal pressure and an external rationale for increasing salaries and benefits. In addition, these few independent schools are currently of little interest to teacher's unions because they would have to be unionized one at a time. However, if vouchers become substantial and raises are possible and likely, unions may well propose unionizing a large set of voucher-receiving schools. This is even more likely if and when parochial schools are added. In that event, one could propose a union organization covering a hundred or more schools. With vouchers approaching public school expenditure levels, that would be an appealing target for union organizers. Thus cost estimates using beginning voucher levels and a highly restricted set of schools may be of little use in understanding the long-term dynamic costs of an open-ended voucher system.

## Private School Failures

During the first six years of the MPCP, three schools failed in midyear, and one other school, the Waldorf School of Milwaukee, closed its doors during the summer of 1996. The first school failure, Juanita Virgil

Academy, occurred in the first year of the program in February 1991. Although the scheduled case study of that school was never done because of the closure, we were able to investigate the problems at Juanita Virgil. The other failures and closing of the Waldorf School occurred in 1995–96 after we stopped collecting data, so the only information on those schools comes from Department of Public Instruction documents and newspaper accounts.

There is little quantitative information on Juanita Virgil Academy, which enrolled seventy-one MPCP students in the fall of 1990. This is because that after the first semester, the school petitioned the Department of Public Instruction to be removed from the program. The reason given was that they wanted to reinstate religious training in the school. The petition was granted; however, several weeks into the new semester the school filed for bankruptcy and closed. The majority of students entered the MPS.

Based on several visits to the school, parent surveys and interviews, and a long interview with the executive director of Juanita Virgil, it was clear that the school was in turmoil from the beginning of the year. The principal was new, having arrived from an unsuccessful term as a principal in the MPS. When I talked with her in September 1990, she said she did not have knowledge of the school's curriculum, knew very few of the teachers, and had no knowledge of any standardized testing. Although classes had been in session for several weeks, she said, "I just arrived."

She did not last long. The executive director indicated she fired the principal in late October. Another administrator had left earlier after a conflict with both the principal and executive director. Although an existing administrator took over day-to-day leadership, there was no indication that a new permanent principal was hired before the school withdrew from the program and later closed.

Parents complained about transportation, food service, the lack of books and materials, space problems, overcrowded classrooms, cleanliness, and a major lack of discipline. One parent wrote on the back of our survey:

> I'm extremely dissatisfied with the academic performance of the school, administrator changed November, 1990 without notification to parents, spanking of children, poor quality atmosphere, transferring child back to public school, January 1991, lack of cooperation from school administration, in regards to curriculum and after school activities—never met registration promises.

There were also allegations of theft and mismanagement of money; however, no external financial audit was available. There was no governing structure in the school beyond an "advisory board," consisting of three friends of the executive director. And it never met. During my interview with the executive director (after the school closed) she specifically stated that she never worked with executive boards because they can "take over and even fire the executive director."

According to the executive director, the school closed due to a lack of funding. She also said they asked to withdraw from the MPCP because tuition-paying parents were not happy with the school situation and that they had lost their Bible classes in qualifying for the MPCP.

In summary, there is no way to interpret the Juanita Virgil experience in a positive light. It failed as a school in the middle of the year following what had to be a questionable educational experience for over one hundred students in the prior months. Recommendations in our evaluation reports for required school governance, financial accountability, and state assessment and reporting consistent with that required of public schools were meant to avoid the Juanita Virgil experience in the future. At a minimum, parents should be assured in making their school choices that a school will be able to last through the year and provide an adequate educational environment for their child.

Two other schools failed in midyear in the 1995–96 school year. One of the schools, Exito, had been an at-risk school in the program for two and one-half years. The principal of that school had begun at Bruce Guadalupe in the fall of 1990, leaving the school suddenly in November. When Exito closed, the principal was charged with several criminal counts, including drug charges and embezzling funds. He fled to Michigan but was returned to Wisconsin. He is currently serving a prison sentence of four and one-half years. The second school, Milwaukee Preparatory, had begun in 1995. The founder and director was also charged with mishandling public funds and fraud. He fled to Mississippi where he was arrested. However, he was later found innocent in a fraud trial. Three hundred and fifty-six students were enrolled in Exito and Milwaukee Preparatory. At best the students had a major disjunction in their education that year, and at worst they lost the better part of a year's education. The state lost an estimated $390,000 in voucher funds, which were paid for education that never occurred (*Education Week*, 21 February 1996, p. 3; *Milwaukee Journal Sentinel*, 21 February 1996, p. B1).

Finally, in the summer of 1996 the Milwaukee Waldorf School closed, with some of the parents trying to continue by forming their own school. There was clearly acrimony between parents and staff, and the number of students had declined since we did a case study of the school in 1993.

The lessons of these failed schools, with four of the eighteen schools that enrolled MPCP students over the life of the program collapsing, underscores two points. First, as with many other aspects of the private schools, extreme variation in quality characterizes inner-city private schools much as it does inner-city public schools. Second, these failures should at least produce a pause for those who champion private schools as the unqualified salvation for the woes of inner-city education. And that point needs elaboration.

## Conclusions

This chapter introduced a number of themes. First, private schools vary a great deal in their form and mission. And they vary in their quality. Second, all of the schools were extremely independent both in their governance and in their day-to-day operations. Third, our study of schools led me to conclude, as with other aspects of vouchers, that private schools need to be evaluated in realistic ways, set within the inner-city context. Doing so makes me suspicious of dramatic claims that private schools hold some sort of magic key to solving the long-standing problems of inner-city education in America.

### Variance and Innovation among Private Schools

A wonderfully refreshing aspect of private independent schools is their unique and diversified nature. The schools we studied differed considerably from one another and often excelled in their specific educational format. They were the theoretical equivalent of Charter schools, although they were even more independent than most Charter schools across the country.[5] John Dewey would have been proud of the systemic innovation represented by the array of schools in the MPCP.

However, a nagging thought also troubles me and it is not a criticism of the schools per se. The specialized, independent approaches of these schools are generally effective for a handful of schools. But our inner-city areas must educate hundreds of thousands of students. Does it

---

[5] In an ironic twist, in October 1997, the state legislature passed legislation modifying the state charter school law to allow the city of Milwaukee, led by its pro-voucher Mayor John Norquist, to charter schools without any involvement of MPS. This was an exception to the general charter school law that required charters to be granted by school district boards. The charter schools were to receive approximately $1,000 more per student than in the MPCP. All of the existing MPCP schools applied for charter status, and four were selected. Because selection as a charter school would have invalidated a $1 million contract for MPS students, Bruce Guadalupe, one of the four, as of this writing was considering withdrawing its application for a charter.

make sense to rely on a very large number of stand-alone, independent schools to try to educate so many students? And, since one of the unique characteristics of these schools was their manageable size, can we afford to replicate these small schools on a systemwide basis?

If 400 students was a manageable size, and most of the MPCP schools were much smaller, 250 schools would be required to educate 100,000 students. That is nearly double the current number of public schools in Milwaukee. Each school would be independent of the others, and uniquely managed and run without centralized support, guidance, or oversight. The point of market-based approaches to education is to eliminate or severely reduce centralized "system" control. However, scaling up to a complete system of independent schools would be a daunting task. But, at least in theory, that is the most common image of the market-based model of American education.

### Lessons

A number of attributes of the private schools we studied were worthy of emulation. The governance systems varied from school to school, but all operated very independently, so decision-making powers were real. In addition, they all involved a combination of parents and staff, and usually also community members. For the most part they worked — a far cry from the impotence of most organizations involving our public schools. Even in the most successful of the Chicago Local School Councils (LSC), the most radical reform in school governance in this century, there are severe system restraints that constrain powers and deflate enthusiasm of elected LSC volunteers. A large proportion of LSCs are simply ineffectual (Ryan et al., 1997). Moreover, most school districts have no local school governance at all.

A second positive lesson, with some offsetting cautions, is the degree of independence given the teachers and administrators in these schools. In general, teachers were allowed to teach. They were not required to follow externally prepared curriculum guides, teaching methods, subject time requirements, or testing procedures (other than required by the MPCP). School administrators were allowed to lead, and that included hiring and firing of teachers and disciplinary actions toward students. In addition, reporting requirements and paperwork were minimal.

### A Reality Check

As we have seen, and will return to in the next chapter, the MPCP aided most schools and in several cases not only saved the schools, but provided the foundation for truly remarkable changes. However, the MPCP did not change the underlying conditions in which these schools operate, and it did not prevent a number of truly miserable schools from entering the program. Neither point is trivial.

In one of the first interviews I conducted with a principal in one of the original MPCP schools, when I asked him what was his most serious problem, this is what he said:

> The hardest problems are to find a safe, stable environment at home and at school. If either are not safe or stable they (children) are in trouble, at-risk. Most of our kids come from dysfunctional families — alcohol, drugs, and physical and sexual abuse. Children can't follow academic pursuits when affected domains are in disarray.

At the time he said these words, his school was in disciplinary chaos, partly due to MPCP students, but mostly due to out-of-control MPS contract students.

But his comments were not isolated. Everywhere we went, we heard and witnessed similar problems. We also know that many of the schools were wary of parents who failed to live up to school expectations. The concept of expelling the parents captured that point very well. Moreover, no one we spoke with used words like "miracle school," or claimed to have the key to solving the array of problems that arrived with the students each morning.

Failed schools will likely be a price that will have to be paid in voucher programs. The cash nexus can be very strong if salaries remain low, vouchers high, and schools essentially free from regulation. Administrators and teachers will not necessarily be certified or be required even to have prior experience. That will lead to some schools being run without professional leadership.

For some choice advocates, this winnowing process is natural and the parallel to failing businesses of all kinds. But if that is the case, at the very least the rhetoric needs to reflect the reality. Vouchers will not always aid all students, and voucher schools will not always be the shining, innovative havens from the public school system that advocates for choice make them out to be. At times they will be run by incompetents or criminals, and the result will be lost months or even years of education for innocent children whose parents simply made the wrong choice.

The good counterargument is that the same types of schools exist in public school districts, but the schools remain open. Clearly, public schools need to address that issue through more stringent evaluations and consequences for incompetent administrators and poor teachers. Mechanisms for closing failing public schools should be explored. However, that does not change the reality that failures also afflict private schools. They simply may be dealt with more easily.

# 6

## Outcomes of the Milwaukee Voucher Program

THIS CHAPTER contains a healthy portion of quantitative data on the outcomes of the Milwaukee voucher program. It also includes some nonquantitative results, which may stay longer in the minds of the reader, but unfortunately have less serious impact. What troubles me is that most of what I suspect is important about education is not easily adaptable to quantitative analysis because it occurs in a quiet way, over a period of time that is not subject to rigorous observation.

For example, consider a school as a place — a place that provides a space for a child simply to be safe and secure; or a place to learn discipline, social behavior, and respect; or a place that provides a chance to catch up or to recoup lost time, or build skills in basic subjects; or simply a place to be happy and then, perhaps, to be happy about learning. I have been in schools like this, and I know they produce these results, but I cannot produce quantitative evidence to support that.

Even more frustrating, if we were to consider theoretical measures of educational outcomes, our first preferences surely would be more functional and relevant than achievement test scores. The thought that education should prepare one for a successful economic and social life is not a romantic idea — it is sensible and what most parents want for their children. The rewards of educational attainment are higher lifetime income and all that is correlated with it.

Unfortunately, the analysis of most public policy programs cannot deal with these broad, long-term results — and that is also the case with the Milwaukee Parental Choice Program. In some other ways, however, the program offered a very promising experimental study. It offered open application so that we could analyze the characteristics of families who might apply for vouchers. We saw the results and cautious conclusions to be drawn from that process in chapter 4. We were able to monitor and track changes in schools, not always with the hard measures we might prefer, but with some uncontestable stories that are lasting. We also know a lot about what parents thought of the program, the schools their children attended, and the reasons some of these parents decided to abandon the program and the private schools.

In terms of individual student achievement, this was a multiyear experiment that allowed the tracking of individual students; thus we do not have to rely on the standard cohort measures. Prior measures of achievement (i.e., standardized test scores) existed for the Choice students and the MPS random sample of students. This allowed us to control for prior achievement and apply value-added models, which assess not what student cohorts (which may change in composition) achieve, but rather the amount of added learning that respective school experiences produce for individual students.[1]

The program also required random selection from among applicants (with modest caveats), and this ostensibly allowed for a natural experiment, controlling for unmeasured selectivity bias — either the result of families or schools. Unmeasured selectivity for families means that after we measure and try to control for all those variables that might affect learning, some factors remain and are not measured. The same problem applies to schools if they are allowed to screen and select students. Also of relevance for this study, we cannot dismiss the possibility that those unmeasured factors are correlated with application to or selection by private schools of Choice applicants. The previous two chapters explored family and school selection in various choice settings, and it was clear that selection was a crucial aspect of both policy design and achievement outcomes.

The presumption implied by random selection was that students and families who were accepted and those who were rejected were similar on these unmeasured factors, and thus a comparison of Choice and Reject students would be a pure experimental comparison. Unfortunately, as we shall see, the experiment failed for reasons that will be beyond the control of most other random assignment, education choice policy experiments. That problem will be further addressed in the final chapter.

A second useful comparison group consists of nonchoosing but choice-eligible MPS students. This comparison group becomes more important as the program expands because in the market-based theory, with uni-

---

[1] There are many examples of cohort analyses that make claims about changes in educational outcomes based on changes in cohort achievement measures. One especially egregious example in the choice debate is the "Miracle in Harlem" case of District 4 in New York City. A great deal of undoubtedly positive change occurred in that district, which was the poorest school district in New York. However, what caught everyone's attention was when the *New York Times* proclaimed remarkable changes in achievement scores of the district. They based their claim for this "miracle" on changes in cohort scores. They never considered the possibility that the student population in District 4 had changed considerably — and clearly for the positive as students were drawn from around the city to the new magnet-type schools that had been created. The issue is not that something positive happened in this Harlem district; it is that the leading newspaper in the world did not understand the problem of translating cohort scores into claims of educational gains (see Fliegel and MacGuire, 1993).

versal vouchers, all students would become choosers. The question of the adequacy of comparison groups and the randomization process have become the center of controversy over test score results. Several other researchers, using the data we made available in 1994 on a web site, have reached conclusions different from mine. Their conclusions tend to favor students in the private schools, ranging from very extreme claims (Greene, Peterson, and Du, 1996) to quite modest differences from my own (Rouse, 1998). The details of those controversies are discussed in detail below.

The outcomes of the Choice program are multidimensional. In the end, that will make for less parsimonious conclusions than many would prefer. The progression of the chapter is from the effects of the MPCP on schools, then on families — as conveyed by parents, and finally on students. The first section focuses primarily on the benefits of the program for private schools; the second on parental involvement and parental attitudes toward private schools and the Choice program; and the last on student achievement and attrition from the program.

## Outcomes for Schools

The theory and rhetoric surrounding vouchers dwell on the effects parent choices have on schools — both public and private. Those favoring vouchers see the influx of money and new customers as a salvation for stressed private schools, especially in the inner city. They also proclaim that competition will improve public schools. Theories opposing vouchers also foresee effects on schools. They predict a monetary windfall for private schools and a further opportunity to expand their preferential selection practices due to the increased demand. They also predict that remaining public schools will lose resources, and that segregation by achievement, economic class, and race will increase.

The problem is that few of these theoretical claims deal specifically, if at all, with troubling details of program characteristics, the scale of voucher programs, or the organizational baggage and historic traditions of education in America. There are some exceptions, such as the work of Paul Teske and his colleagues who have analyzed several choice programs with an eye on the problem of scale and the marginal effects of even small increases in choice (Teske et al., 1993). Jeffrey Henig has made the most forceful argument that the metaphor of choice seems to carry its own validity even in the absence of any detailed theory or consistent evidence (Henig, 1994).

My contributions to this debate will be modest. I find it essentially impossible to determine the effects of the MPCP on Milwaukee public schools. The effects on private schools are mixed, but generally positive, but they are not the effects that many choice advocates may be looking for. What happened in Milwaukee was that private schools, many under considerable financial stress, received money, and that money improved their schools. In several cases, that allowed the schools to survive as options for families — some of whom would not have been able to take advantage of that option without vouchers. Those are not trivial results in the microworld of this program. But it is very difficult to see how those results predict what would happen to the full system of schools in a universal voucher system.

### Effects on Public Schools

Ideally, an analysis of a voucher program would include a study of the impact of vouchers on both private and public schools. There are unfortunately several research problems that make such a study difficult if not impossible in the Milwaukee case and possibly for a much larger and less targeted voucher program as well. First, in the case of Milwaukee (and now Cleveland), the program is simply too small to have discernible direct effects on the school system. There was no doubt that with the hundreds of media presentations about Milwaukee, usually prefaced by anguished examples of failures of the public schools, the program provided a bully pulpit for public school critics. This may have had indirect effects on MPS. However, given that the number of students enrolled barely reached 1 percent of the MPS enrollment, direct competition for students was not likely.[2]

The problems of determining the effects of vouchers on public schools are not only a question of program sizes, however. Large inner-city school districts are constantly reforming, experimenting, and reorganizing their schools and systems, often in reaction to the political pressures they experience.[3] The effect is that change is ongoing, and trying to

[2] During the first years of the program, the reverse may have occurred. MPS were overcrowded and very early in the semester in each of the first two years, the MPS administration wanted lists of students enrolled in choice private schools, because a number of those students had also signed up for MPS schools. The administration wanted to know who enrolled in the private schools so they could release seats of Choice students and give them to other students.

[3] I was critical of the methodological and statistical problems of John Chubb and Terry Moe's extremely visible book, which surely pushed the choice debate to the top of the educational agenda (Chubb and Moe, 1990; Witte, 1992). However, my most serious criticism of their book has to do with their apparent misunderstanding of the fundamental politics of big-city school districts. They argued that political accountability somehow stifles change and creates bureaucratic ossification of school districts. My experience, and

causally distinguish routine changes from those specifically tied to the onset of a voucher program will be very difficult if not impossible.

### Effects on Private Schools

As described in the last chapter, there were numerous positive effects of vouchers on the private schools in the program. Financially, they became more secure. Personnel turnover declined for both teachers and administrators. Staff diversity improved in the first several years of the program as, presumably, higher wages allowed schools to hire and retain male and minority teachers. Finally, the physical plants, equipment, and materials in the schools improved, with one school building a new, modern building that was expanded further in 1998. In several cases, including Bruce Guadalupe and Harambee, the financial turnaround was dramatic—from the brink of bankruptcy to financial solvency.

Although there was major curriculum development and improvement in one of the largest schools, in general the effects of vouchers did not produce radical changes in how the schools operated, taught, or were organized. One of the reasons for this was that they were either quite traditional elementary schools or they were already specialty schools with prescribed pedagogy, such as Montessori or Waldorf schools. In several schools the improved financial conditions allowed the schools to enhance programs (language, arts, music) or add technology (usually computers) to the instructional program. These positive effects on private schools were marred by the bankruptcy, closing, and criminal allegations against administrators in three schools. Several other schools that joined the program after the legislative changes in 1995 have repeatedly been rumored to be on the verge of closing (Molnar, 1997).

Given tacit court approval, the MPCP will expand to a maximum of 15,000 students, including religious schools and students enrolled previously in private schools. Given expanded state aid, the voucher will increase to well over $5,000. As that happens, there is little doubt that vouchers will strengthen many more private schools in Milwaukee. Certainly four inner-city Catholic elementary schools, which the church has indicated would be closed, will survive.[4] In addition, the PAVE program

---

that of others who have been in these districts, is exactly the opposite—they try everything that comes across their desks, trumpeting the changes they inaugurated under their regime (Cuban, 1990). What is striking about the Chubb and Moe argument is that they seem to disregard an enormous amount of political science research, as well as common sense, that suggests this type of activism is exactly what we would predict from political regimes under stress (Smith and Meier, 1995).

[4] When the court ruled that the 1995 changes admitting religious schools to the pro-

either will no longer be needed, and the supporting philanthropy can be used for other purposes, or PAVE will be able to shift its focus to students who do not qualify for vouchers.

However, as we will see in the next two chapters, it is not clear how these benefits will be distributed across private schools, or how the general results can be interpreted. The expanded program, moving quickly toward a universal voucher system, could be seen as continuing to provide vital options for disadvantaged children, or ultimately as a subsidy for middle- and upper-class families to support their children going to specialized or religious schools they probably would have attended anyway.

## Parent Outcomes

### Parental Satisfaction

Given that the theory of choice places considerable emphasis on family choices as the means of accountability, effects on parents matter a great deal. Parents of Choice students were surveyed as they applied to the program and at the end of each subsequent year. Thus I have been able to ascertain their attitudes toward their prior schools as compared with their attitudes toward the Choice private schools. All of those attitude comparisons are extremely positive.[5]

Satisfaction of Choice parents with private schools was just as dramatic as dissatisfaction was with prior public schools. As noted in chapter 3, Choice parents were much less satisfied with their public schools than either the average MPS parent or the low-income group. Exactly the reverse occurred when parents responded to the same questions for private schools. Table 4.4 indicated the level of school dissatisfaction with prior public schools and, for Choice students, the cumulative dissatisfaction over five years with private schools. The relevant scale is A6 at the end of the table.

As described in chapter 4, Choice parents expressed high levels of dissatisfaction with prior public schools. However, that turned around when they were asked the same questions about the Choice private

gram were to be withdrawn pending court appeals, the Catholic church in Milwaukee agreed to keep those schools open and absorbed a considerable financial loss as a result. Catholic Choice families began receiving voucher payments in the fall of 1998.

[5] Surveys of Choice parents, conducted in June of each year, were returned by an average of 46 percent of the parents. All surveys, pre- and post-, were sent twice. It is difficult to determine biases in the responses. Would more pleased or angry parents be more likely to respond? Even if the response bias favors more favorably disposed parents, the reported differences between pre- and post-attitudes were extremely large.

schools their children attended. There were eight questions in the school-satisfaction scale: the four-point Likert ratings ranged from "very satisfied" (1) to "very dissatisfied" (4), with a range from 8 to 32. Thus the mean for Choice private schools was 13.6, indicating that most parents ranged from "very satisfied" to "somewhat satisfied" with the private schools on all measures. This compares with a mean of 16.4 for their prior public schools. The difference of means between Choice parents' dissatisfaction with prior public schools and their dissatisfaction with Choice schools was statistically different at the .001 level. Interestingly, the two measures on which parents were least satisfied in the public schools — educational environment and discipline — were the areas of greatest satisfaction in the private schools.

These results were consistent with several other indicators of satisfaction. On both pre- and post-surveys, parents were asked to grade their schools on an A to F scale. The comparative results from prior schools again indicated much greater satisfaction with the private schools. To recall from chapter 4, on a 4.0 scale, the average grade for prior schools for both Choice applicants and those who enrolled was 2.4. This compared to an average grade for the MPS control groups of 2.8. The results for Choice parents evaluating their child's private schools were considerably different. In every year they were considerably more positive than they were for their child's prior public school. The averages from 1991 to 1995 were: 3.0, 2.9, 2.8, 3.1, and 3.1.

In each year, there was also overwhelming support among participants that the MPCP should continue. The positive responses averaged 98 percent, even in the first year when a school went bankrupt and over seventy students ended their year in MPS schools (Witte et al., 1994, p. 20).

### Parental Involvement

Finally, parental involvement, which was clearly very high for Choice parents before they enrolled in the program, increased while their children were in private schools. Comparing the prior involvement of parents of students who enrolled in the Choice program (fall) to private school involvement, parental involvement increased on all dimensions. Table 4.4 (see chapter 4) provides the means and standard deviations of the scales for the applicants from 1990 to 1994 and the comparable scale scores for Choice parents from 1991–1995 June surveys. Table 4.5 provides statistics on differences of means between relevant groups.

For the four types of educational involvement we measured, already relatively high levels of prior parental involvement for Choice parents significantly increased in the private Choice schools. These include parents contacting schools, schools contacting parents, and parental involvement in organized school activities. The increases were significant at the .001 level. The one exception was parental involvement in educational activities at home (scale A5), for which involvement increased but the increase was not statistically significant. These results were also confirmed independently in each of the five years of the program. Part of the reason for this increase may have been that some of the private schools required participation and made parents sign parental involvement agreements. However, these parents were involved from the beginning and at best the contracts would have been a marginal incentive.

### Summary

The evidence based on parental attitudes and involvement in the schools and in the education process was positive. Those parents responding to followup surveys rated the private schools higher than their prior public schools on all measures, they were very positive about the Choice program, and parental involvement was reported as even higher than in their prior public schools.

## Student Outcomes

### Attendance

Attendance is not a very discriminating measure of educational performance in elementary grades because attendance is very high for all students and thus there is little school-to-school variation. For example, from 1991 to 1994, average attendance in MPS elementary schools was 92 percent in each year. Middle school attendance for the same years averaged 89 percent, 88 percent, and 89 percent. Attendance of Choice students in the private schools (excluding alternative schools) averaged 94 percent in 1990–91; 92 percent in 1991–92, 92.5 percent in 1992–93; and 93 percent in 1993–94. It can be concluded that overall attendance was satisfactory and on average not a problem in either Choice or comparable MPS schools.

### Achievement Test Scores

The estimation of educational achievement, as measured by scores on standardized tests, is often overemphasized in evaluations of education innovations. However, it is also a legitimate and necessary form of analysis. Test scores take on even more importance at the elementary school level where other quantitative measures such as course grades, disciplinary measures, and course and grade completion have little validity. The problem is that any analysis of achievement gains and comparisons between groups is inherently complex. In the case of the Milwaukee Parental Choice Program, that complexity extends to: (1) the appropriate comparison groups; (2) different data bases, which provide varying sets of control variables; and (3) various statistical modeling techniques. What this means is that what follows is necessarily complicated. To alleviate some of the complexity, I have relegated one important but technically difficult issue to a chapter appendix. Several of the more technical issues are treated in even more detail in other publications (Witte, 1997; Rouse, 1998).

The initial complication in the chapter is the relevant comparison group for Choice students. The three experimental groups are portrayed in table 6.1, which defines the groups, indicates to whom appropriate generalizations of findings can be made, and identifies the potential problems with each group. The experimental Choice group is comprised of students selected into and enrolling in a private school for some period of time. If they leave the private school, only their period in the program is considered part of the experiment.[6] In one sense the best potential comparison group is composed of the Rejected applicants. They would be the best because in comparison to Choice students, they provide a natural control on unmeasured selectivity bias (see above, p. 113). The basis for generalization for Choice and Reject comparisons is low-income families. On the other hand, while the nonapplicant MPS students do not provide a control on unmeasured selectivity bias, they can serve as a basis for generalization to all students. And, if only free-lunch qualified students are used, the results may also be generalized to comparisons involving Choice or Reject students.

For each group, there are potential problems. For Choice and Rejects, if nonrandom factors affect selection or nonselection, the randomness of the experiment is affected. The sibling rule, exempting Choice applicants from random selection when a sibling already attended the private school, could potentially contaminate the experimental group. Disabled Rejects not accepted in the private schools, and for whom no records were kept, create a serious potential problem for that group. For all three groups, if attrition (leaving the program prematurely) is biased either in favor of or against better students, difficulties also emerge. Finally, expansion of the program, either by removing income limits or

---

[6] Other researchers using our data have kept these students in the program, and considered their subsequent scores part of their Choice record even if after leaving the private schools they were educated and tested in MPS (see Rouse, 1998).

**TABLE 6.1**
Experimental and Control Groups for the Milwaukee Voucher Program

| Experimental Groups | Groups Defined | Basis for Generalization | Potential Problems |
|---|---|---|---|
| Choice | Choice applicants who enrolled in a private school | To programs with comparable income limits and nonsectarian private schools | (1) Nonrandom selection into the program (e.g., sibling rules) (2) Nonrandom attrition (3) Expansion of the program to higher income groups and sectarian schools |
| Rejects | Choice applicants who were not selected and did not enroll in a private school | To programs with comparable income limits | (1) Nonrandom selection out of the program (e.g. disabled students) (2) Nonrandom attrition (3) Expansion of the program to higher income groups |
| MPS random sample | Randomly selected MPS students who did not apply to the Choice program | To programs with or without income limits | (1) Nonrandom attrition (2) Unmeasured selectivity bias |

including sectarian schools, would invalidate the experimental group. As explained below, some of these problems can be compensated for statistically; others cannot.

I begin with what I will argue turns out to be the only appropriate comparison for this experiment—a large, random sample of nonchoosing MPS students. Most of my analysis relies on this comparison. However, I also examine the possibility of using the Rejects as a comparison group. As indicated above, this comparison is potentially very valuable. However, my main analysis of the Rejects will demonstrate why, in this case, they do not turn out to be a legitimate comparison group.

Within each of these analyses I employ multiple levels of data based first on student records and then on student records plus family survey data. The latter provide richer sets of control variables, but with reduced sample sizes because not all families completed surveys. The analyses, both in the chapter and appendix, also employ a number of statistical models at varying levels of sophistication and capturing different ways of conceptualizing student learning.

Despite the complexity, my analysis reaches a consistent conclusion: there is no reliable evidence that Choice students achieved more than comparable MPS students. If anything, there was a possible advantage for MPS students on reading, but no differences on math. On a positive note, cohort estimates for both samples, while always below national norms, do not substantially decline as students enter higher grades. This is not the normal pattern in that inner-city student average scores usually decline relative to national norms in higher grades. That both Choice and MPS students held their own is a positive result for the city as whole.[7] For reasons explained, Rejects unfortunately turned out to be an inappropriate comparison group and provided no useful information.

### Choice Compared to MPS Students

Because of the income limitation of the Choice program, the comparable income group in MPS was students who qualified for free or reduced-free lunch. However, because potentially the entire Milwaukee student population may be eligible for vouchers, I present data that can be interpreted for all MPS students. By including an indicator variable to control for free-lunch eligibility or alternatively a continuous income variable, the models allow us to estimate the effects of income on achievement. At the same time, by controlling for income, we factor out the effect of income and allow an appropriate test of how the MPS students performed against Choice students regardless of income. Somewhat different models in the appendices exclude non–free-lunch qualified MPS students altogether. The results of these different approaches are very similar, and both approaches support my general conclusions that there were no consistent differences between Choice and MPS students.

The achievement tests reported throughout are the Iowa Tests of Ba-

---

[7] It is not as clear that the Choice students held their own as it is for the MPS students. The reason is that the original MPS sample was unchanged, except for attrition, while new students entered the Choice program each year. Because Choice students were admitted in the very lowest grades, the MPS sample aged more than the Choice sample. Also, for both groups there is some indication that, within groups, students in higher grades did less well than students in lower grades.

sic Skills for reading and math, which were described in detail in chapter 4. I begin with descriptive statistics and move to more complex, multivariate models. Still more complex models are used in the analysis of Choice versus Reject students and in the appendix. The results of the more complex presentations, however, do not alter in any way the conclusions drawn from the core data presented in tables 6.2 to 6.6.

Table 6.2 provides the aggregate test results from 1990 to 1994 for Choice students and for students taking tests in MPS in the respective years. Tests were administered in April or May of each year. Only students taking tests in two subsequent years are included, thus allowing us to focus on achievement gains and losses expressed as change scores.[8] The results in the table are based on differences in NCEs, subtracting the first-year score from the second.[9] We caution the reader that sample sizes in some years are quite small for Choice students. For these descriptive statistics, the most relevant comparisons are with the low-income MPS subsample.

For the first year, the positive result was that the averages for all groups, except math scores for Choice students, improved. For the Choice students, the reading gain was considerable, although not significant (due to small sample sizes). Math scores stayed essentially the same. The MPS numbers indicate considerable, statistically significant improvement in average math scores, with smaller gains in reading. Both low-income and non-low-income MPS students gained in math. Three of these gains were statistically significant.

There were quite different effects in the second year. Change scores for Choice students in math and for MPS students in both reading and math were not appreciable. None of these differences approached standard levels of statistical significance. In contrast to the first year, however, reading scores dropped 3.9 NCE points (approximately 20 percent of a standard deviation) for Choice students. The decline was statistically significant at the .001 level.

The results shifted again in the third year. Choice students declined slightly in reading, which was not significant. On the other hand, for the first time, math scores for Choice students improved. The mean

---

[8] Please note that the cohort population described in chapter 4 is not identical with students for whom we have change data from one year to the next. Thus, tables 4.6 and 6.2 are not directly comparable.

[9] Normal Curve Equivalents are used because National Percentile Rankings are not interval level data. One of the problems with the transformation from NPRs to NCEs is that the very lowest and highest ends of the distribution are compressed. This tends to inflate very low-end scores and deflate very high-end scores. The lower-end inflation may affect this population, which has quite a few test scores below the 10th National Percentile. NCEs are, however, the national standard for reporting results across populations and grades for Chapter 1 of the Primary and Secondary Education Act and other programs.

**TABLE 6.2**
Mean NCEs, Iowa Test of Basic Skills, 1990–94

| | Choice | | Low-Income MPS | | MPS Control | |
|---|---|---|---|---|---|---|
| | R | M | R | M | R | M |
| *1990–1991* | | | | | | |
| 1990 | 40.0 | 39.2 | 37.5 | 39.5 | 39.5 | 41.6 |
| 1991 | 41.8 | 39.1 | 38.2 | 42.2 | 40.5 | 44.2 |
| Change score | +1.8 | −.1 | +.7 | +2.7*** | +1.0* | +2.6*** |
| (N)[a] | (84) | (88) | (812) | (792) | (1,048) | (1,029) |
| *1991–1992* | | | | | | |
| 1991 | 39.8 | 39.0 | 38.0 | 41.6 | 40.0 | 43.4 |
| 1992 | 35.9 | 38.4 | 38.4 | 41.3 | 40.5 | 43.1 |
| Change score | −3.9*** | −.6 | +.4 | −.3 | +.5 | −.3 |
| (N) | (192) | (198) | (911) | (895) | (1,173) | (1,148) |
| *1992–1993* | | | | | | |
| 1992 | 38.7 | 38.3 | 39.5 | 42.2 | 40.8 | 43.2 |
| 1993 | 38.3 | 42.7 | 38.8 | 41.0 | 40.1 | 42.0 |
| Change score | −.5 | +4.4 | −.7 | −1.2 | −.7 | −1.2 |
| (N) | (282) | (288) | (873) | (842) | (973) | (938) |
| *1993–1994* | | | | | | |
| 1993 | 37.6 | 44.0 | 38.8 | 41.8 | 40.1 | 42.8 |
| 1994 | 37.5 | 42.0 | 35.6 | 41.5 | 39.9 | 42.7 |
| Change score | −.1 | −2.0** | −.2 | −.3 | −.2 | −.1 |
| (N) | (289) | (281) | (688) | (678) | (766) | (755) |

[a](N) means the number of students tested in both 1990 and 1991. Only Choice students enrolled in private schools for the full year were included.

*probability < .05 that change score differs from 0

**probability < .01 that change score differs from 0

***probability < .001 that change score differs from 0

math NCE went from 38.3 to 42.7 for a 4.4 NCE gain that was statistically significant. Scores for MPS students, on the other hand, declined for both tests and for both groups. Because of relatively large sample sizes for the MPS control group, the decline in math scores was significant and estimated to be 1.2 NCEs for both the total MPS control group and the low-income sample.

The results for 1994 again shifted for both groups. For all groups, reading scores effectively did not change. The same was true of math scores for the MPS groups, although the low-income MPS scores declined slightly more than the non–low-income group. For the Choice students, after a large math increase in 1993, there was a decline of 2 NCE points in 1993.

To summarize over the four years, for Choice students, five of the eight change scores did not significantly differ from zero, while three did — one negative reading score and one positive math score. For both MPS samples, the results were similar. For low-income MPS students, two of the eight scores differed from zero, one positive and one negative math score. For the full MPS sample, there were parallel positive and negative scores in math, but also a positive gain in reading in the first year. Averaging the change scores across the four years results in the following: Choice ($R = -.67$; $M = +.42$); Low-Income MPS ($R = +.05$; $M = +.22$); MPS ($R = +.15$; $M = +.25$). The Choice advances in math were the result of third-year gains, and the MPS positive math scores were based on first-year gains. Similarly, the Choice decline in reading was primarily due to the poor performance of Choice students in the second year. However, the overall impression is that annual change scores are modest, not appreciably differing from zero.[10]

Test score differences could be based on a number of factors, which could be distributed differentially between Choice and MPS students. Thus, to provide an accurate and confirming picture of test achievement, it is necessary to control statistically for factors other than whether students were in MPS or Choice schools. Those controls are provided by multivariate regression analysis of the combined MPS and Choice samples. Using these controls, there are a number of ways to model achievement gains.

Various multivariate models are reported in tables 6.3 to 6.6. The models vary in several ways. First, tables 6.3, 6.5, and 6.6 include only control variables taken from Student Record Data Bases (SRDB), and do not include any variables obtained from our surveys. Because not all families responded to surveys, table 6.4 includes fewer students but a richer set of control variables than the other tables.

Also captured in tables 6.3 to 6.6 are a number of different ways to model the effects of the Choice program. Tables 6.3 and 6.4 combine all four years of data and provide two models for testing the significance of Choice program effects. The first and most straightforward method in tables 6.3 and 6.4 is simply to include participation in Choice rather

---

[10] This impression may change if these annual changes are extended over twelve years. Then the reading decline of Choice students would be $-7.8$ NCEs or approximately 40 percent of a standard deviation compared to national norms. This would be offset by approximately 25 percent of a standard deviation gain in math.

**TABLE 6.3**
Estimated Iowa Test of Basic Skills, 1991–94, Student Record Data Base
Variables Only ($b$, std. error of $b$)

| Independent Variable | Reading | | Math | |
|---|---|---|---|---|
| | Choice Indicator | Choice Program Years | Choice Indicator | Choice Program Years |
| Prior reading | .49*** | .49*** | .55*** | .55*** |
| | (.01) | (.01) | (.01) | (.01) |
| Prior math | .17*** | .17*** | .17*** | .17*** |
| | (.01) | (.01) | (.01) | (.01) |
| Test grade | −.18 | −.17 | −1.09*** | −1.09*** |
| | (.09) | (.09) | (.10) | (.10) |
| Gender (1 = female) | 1.56*** | 1.56*** | −.07 | −.07 |
| | (.37) | (.37) | (.40) | (.40) |
| African American | −3.91*** | −3.91*** | −4.18*** | −4.18*** |
| | (.55) | (.55) | (.60) | (.60) |
| Hispanic | −1.60* | −1.62* | −1.55 | −1.57* |
| | (.73) | (.73) | (.79) | (.80) |
| Other minority | −2.43* | −2.44* | .29 | .28 |
| | (1.047) | (1.047) | (1.151) | (1.152) |
| Low income | −2.51*** | −2.51*** | −1.43* | −1.43* |
| | (.58) | (.58) | (.63) | (.63) |
| Choice indicator | −.57 | — | −.11 | — |
| | (.48) | | (.53) | |
| Choice program year 1 | — | .10 | — | −.68 |
| | | (.82) | | (.89) |
| Choice program year 2 | — | −1.20 | — | .06 |
| | | (.73) | | (.80) |
| Choice program year 3 | — | −.09 | — | .56 |
| | | (.87) | | (.95) |
| Choice program year 4 | — | −1.39 | — | −.82 |
| | | (1.41) | | (1.54) |
| Constant | 18.13*** | 18.12*** | 22.26*** | 22.25*** |
| | (.97) | (.97) | (1.06) | (1.06) |
| Adj. $R^2$ | .46 | .46 | .46 | .49 |
| F Statistic | 446.32 | 441.23 | 498.60 | 487.23 |
| Probability F = 0 | .000 | .000 | .000 | .000 |
| Dependent mean | 40.09 | 40.09 | 42.48 | 42.48 |
| Dependent st. dev. | 16.98 | 16.98 | 18.83 | 18.83 |
| (N) | (4,716) | (4,716) | (4,653) | (4,653) |

***Probability < .001 that $b$ = 0
**Probability < .01 that $b$ = 0
*Probability < .05 that $b$ = 0

**TABLE 6.4**
Estimated Iowa Test of Basic Skills, 1991–94, Full Variables Set
($b$, std. error of $b$)

| Independent Variable | Reading | | Math | |
|---|---|---|---|---|
| | Choice Indicator | Choice Program Years | Choice Indicator | Choice Program Years |
| Prior reading | .43*** | .44*** | .53*** | .53*** |
| | (.03) | (.03) | (.02) | (.02) |
| Prior math | .18*** | .17*** | .15*** | .15*** |
| | (.02) | (.02) | (.03) | (.03) |
| Test grade | −.02 | −.04 | −1.29*** | −1.30*** |
| | (.17) | (.17) | (.19) | (.19) |
| Gender (1 = female) | 2.51*** | 2.52*** | 1.49* | 1.49* |
| | (.66) | (.66) | (.75) | (.76) |
| African American | −3.74*** | −3.76*** | −5.11*** | −5.13*** |
| | (.93) | (.93) | (1.08) | (1.08) |
| Hispanic | −1.14 | −1.03 | −2.45 | −2.39 |
| | (1.17) | (1.17) | (1.36) | (1.36) |
| Other minority | −3.22 | −3.19 | −3.38 | −3.37 |
| | (2.34) | (2.34) | (2.69) | (2.69) |
| Income ($1,000) | .09** | .09** | .11** | .11** |
| | (.03) | (.03) | (.04) | (.04) |
| Mother's education | .49** | .50* | .01 | .01 |
| | (.26) | (.26) | (.30) | (.30) |
| Married (1 = yes) | −.27 | −.30 | −.52 | −.53 |
| | (.79) | (.79) | (.91) | (.91) |
| PI-Schl. Cont. | −.11 | −.11 | −.22* | −.21* |
| | (.09) | (.09) | (.10) | (.10) |
| PI-Par. Cont. | .08 | .08 | .30 | .30 |
| | (.15) | (.15) | (.18) | (.18) |
| PI-Schl. Organ. | .48 | .47 | −.20 | −.20 |
| | (.27) | (.27) | (.31) | (.31) |
| Edu. Expectations | .17 | .18 | .74 | .75 |
| | (.35) | (.35) | (.40) | (.40) |
| Choice indicator | −2.15** | — | .09 | — |
| | (.75) | | (.86) | |
| Choice program year 1 | — | −1.38 | — | .28 |
| | | (1.09) | | (1.26) |
| Choice program year 2 | — | −3.85*** | — | −.46 |
| | | (1.02) | | (1.19) |
| Choice program year 3 | — | −1.26 | — | .19 |
| | | (1.23) | | (1.41) |
| Choice program year 4 | — | −.41 | — | 1.30 |
| | | (1.85) | | (2.13) |

TABLE 6.4 (*cont.*)

| Independent Variable | Reading | | Math | |
| --- | --- | --- | --- | --- |
| | Choice Indicator | Choice Program Years | Choice Indicator | Choice Program Years |
| Constant | 14.95*** | 14.97*** | 22.56*** | 22.57*** |
| | (2.17) | (2.17) | (2.50) | (2.51) |
| Adj. $R^2$ | .50 | .50 | .53 | .53 |
| F statistic | 86.15 | 73.03 | 97.02 | 81.60 |
| Probability F = 0 | .000 | .000 | .000 | .000 |
| Dependent mean | 42.95 | 42.95 | 45.37 | 45.37 |
| Dependent st. dev. | 16.47 | 16.47 | 19.53 | 19.53 |
| (N) | (1,385) | (1,385) | (1,372) | (1,372) |

***Probability < .001 that $b = 0$
**Probability < .01 that $b = 0$
*Probability < .05 that $b = 0$

than the MPS control group as a dichotomous, or indicator, variable. This variable measures the mean effect of students being in Choice over four years. The second method breaks the indicator variable into relevant year indicator variables (year 1 = 1990–91, etc.) comparing effects for each Choice year against the control group. This allows us to ascertain the effects over the years while controlling for other factors. The final method, as exemplified in tables 6.5 and 6.6, is to determine if there is a longitudinal effect of students being in a choice school over a number of years.

All of these models have relevance in evaluating program success. Policymakers certainly would be interested in understanding the overall effect of a program intervention. However, they might also be interested in the trend in the program. Does it show variance from year to year, or are the results stable over time? Finally, we would also be interested in a learning curve or trend effect for individual students. It could be that students need time to become acclimated to the different approaches applied in the private schools and thus achievement gains might be delayed. It could also be that as initial enthusiasm with a new school wears off, or a student fails to adjust to a different educational style, achievement could drop.

The basic results mirror the descriptive statistics. Table 6.3, which includes more students but fewer control variables, indicates that the control variables all acted as anticipated.[11] The two prior tests were

[11] The results in tables 6.3 and 6.4 are stacked, and thus a student may appear more than once in different years. This could violate the Ordinary Least Squares (OLS) assumption of independence of error terms. The standard correction for this is to use the Huber/

TABLE 6.5

Estimated Iowa Test of Basic Skills *Reading* Score, Including Student Choice
Year: 1991, 1992, 1993, 1994 (*b*, std. error of *b*)

| Independent Variable | 1991 | 1992 | 1993 | 1994 |
|---|---|---|---|---|
| *Prior reading* | .48*** | .49*** | .49*** | .49*** |
| | (.03) | (.03) | (.03) | (.03) |
| Prior math | .18*** | .16*** | .16*** | .19*** |
| | (.03) | (.02) | (.02) | (.03) |
| Test grade | −.52** | −.54** | .53** | −.14 |
| | (.19) | (.17) | (.17) | (.21) |
| Gender | 1.13 | 1.85** | 1.32* | 2.34** |
| | (.76) | (.71) | (.68) | (.76) |
| Low income | −3.72** | −2.08 | −2.37 | −4.11** |
| | (1.28) | (1.27) | (1.41) | (1.65) |
| African American | −2.85** | −5.52*** | −4.21*** | −2.84* |
| | (1.06) | (1.05) | (1.05) | (1.23) |
| Hispanic | −3.00* | −1.53 | −3.23* | −.17 |
| | (1.52) | (1.51) | (1.38) | (1.49) |
| Other minority | −1.63 | −1.57 | −5.21** | −.28 |
| | (2.11) | (2.00) | (1.93) | (2.36) |
| Student choice year 1 | 2.05 | −1.44 | .57 | −1.79 |
| | (1.41) | (1.30) | (1.24) | (1.52) |
| Student choice year 2 | NA | −2.45* | 1.99 | −.57 |
| | | (1.28) | (1.16) | (1.38) |
| Student choice year 3 | NA | NA | .39 | −.13 |
| | | | (1.29) | (1.28) |
| Student choice year 4 | NA | NA | NA | −.67 |
| | | | | (1.52) |
| Constant | 21.30*** | 20.82*** | 15.18*** | 16.92*** |
| | (2.02) | (1.97) | (2.03) | (2.49) |
| $R^2$ | .44 | .44 | .48 | .46 |
| F(df) | 97 | 105 | 105 | 78 |
| | (1,075, 9) | (1,313, 10) | (1,274, 11) | (1,121, 12) |
| Probability F = 0 | .000 | .000 | .000 | .000 |

***Probability that *b* = 0 < .001
**Probability that *b* = 0 < .01
*Probability that *b* = 0 < .05

always highly significant, with a much larger coefficient on the matched
prior test (i.e., reading for reading). Test grade was always negative,
indicating students in higher grades did less well, but it was only signifi-

White corrections to recompute standard errors of the estimators. Application of that
correction had no appreciable effect and therefore ordinary OLS estimates are reported
(see Huber, 1967; White, 1980).

TABLE 6.6
Estimated Iowa Test of Basic Skills *Math* Score, Including Student Choice
Year: 1991, 1992,1993, 1994 (*b*, std. error of *b*)

| Independent Variable | 1991 | 1992 | 1993 | 1994 |
|---|---|---|---|---|
| Prior math | .58*** | .59*** | .49*** | .54*** |
| | (.03) | (.03) | (.03) | (.03) |
| Prior reading | .13*** | .14*** | .19*** | .20*** |
| | (.03) | (.03) | (.03) | (.03) |
| Test grade | −1.33*** | −1.18*** | −1.19*** | −.51 |
| | (.20) | (.18) | (.19) | (.24) |
| Gender | −.59 | .11 | −.06 | .24 |
| | (.80) | (.77) | (.75) | (.85) |
| Low income | −3.42** | −1.17 | −2.11 | −3.94* |
| | (1.33) | (1.37) | (1.55) | (1.86) |
| African American | −3.26** | −4.63*** | −4.42*** | −2.07 |
| | (1.10) | (1.13) | (1.16) | (1.37) |
| Hispanic | −3.68* | −.44 | −1.89 | .57 |
| | (1.59) | (1.62) | (1.52) | (1.66) |
| Other minority | −.47 | 2.01 | .00 | −.47 |
| | (2.24) | (2.14) | (2.12) | (2.64) |
| Student choice year 1 | −2.33 | −1.63 | 1.81 | −2.23 |
| | (1.48) | (1.39) | (1.38) | (1.70) |
| Student choice year 2 | NA | −1.58 | 3.03* | .85 |
| | | (1.37) | (1.27) | (1.53) |
| Student choice year 3 | NA | NA | 2.66* | .12 |
| | | | (1.39) | (1.42) |
| Student choice year 4 | NA | NA | NA | −.84 |
| | | | | (1.69) |
| Constant | 24.53*** | 21.08*** | 24.24*** | 18.77*** |
| | (2.10) | (2.13) | (2.23) | (2.80) |
| $R^2$ | .52 | .50 | .48 | .47 |
| F(df) | 132 | 131 | 106 | 81 |
| | (1,067, 9) | (1,300, 10) | (1,246, 11) | (1,106, 12) |
| Probability F = 0 | .000 | .000 | .000 | .000 |

***Probability that *b* = 0 < .001
**Probability that *b* = 0 < .01
*Probability that *b* = 0 < .05

cant for math. Girls did better on reading, but not on math. Minority
students did less well than whites, and low-income students did less well
than non–low-income students. With all these variables controlled,
none of the choice variables were significant, and only the second-
year reading score even approached significance (-1.2 with a *t*-value of
−1.6).

Table 6.4, with more variables included, tells a similar story, but the reading result is now significant and favoring the MPS students. Again the control variables are almost all in the expected direction, with some less significant and some more significant than in table 6.3. Of the new variables in this table, income and mother's education were in the direction expected. Some parental involvement scales seemed to be counter to expectations, which indicates a possible connection between the prior involvement and difficulties these children experienced or their frustration with prior schools. The negative signs on parental involvement at home, which were significant for math, are hard to interpret.

The results of the Choice indicator variables in table 6.4 were in the same directions as in table 6.3 and generally were not significantly different from zero. The one exception was the negative Choice effect on reading, which at $-2.15$ was 1.58 points lower than in table 6.3. This means that controlling for all variables, including income, the Choice students did worse on reading than the MPS students. The result was statistically significant at the .01 level. However, when we look at the year effects, and compare them with change scores in table 6.2, it is quite clear that the entire effect is driven by a bad second year in the Choice schools. Change scores in table 6.2 indicate a decline in year 2 reading of $-3.9$ NCEs. The second-year indicator variable in Table 6.4 is almost identical at $-3.85$. The reason Choice students did worse in this model than when only SRDB variables were included (see table 6.3) was undoubtedly the inclusion of mother's education, which was higher in Choice families, thus setting up higher expected scores. As will be discussed below, the reason for the effect in this single year is probably connected to attrition from the program.

The trend over time in student performance has been a very controversial aspect of the MPCP. Several other authors have claimed a trend effect favoring Choice students. Specifically, they argue, using Rejects as a control, that third- and especially fourth-year Choice students make remarkable gains in math, but (with no explanation) no statistically significant gains in reading (Greene, Peterson, and Du, 1996). That result will be addressed below.

The analyses presented in tables 6.5 (for reading) and table 6.6 (for math) provide trend data in comparison to the MPS control group. Because the data indicate trends for each of the four years, only SRDB variables are included. Sample sizes, especially of Choice students, would be very small if survey variables were also incorporated. Inclusion of those variables tended to reduce the levels of significance of the findings in tables 6.5 and 6.6 because of inflated standard errors. Data in these tables are not stacked (see note 11). That means that for 1994, Student Choice Year 1 gives the estimated effects for Choice students who began in the program in August 1993. Student Choice Year 4 indicates the results for the Choice students who have remained in the program for all four years, having first enrolled in the MPCP in August 1990.

The results again tend to support the conclusion that there was no consistent pattern in achievement score differences across the different tests and years. For reading scores in table 6.5 there is only one significant coefficient: a $-2.45$ NCE disadvantage for the second-year Choice students in the second year of the program. This result reinforces the pattern indicated in Tables 6.2 and 6.4, where the negative reading result seemed to be the result of the second program year. The only other score in the table that approached statistical significance was the second-year cohort's $+1.99$ points in the third year (1993). It appears that this Choice cohort (1991–92) had better students on average than the other cohorts. This result carries over to math scores in table 6.6.

Consistent with the descriptive results in table 6.2, there appears to be a positive Choice effect for math in the third year for all Choice students. The results for second- and third-year Choice students in 1993 in table 6.6 were statistically significant at the .05 level. However, again reinforcing the "no consistent difference" conclusion, these results were not repeated in the fourth year of the program (1994). In that year, nothing approached significance except for the newly admitted Choice cohort (Year 1), and they did worse than MPS students (-2.23 NCE).

Thus, combined with the reading results that are in the opposite direction, these results confirm the general conclusion that there was no consistent difference between the MPCP students and the control group. This was true for the descriptive statistics, mean effects, program year effects, and student trends. The few significant results that did emerge will be at least partly explained by attrition from the program as described below.

Because of potential problems with selection into and out of both the MPCP sample and the MPS control group, specific attention needed to be paid to those possibilities. The methods of controlling for selection effects unfortunately are quite complex statistically, so that analysis is contained in the appendix to this chapter. The appendix also provides yet another set of methods for modeling achievement and includes only the low-income MPS students as a control group. However, the results of these multiple analyses also reinforce the general finding that there were no consistent achievement differences between MPCP and MPS students.

## Choice Students Compared to Rejected Choice Students

As noted above, the rejected students were potentially a very valuable control group, theoretically providing a natural control on selection bias. The logic was that they had committed to choice, and thus retained all the unmeasured characteristics of choosers, but were *randomly not selected into the program*. Unfortunately, there were problems with this experimental arrangement from the beginning. Despite the limitations, however, this comparison clearly requires attention, especially given the public relations efforts and media attention given to a paper released in August 1996 touting the enormous successes of the MPCP (Greene, Peterson, and Du, 1996). That paper was released several days prior to Paul Peterson's appearance before a Wisconsin court in which he uncategorically supported the MPCP program, with testimony relying heavily on evidence from the paper. It was also released on the eve of the Republican National Convention in August 1996, and the results were subsequently reported in over fifty newspapers and on most television networks. Based solely on comparisons with the rejects sample, the paper proclaimed undeniable advantages for MPCP students who remained in the program for three years and even greater advantages if they remained for four years. That finding led the authors to an extraordinary conclusion: "If similar success could be achieved for all minority students nationwide, it could close the gap separating white and minority test scores by somewhere between one-third and one-half" (Greene et al., 1996, p. 4). In a *Forbes* magazine article, Peterson became even more optimistic: "If one extrapolated these results over twelve years, the difference between white and minority math scores would disappear entirely, and the difference between reading scores would be almost eliminated" (Lee and Foster, 1997, p. 146). These generalizations were based on a fourth-year math score estimated for Choice versus Reject students, and reading scores said to favor MPCP, although not statistically significant by conventional standards.[12]

My approach to the analysis of Choice versus Reject students was quite different from the original Peterson/Green approach. Rather, I followed the more appropriate techniques used by economist Cecilia Rouse (Rouse, 1998). To provide a comparison with the modeling approaches of Rouse, and to provide readers with yet another approach to modeling achievement trends, I analyzed the Choice/Reject comparison using the estimation models for analysis of selection bias given in the chapter appendix. Thus the modeling approach used in tables 6.7, 6.8, and 6.9 includes simple treatment effects, parallel to the Choice indicator variable in the previous section. However, as in the selection bias analysis in the appendix, only low-income MPS students are included. The analysis also includes two trend effects, controlling both

[12] Peterson and Greene have subsequently found similar "success" in the Cleveland program, again in the face of an independent evaluation that found no differences between voucher and nonvoucher schools (see Greene, Howell, and Peterson 1997; Metcalf et al., 1998; Metcalf, 1998).

for trends in Choice students and years in the program for Reject students. The first trend for Choice is as a continuous variable; the second breaks the trend into years as was done in the main body of the chapter. These methods are close to those used by Rouse, and the results have some similarities with both Rouse's outcomes and those of Green, Peterson, and Du. However, my analysis looks very carefully at the validity of the Reject sample and subsequently reaches a very different conclusion.

The first Choice/Reject comparisons are presented in table 6.7. In this table, the treatment group is Choice. Thus the overall effect of being in Choice rather than the Reject group is the Treatment variable, and the trend effect for Choice students is the Treat*Yrs variable. The YrsInPrg variable represents the trend for the Reject group, and the TreatYR1, TreatYR2, etc., variables indicate the effects of students being in the Choice program in each successive year.

As in the MPS/Choice comparison, reading seems to be a wash in all analyses. None of the treatment or trend coefficients in either the SRDB or Full Variable analyses approach a level of probability that would justify concluding that they differ from zero. Thus columns 1 to 3 in both the top and bottom panels indicate no significant effects.

Math is somewhat different. For the reduced (SRDB) variable set, with a larger sample size, the straight treatment effect (column 4) was significant and indicated that Choice students were on average 2 NCEs better than Reject students. When treatment and program trends are taken into consideration (column 5), nothing remained close to significant. When year dummies were used to represent treatment effects (column 6), only the third-year effect was significant. The coefficients for years 2 to 4, however, were positive and over 2.0 NCEs.

When the full set of variables are used as controls, including family income, mother's education, employment, marital status, and expectations for the child's future education, the treatment coefficients increased considerably. The straight treatment effect (column 4, lower panel) more than doubled; the year-treatment trend variable (column 5), which denotes the linear gain per year for Choice students, was estimated at a remarkable 3.25 with a standard error of 1.6; and the year treatment dummy variables (column 6) went straight up from 4.4 after two years to 8.5 and 10.9 in the third and fourth years.[13] This finding

---

[13] Heckman corrections used in appendix 6 had essentially no impact on the SRDB model estimations given above, but had reasonable model specification indicators. However, for the Full Variable models they encountered serious specification problems. In many of the equations the iterations began with a Rho of .99, encountered nonconcave functions, and in three instances did not complete the maximum likelihood iteration process. Thus Heckman estimates are not presented in the Choice-Reject analysis.

**TABLE 6.7**

Regression Results, 1991–94, *Choice* (Treatment) and *Rejects* (*b*, std. Error of *b*)[a]

| | SRDB Only | | | | | |
| --- | --- | --- | --- | --- | --- | --- |
| | Reading | | | Math | | |
| | (1) | (2) | (3) | (4) | (5) | (6) |
| Treatment | −.44 | .35 | — | 1.98* | .35 | — |
| | (.89) | (2.25) | — | (1.00) | (2.25) | — |
| Treat*Yrs | — | .83 | — | — | .83 | — |
| | — | (1.05) | — | — | (1.05) | — |
| YrsInPrg. | — | −.66 | −.33 | — | −.63 | −.61 |
| | — | (.95) | (.83) | — | (.95) | (.95) |
| TreatYR1 | — | — | −.09 | — | — | .91 |
| | — | — | (1.42) | — | — | (1.48) |
| TreatYR2 | — | — | −.69 | — | — | 2.07 |
| | — | — | (1.01) | — | — | (1.19) |
| TreatYR3 | — | — | .05 | — | — | 3.67* |
| | — | — | (1.44) | — | — | (1.65) |
| TreatYR4 | — | — | −1.08 | — | — | 2.05 |
| | — | — | (2.17) | — | — | (2.69) |
| $R^2$ | .34 | .34 | .34 | .42 | .42 | .42 |
| MSE | 12.54 | 12.54 | 12.55 | 13.44 | 13.45 | 13.45 |
| Reading: N = 1,158 | | | Math: N = 1,106 | | | |

| | Full Variable Set | | | | | |
| --- | --- | --- | --- | --- | --- | --- |
| | Reading | | | Math | | |
| | (1) | (2) | (3) | (4) | (5) | (6) |
| Treatment | .22 | −2.59 | — | 4.70** | −1.74 | — |
| | (1.50) | (3.25) | — | (1.52) | (3.71) | — |
| Treat*Yrs | — | 1.43 | — | — | 3.26* | — |
| | — | (1.50) | — | — | (1.59) | — |
| YrsInPrg. | — | −1.16 | −1.16 | — | −2.91* | −2.90* |
| | — | (1.38) | (1.38) | — | (1.47) | (1.47) |
| TreatYR1 | — | — | −.64 | — | — | 1.66 |
| | — | — | (2.13) | — | — | (2.46) |
| TreatYR2 | — | — | −.40 | — | — | 4.45** |
| | — | — | (1.66) | — | — | (1.71) |
| TreatYR3 | — | — | 1.97 | — | — | 8.46*** |
| | — | — | (2.39) | — | — | (2.22) |
| TreatYR4 | — | — | 3.54 | — | — | 10.86** |
| | — | — | (3.57) | — | — | (3.63) |
| $R^2$ | .32 | .32 | .32 | .46 | .47 | .47 |
| MSE | 12.43 | 12.44 | 12.45 | 13.31 | 13.28 | 13.30 |
| Reading: N = 608 | | | Math: N = 590 | | | |

***Probability that $b = 0 < .001$

**Probability that $b = 0 < .01$

*Probability that $b = 0 < .05$

[a]Standard errors are robust using the White/Huber estimation procedure to account for clustering. Also included in the *SRDB* equation are prior tests for reading and math, test grade, and race and gender indicator variables. In addition to the *SRDB* variables, the *Full* Variable set adds log income, mother's education, employment, educational expectations, and marital status.

has been held up by Peterson and company as the savior of minority education in America.

Why the discrepancy in math results between the MPS and the Reject control groups? A ten-point math advantage is over one-half of a standard deviation increase in one year. If that were indicative of the general achievement advantages of Choice students, and whatever is being done in the private schools could be replicated, racial gaps would indeed be closed very quickly. If one believes these results, and extrapolates these gains over twelve years, private schools would have increased achievement approximately six standard deviations relative to public school students. However, the annual gain of ten points is between five and ten times larger than any similarly reported achievement gains based on public and private school comparisons in national databases (Witte, 1992, 1996). Common sense suggests that for large inner-city populations the educational problems are deep and sticky, and that one needs to be suspicious of these types of gains. That is the case with this result.

I question the Choice/Reject math results based on three problems. First, the selection processes were, in an experimental sense, inadequate in several ways.

1. Random selection was used only for students in certain grades in particular schools where there was oversubscription. For example, one African American school usually admitted everyone, while the other black school always had waiting lists.

2. A significant proportion (52 percent) of rejected students disappeared for programmatic purposes — meaning there was no subsequent test information on them after they were rejected.

3. There was no oversight of the random selection process, or accounting for students who were rejected because of disabilities.

4. There was a sibling rule, and no data existed on who was admitted under the rule and how that may have affected the randomization of the selection process.

5. After the first year, Choice students were allowed to enter from waiting lists after the beginning of the year. No rules existed as to how those lists were maintained.

Second, small sample sizes were a problem, particularly when we are focusing primarily on single-year effects. In Year 4 (for the original 1990 cohort) there were only eighty-five Choice students and twenty-seven Rejects remaining who had both 1993 and 1994 tests.

A third issue is the initial loss of Reject students from the control group. Were the Rejects who left the experiment systematically different from those who stayed? And, if different, were the differences likely to affect future achievement?

I looked at selection and samples size problems in two ways. First, I focused on the 52 percent of the Reject students who walked away from the experiment. Because most Rejects were very young, there was little prior test or SRDB information on them. However, all applicants were sent surveys, so information existed on both those who later returned to MPS and those who did not. When we initially compared all Rejects with Choice enrollees, we found few differences between the groups. The most notable were that Rejected-student parents had lower educational expectations for their children than parents of selected students, and that Rejected-student parents were not as happy with the administration of the program as Choice parents (see chapter 4). The latter finding was understandable given their disappointment, but the former may have reflected some of the selection problems outlined above. Private schools would have been very interested in the expectations of parents for their child.

However, the Choice/Reject comparison of applicants (see chapter 4) did not include an analysis of the differences between rejected students who returned to MPS, and thus in effect continued in the experiment, and those who did not. Logistic regression comparing Rejects who "left" the experiment with those who went back and continued to be tested in MPS provide such an analysis. Logistic regressions were explained and used in chapter 4 to estimate differences in those who applied and did not apply to the Choice and Chapter 220 programs. The results of a logistic regression estimating the characteristics of Reject students who "remained" in the experiment—meaning returned to MPS and had any subsequent test record—are given in table 6.8.

The results are not trivial. Although with reduced sample sizes not all coefficients are significant at the conventional .05 level of probability, the direction of all of the coefficients indicate that the rejected students who remained in the study were: (1) poorer; (2) in higher grades; and (3) from families whose parents were likely to be less educated and were less involved in their children's education than students who disappeared from the program. This makes sense. Rejects were looking to leave MPS in the first place. If not selected for Choice, and if they had the means (especially if their children were young), they left for private schools—either on their own or with the help of privately funded vouchers; or they went to another public school district. Thus the Reject "control group" that remained behind in MPS was hardly a random sample of those who applied and were rejected. All indications suggest those remaining in the experiment were likely to be an educationally weak representation of the initial group.

Small samples are a second problem with the Choice/Reject comparison, especially when the results focus on one or two years. In such a

**TABLE 6.8**
Logistic Regression on Rejects Having Any Postapplication Test, 1991–94*

| Variables | B | SE B | EXP(B) |
|---|---|---|---|
| LogInc$ | −1.01 | .51 | .37 |
| Mother's education | −.05 | .14 | .95 |
| Gender (1 = fm) | .62 | .37 | 1.86 |
| Grade at application | .60 | .09 | 1.82 |
| African American | .24 | .84 | 1.27 |
| Hispanic American | −.31 | 1.00 | .73 |
| Parental involvement scale (High = more) | −.11 | .13 | .89 |

*Model Chi-sq. = 77.34, $p < .000$; 81.3 percent of the cases were correctly assigned; N = 192.

situation, the scores of a few students could influence the general results. On closer investigation, that was clearly the case in the data presented in table 6.7. As one might anticipate, the Rejects were the problem. As indicated earlier, the critical fourth-year Choice/Reject comparison was based on a small number of students. The large math difference in table 6.7 (bottom panel, column 6, TreatYR4 variable) was based on eighty-five Choice students (of the original 341 in 1990–91) and twenty-seven Reject students. Of the twenty-seven reject students, five students (18.5 percent) received a score of 1 on the math test. A 1 NCE is the lowest recorded score on the Iowa Test of Basic Skills. It often results from a student's *simply not filling in the dots* on the test form. The data do not contain the original answers to each question, so it cannot be determined if students missed all the questions or large blocks—which would be indicators of not filling in the dots. However, adding to the spectulation that these students simply did not do the test is that those same five students scored an average of 31 on their math tests in the prior (1993) year. There were no similar 1 scores in the Choice schools. The lowest Choice score was 4.

To test the sensitivity of the models in table 6.7, I re-estimated the results taking out the students from both groups who had scores less than 5 NCEs. The results are presented in table 6.9. Comparing the N's in tables 6.7 and 6.9, this meant I dropped twenty-nine and forty-three students for reading and math respectively for the SRDB models over all the years. For the Full Variable models I dropped nine reading and twenty-four math scores. For the fourth year, math with Full Variables—where we get the big kick in table 6.7—that meant dropping only five Reject and two Choice students.

The results are quite extraordinary. First, the reading estimates (columns 1 to 3) are unaffected—still no signs of life there. For math, both the SRDB and the Full Variables panels are dramatically affected. For the larger SRDB sample, the average treatment effect in table 6.7 (column 4) was 1.98 points and was significant at conventional levels. With the lowest scoring students removed from both samples, it was insignificant and dropped to .89 NCEs (table 6.7, column 4). Similarly, the significant trend effect in the SRDB model (for TreatYR3) dropped from 3.67 to 1.58 (column 6 in each table) and was not even close to significant. The same shifts occurred using the Full Variables model. The overall treatment effect (column 4) was statistically eliminated, and the only trend effect that remained was the third-year effect (column 6). The coefficient representing the big fourth-year finish (TreatYR4, column 6)was reduced by 40 percent and was no longer significant by conventional standards. *These results were accomplished by eliminating only seven students who scored the lowest scores on the math test.*[14]

A final way of looking further at the Rejects as a treatment group is to compare them to the MPS random sample. If the Rejects are truly representative of education in the Milwaukee public schools, which is the Peterson et al. position, one would hypothesize that the Reject/MPS comparison should be a wash. If this is not the case, generalizing results to national inner-city populations as they have done would be absurd.

As revealed in table 6.10, the Reject/MPS comparison is hardly a wash. In this table, *with Rejects being the treatment group, negative coefficients mean the MPS students did better than Rejects.* Again, for the critical math scores, there were many large, significant, negative coefficients. A comparison with table 6.7 is instructive. Perhaps the most remarkable results are for the SRDB models in the top panel. The general treatment effect was worse for Rejects when compared to MPS than when Rejects were compared to Choice (column 4). In addition, a first-year effect emerged, and the fourth-year effect, which was not significant in table 6.7, is over 8 points in table 6.10. With the Full Variable model, all of these coefficients at least doubled, and the fourth-year effect of being a random, nonchoosing MPS student was an amazing 17.38 points math advantage over our poor Reject group.

Obviously the same types of low-scoring student biases that affected the Choice/Reject comparison will also affect these results. A re-estimation, comparable to table 6.10 (excluding students with scores below 5 NCEs), as expected, reduced the statistical significance of many treatment variables. However, the fourth-year math effect, with Full Variables, remained a robust 13.3 NCEs — and was significant at the .001 level.

Thus fourth-year Rejects performed very poorly in comparison to

[14] Eliminating two Choice students raised the math average of the remaining eighty-three students' 1994 posttests by only .9 NCEs. However, eliminating five Reject students raised the average of the remaining twenty-two students by 6.5 NCEs.

**TABLE 6.9**

Regression Results, 1991–94, *Choice* (Treatment) and *Rejects*—Excluding Lowest Scoring Students (NCE < 5) (*b*, std. Error of *b*)[a]

|  | SRDB Only | | | | | |
|  | Reading | | | Math | | |
|  | (1) | (2) | (3) | (4) | (5) | (6) |
|---|---|---|---|---|---|---|
| Treatment | −1.01 | −1.01 | — | .89 | .65 | — |
|  | (.85) | (2.04) | — | (.93) | (2.15) | — |
| Treat*Yrs | — | .03 | — | — | .11 | — |
|  | — | (.89) | — | — | (.94) | — |
| YrsInPrg. | — | −.25 | −.25 | — | −.01 | .00 |
|  | — | (.78) | (.78) | — | (.83) | (.83) |
| TreatYR1 | — | — | −.75 | — | — | .32 |
|  | — | — | (1.37) | — | — | (1.44) |
| TreatYR2 | — | — | −1.39 | — | — | 1.22 |
|  | — | — | (.97) | — | — | (1.08) |
| TreatYR3 | — | — | −.49 | — | — | 1.58 |
|  | — | — | (1.36) | — | — | (1.39) |
| TreatYR4 | — | — | −1.15 | — | — | −.47 |
|  | — | — | (1.98) | — | — | (2.36) |
| $R^2$ | .34 | .34 | .34 | .41 | .41 | .41 |
| MSE | 11.75 | 11.76 | 11.77 | 13.44 | 12.53 | 12.53 |
| Reading: N = 1,129 | | | | Math: N = 1,063 | | |

|  | Full Variable Set | | | | | |
|  | Reading | | | Math | | |
|  | (1) | (2) | (3) | (4) | (5) | (6) |
|---|---|---|---|---|---|---|
| Treatment | −.41 | −3.42 | — | 2.67 | −1.69 | — |
|  | (1.43) | (3.15) | — | (1.45) | (3.75) | — |
| Treat*Yrs | — | 1.51 | — | — | 2.24 | — |
|  | — | (1.46) | — | — | (1.59) | — |
| YrsInPrg. | — | −.98 | −.97 | — | −2.16 | −2.15 |
|  | — | (1.35) | (1.35) | — | (1.48) | (1.48) |
| TreatYR1 | — | — | −1.55 | — | — | .38 |
|  | — | — | (2.05) | — | — | (2.44) |
| TreatYR2 | — | — | −.96 | — | — | 2.91 |
|  | — | — | (1.58) | — | — | (1.56) |
| TreatYR3 | — | — | 1.47 | — | — | 5.29* |
|  | — | — | (2.32) | — | — | (2.07) |
| TreatYR4 | — | — | 2.67 | — | — | 6.63 |
|  | — | — | (3.47) | — | — | (3.55) |
| $R^2$ | .32 | .32 | .32 | .43 | .43 | .43 |
| MSE | 11.81 | 11.81 | 11.83 | 12.44 | 12.44 | 12.46 |
| Reading: N = 597 | | | Math: N = 590 | | | |

***Probability that $b = 0 < .001$

**Probability that $b = 0 < .01$

*Probability that $b = 0 < .05$

[a]Standard errors are robust using the White/Huber estimation procedure to account for clustering. Also included in the *SRDB* equation are prior tests for reading and math, test grade, and race and gender indicator variables. In addition to the *SRDB* variables, the *Full Variable* set adds log income, mother's education, employment, educational expectations, and marital status.

**TABLE 6.10**

Regression Results, 1991–94, Rejects (Treatment) and MPS ($b$, std error of $b$)[a]

|  | SRDB Only | | | | | |
|---|---|---|---|---|---|---|
|  | Reading | | | Math | | |
|  | (1) | (2) | (3) | (4) | (5) | (6) |
| Treatment | −.33 | .35 | — | −2.25* | −.69 | — |
|  | (.80) | (1.92) | — | (.94) | (2.02) | — |
| Treat*Yrs | — | −.42 | — | — | −.89 | — |
|  | — | (.84) | — | — | (.98) | — |
| YrsInPrg. | — | −.33 | −.33 | — | −.29 | −.28 |
|  | — | (.20) | (.20) | — | (.22) | (.22) |
| TreatYR1 | — | — | .23 | — | — | −2.91* |
|  | — | — | (1.38) | — | — | (1.38) |
| TreatYR2 | — | — | −.63 | — | — | −.14 |
|  | — | — | (1.39) | — | — | (1.61) |
| TreatYR3 | — | — | −2.23 | — | — | −2.55 |
|  | — | — | (1.71) | — | — | (2.09) |
| TreatYR4 | — | — | 1.12 | — | — | −8.15* |
|  | — | — | (2.48) | — | — | (3.37) |
| $R^2$ | .41 | .41 | .41 | .45 | .45 | .45 |
| MSE | 12.59 | 12.58 | 12.59 | 13.77 | 13.77 | 13.76 |
| Reading: N = 3,425 | | | | Math: N = 3,331 | | |

|  | Full Variable Set | | | | | |
|---|---|---|---|---|---|---|
|  | Reading | | | Math | | |
|  | (1) | (2) | (3) | (4) | (5) | (6) |
| Treatment | −1.69 | −1.81 | — | −4.88** | .25 | — |
|  | (1.35) | (2.87) | — | (1.54) | (3.29) | — |
| Treat*Yrs | — | −.06 | — | — | −2.70* | — |
|  | — | (1.24) | — | — | (1.42) | — |
| YrsInPrg. | — | −.65 | −.65 | — | −.49 | −.49 |
|  | — | (.38) | (.38) | — | (.46) | (.46) |
| TreatYR1 | — | — | −2.26 | — | — | −4.87* |
|  | — | — | (2.28) | — | — | (2.43) |
| TreatYR2 | — | — | −1.62 | — | — | −2.39 |
|  | — | — | (2.46) | — | — | (2.36) |
| TreatYR3 | — | — | −.99 | — | — | −2.89 |
|  | — | — | (3.17) | — | — | (3.42) |
| TreatYR4 | — | — | −3.83 | — | — | −17.38*** |
|  | — | — | (2.82) | — | — | (3.55) |
| $R^2$ | .45 | .45 | .45 | .51 | .51 | .51 |
| MSE | 12.20 | 12.19 | 12.21 | 13.96 | 13.93 | 13.89 |
| Reading: N = 920 | | | | Math: N = 899 | | |

***Probability that $b$ = < .001

**Probability that $b$ = < .01

**Probability that $b$ = < .05

[a]Standard errors are robust using the White/Huber estimation procedure to account for clustering. Also included in the SRDB equation are prior tests for reading and math, test grade, and race and gender indicator variables. In addition to the SRDB variables, the Full Variable set adds log income, mother's education, employment, educational expectations, and marital status.

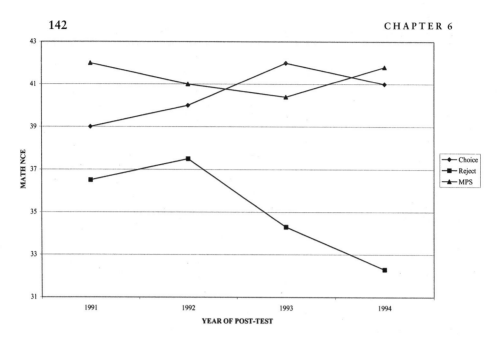

**Figure 6.1** 1990 Cohorts — Math NCEs

their own MPS classmates. They did even worse in that comparison than when compared to the Choice students. What happened to the fourth-year students can be seen in figure 6.1. The figure depicts the original 1990 students in each group as they are tested across the years. As is apparent, the differences between groups were a function of the poor performance of the Rejects — not a dramatic improvement in either Choice or MPS cohorts. As my conclusion predicts, Choice and MPS students are similar in achievement. The Rejects, as would be predicted by the profile of Reject students who returned to MPS, started off worse than both Choice and MPS students. And their later scores declined precipitously. Thus the math phenomenon was conditioned on the Rejects, not on anything happening in either the Choice schools or the larger MPS system. It should be remembered that there are very few Rejects — the yearly N's for the 1990 reject cohort depicted in figure 6.1 were 35, 37, 21, and 27 from 1991 to 1994 respectively.

## Summary

The study of student achievement effects of the MPCP was complex, but I believe the basic conclusion is not. Using different variable sets, student populations, and a range of statistical models and tests, there is no consistent and reliable evidence that the Choice students differed in achievement from randomly selected MPS students or Reject applicants.

In terms of reading, the only significant effect favored MPS students when we included the full variable set based on survey data. However, once we controlled for selection effects, that result became insignificant. There was no evidence of significant differences on reading between Choice and Rejects no matter how the estimates were created.

For math, the story was somewhat different. For the Choice/MPS comparison there was again not a hint of difference between the groups. But for the Choice/Reject comparison, I found a math effect favoring Choice schools, an effect that accelerates if students remained long enough in the Choice schools. I challenged that result, however, based on small sample sizes, nonrandom attrition from the Reject group, and because the results were heavily conditioned on a literal handful of Reject students who scored abysmally low on the math test. Finally, when I compared the Rejects to the random MPS sample, the Rejects did worse than they did against the Choice students. Thus, while there was little evidence of increased improvement in either the Choice or MPS samples, there was evidence of very poor performance from the beginning for the Rejects. The simple conclusion is that the Rejects sample was a small and very poor comparison group. They clearly were not a random sample of Rejects, of Choice, or of MPS students.

## Attrition from the Program

### Attrition Rates

A final concern, as both an outcome measure and a methodological issue, is the level of attrition from the Choice program. For whatever reasons, the attrition rates from the Choice schools were quite high, although they declined over time. The last two rows in table 4.1 in chapter 4 provide the relevant statistics. Attrition was defined as leaving a school before a terminal grade was reached. Because students only had to submit to lottery conditions once, subsequent leaving was the result of either family or school choice. Since the program did not require schools to list nonreadmitted students (and they did not have to readmit Choice students), we cannot distinguish between family choices and school nonadmissions. Regardless of the reasons, the numbers were, in one sense, substantial.

Annual attrition averaged 33.4 percent for all Choice schools, and 30.2 percent if we exclude alternative schools in the Choice program. The numbers are substantial in the sense that if the Choice program is to have a major impact for a number of students, presumably those students would have to remain in the Choice schools for a number of years — and few do. For example, of the initial class of 341 in 1990, four years later in the fall of 1994 there were only 57 students left. Because schools admitted mostly very young students, there were few graduations (Wisconsin Legislative Audit Bureau, 1995, p. 28).

Is attrition itself a measure of Choice school failures? The answer is probably no. Although the numbers appear high, they seem to be in line with the attrition rates in the public schools for the elementary grades. Given data reporting problems on who is in what school in the first month of school, the range of attrition for Kindergarten to eighth graders in MPS was estimated at 22 percent to 28 percent, which is close to that in the Choice program (Witte et al., 1994, p. 22). Thus attrition appears to be a common problem in inner-city school districts, regardless of the type of school.

### Biases in Attrition Students

Who was likely to leave and for what reasons? The characteristics of attrition students varied from year to year, but the four-year profile is interesting and suggestive. A four-year summary is provided in table 6.11. Race and gender statistics represent proportions. Thus 4 percent of continuing students (.04) were white, compared to 7 percent of the attrition students. The general characteristics of continuing, compared to attrition students indicate that whites and blacks were somewhat more likely to leave than Hispanics, and boys more likely to leave than girls. Distance was represented by miles, thus students living farther away from school were more likely to leave.

What is perhaps more important, however, is that attrition students appear to have been underachievers in every sense: lower prior scores, lower post-scores, and lower change scores. The probabilities respresented in column 3 indicate the probability that differences between continuing and attrition students are zero. All of the scores are higher for continuing students than those who left the Choice schools. Math differences are larger, meaning that those who left private schools were worse in math both coming in and leaving than those who stayed. Overall two of the differences were significant at .05 conventional standard, two others were very close (.06 and .07), and the remaining reading scores were still quite high (.11 and .12).

Achievement problems were reflected in a considerably lower opinion of the private school among leaving parents than those who stayed. This is reflected in the school dissatisfaction scale (DisPrScl), on which a

**TABLE 6.11**
Mean Differences between Continuing and Attrition Choice Students, 1990–93

| Variable/Scale | 1 Continuing Students | | | 2 Attrition Students | | | 3 Prob. Diff. = 0 |
|---|---|---|---|---|---|---|---|
| | Mean | Std. Dev. | (N) | Mean | Sd. Dev. | (N) | P |
| Race and gender | | | | | | | |
| African American | 0.72 | 0.45 | 1605 | 0.75 | 0.43 | 684 | 0.097 |
| Hispanic | 0.22 | 0.42 | 1605 | 0.16 | 0.37 | 684 | 0.000 |
| Other minority | 0.02 | 0.13 | 1605 | 0.02 | 0.13 | 684 | 0.821 |
| White | 0.04 | 0.21 | 1605 | 0.07 | 0.26 | 684 | 0.022 |
| Gender (Fem = 1) | 0.56 | 0.50 | 1596 | 0.52 | 0.50 | 673 | 0.049 |
| Distance to school | 3.07 | 2.42 | 1300 | 3.36 | 2.92 | 547 | 0.046 |
| Test scores | | | | | | | |
| Prior RNCE | 38.64 | 15.97 | 832 | 36.87 | 17.68 | 326 | 0.115 |
| Post RNCE | 38.33 | 15.54 | 1142 | 36.62 | 17.01 | 413 | 0.073 |
| RNCE Diff | −0.50 | 14.45 | 805 | −1.86 | 12.76 | 312 | 0.124 |
| Prior MNCE | 40.20 | 18.13 | 844 | 37.95 | 18.83 | 326 | 0.065 |
| Post MNCE | 40.81 | 18.39 | 1191 | 37.80 | 18.07 | 417 | 0.004 |
| MNCE Diff | 0.91 | 15.24 | 818 | −1.79 | 14.95 | 306 | 0.008 |
| Parental Involvement[a] | | | | | | | |
| PiParScl | 10.59 | 4.68 | 644 | 10.18 | 5.20 | 155 | 0.372 |
| PiSclPar | 4.36 | 2.98 | 676 | 4.32 | 3.09 | 164 | 0.896 |
| PiSclOrg | 3.08 | 1.21 | 669 | 2.87 | 1.38 | 159 | 0.088 |
| PiChild | 9.07 | 3.62 | 674 | 8.70 | 3.78 | 164 | 0.256 |
| Parental Attitudes | | | | | | | |
| DisPrScl | 13.21 | 4.26 | 526 | 15.29 | 6.05 | 108 | 0.001 |

[a]For variable abbreviation definitions, see table 4.4.

higher number means greater dissatisfaction. The difference between continuing and leaving parents is approximately 40 percent of a standard deviation and significant at the .01 level. This combination of characteristics makes sense as either an explanation for family choices not to return — the hoped-for educational improvement did not occur — or schools not readmitting lower achieving, nonimproving students, and angry parents.

The four-year pattern of attrition masks important year-to-year variations. Year-to-year data indicate that attrition students in the first two years were very different from one another. After the first year, there was uncertainty about the program in that the courts had not yet decided its validity and the closing of Juanita Virgil Academy had put

TABLE 6.12

Test Scores of Leaving and Returning Choice Students, Spring 1991 and 1992

|  | Leaving Choice Students | | Returning Choice Students | |
|---|---|---|---|---|
|  | R | M | R | M |
| 1991: Mean NCE | 45.3 | 42.2 | 41.6 | 39.7 |
| (N) | (41) | (44) | (129) | (134) |
| 1992: Mean NCE | 35.4 | 35.2 | 38.4 | 37.2 |
| (N) | (87) | (98) | (238) | (248) |

*Source*: Author constructed from Witte et al., 1992, table 20.

political pressure on the program. A number of high-achieving students left that year, presumably pulled out by family decisions. The next year, with the program stabilized, the exact opposite occurred, and this was at least in part induced by the schools not readmitting some of the underachieving and nonimproving students.[15]

The test score means verify these differences. As indicated in table 6.12, there was an extraordinary difference in spring test scores between leaving and returning students in the first two years. The first year, leaving students outperformed returning students by 3.7 NCEs in reading and 2.5 points in math. In the second year, leaving students were 3.0 NCEs *worse* than returning students in reading and 2.0 points *worse* in math.

This difference in attrition is undoubtedly linked to the sharp decline in reading scores for Choice students in the second year, following an increase in reading in the first year (tables 6.2 and 6.4). As indicated in table 6.5, the decline in 1992 was mostly the result of second-year students — those who were indulged for the first year. In the following two years, the remaining students from that first cohort did better in reading, but essentially the same as MPS students. The same phenomenon may well account for the remarkable change in math scores for the first-year cohort. As seen in table 6.6, in 1992, the second-year students had an estimated effect compared to MPS of -1.58 NCEs in math. In 1993, that coefficient changed to a positive (and significant) +2.66 NCEs. Again, and consistent with the reading results, attrition of poor students after the second year could account for this sharp improvement.

[15] The author had a conversation to this affect with the principal of one of the largest schools. He said: "We were very lax the first year because we knew these kids needed readjusting to our style. However, by the end of the second year, it was clear they were not working out, and we let a number go."

These attrition levels suggest several other methodological cautions. First, the small sample sizes allow unique selection decisions, such as one or two schools changing readmission policies, to have quite dramatic effects. Second, the overall attrition of Choice students indicates that if a similar attrition did not occur among the Milwaukee sample, the achievement test results could be biased in favor of Choice students. Over the four-year period, lower-achieving students left the Choice program. But the general lesson is that program attrition is a major problem in terms of both policy conclusions and subsequent evaluations of similar programs.

### Why Students Left

The characteristics of attrition students described above indicate that they were not doing as well and were much less satisfied with Choice schools than students who continued. Followup survey data tend to confirm that conclusion, although the data are far from perfect. Because those who left were not known until the September following the close of school in June, it was extremely hard to track down nonreturning families. The response rates to mailed and phone surveys were only 38 percent. We must assume that the largest bias in these responses was missing families who moved out of the Milwaukee area. Telephone searches were impossible for that group.

Parents were asked two open-ended questions: Why did your child leave the Choice program school? Where is he/she going to school now? The responses to the first question are given in table 6.13. Of the reasons parents gave for leaving, only 15 percent of the responses (and they could give more than one) indicated child- or family-specific reasons—including moving. This category is clearly underestimated, however. Almost all of the remaining responses were critical of some aspect of the Choice program or the private schools. The leading problems with the program were the lack of religious training, school transportation problems, and difficulties in reapplying to the program (including references to not being readmitted). Within-school problems most often cited were unhappiness with the staff (usually teachers), dissatisfaction with the general quality of education, and perceptions that discipline was too strict. The lack of special programs, which might have been available elsewhere, was also cited in 6 percent of the responses. Thus, survey responses fit with the factors that seem to distinguish attrition students from those who remain—distance and transportation problems, less achievement success, and resulting dissatisfaction with the private schools.

TABLE 6.13
Why Choice Students Left the Choice Program, 1991–94

| Responses | (N) | % |
|---|---|---|
| Quality of program | 68 | 30.5 |
| Lack of religious training | 13 | 5.8 |
| Lack of transportation | 17 | 7.6 |
| Income | 9 | 4.0 |
| Application problems | 14 | 6.3 |
| Fee changes | 13 | 5.8 |
| Selection problems | 2 | 0.9 |
| Quality of the choice school | 96 | 43.0 |
| Poor education | 20 | 9.0 |
| Too disciplinarian | 13 | 5.8 |
| Unhappy with staff | 31 | 13.9 |
| Lack of programs for special needs students | 14 | 6.3 |
| Lack of programs for talented students | 2 | 0.9 |
| Too segregated | 1 | 0.4 |
| Child terminated | 3 | 1.3 |
| Lack of teaching materials | 7 | 3.1 |
| Child/family specific | 43 | 19.3 |
| Transportation — too far away | 12 | 5.4 |
| Moved | 15 | 6.7 |
| Pregnancy | 3 | 1.3 |
| Quit school | 4 | 1.8 |
| Child custody change | 2 | 0.9 |
| Miscellaneous | 9 | 4.0 |
| Total | 223 | |

Question: "What were the major reasons your child did not continue in last year's school?" (Respondents could give up to three answers.)


## Where Did Students Go?

Our survey data were very consistent with later efforts by the Wisconsin Legislative Audit Bureau to track attrition students back to MPS. Our survey data indicated that approximately half of the students who left after the second and third years (57 percent) enrolled in MPS schools, 26 percent in other private schools in the area (often for religious reasons), with the remaining 16 percent going to private MPS contract schools, home schooling, or schools outside Milwaukee. The Legislative Audit Bureau confirmed that 51.5 percent of the students had enrolled in MPS after leaving the private Choice schools (Wisconsin Legislative Audit Bureau, 1995, p. 35).

In summary, attrition from the Choice program declined over time and appeared to be similar to the rates of movement between schools for MPS students. However, mobility of students was undoubtedly a problem for both sets of schools. The picture of those who left differed somewhat over the years, but for the four-year period, students who left were not doing as well in Choice schools as those who remained. That was reflected in their parents' dissatisfaction with the schools. It is therefore difficult to interpret attrition from the program in a positive light. The rates were high and poorer students disproportionately returned to the public schools.

## Summary and Conclusions

### Outcome Summary

The outcomes of the Milwaukee Parental Choice Program were multiple, pointed in somewhat different directions, and are, to some degree, open to differing interpretations. The sum of effects on private schools was probably positive. Clearly the major schools in the program benefited financially from the program. Their balance sheets improved, teacher and administrator turnover declined, and buildings were repaired, expanded, and built. On the negative side of the ledger, three schools went bankrupt in the middle of the year, and another closed during the summer. Choice supporters view this as admirable elimination of poorly performing schools; detractors note that serious illegal activities were associated with several school closings and that there was considerable disruption to the education of the students involved.

In general, the effects on parents were positive. On average, they were much more satisfied with the private schools than they were with their former public schools. Although these results could have been affected by response bias to our surveys, we detected little and the shifts in attitudes were robust and consistent across several different measures. Further, the satisfaction seemed to be most rooted in the dimensions that were most troubling in the public schools: educational environment and discipline. In addition, parental involvement in most forms improved from an already high level in their prior public schools. Finally, the parents almost unanimously approved of the program and felt it should be continued.

Student outcomes were the most difficult to assess and interpret. Because the students were either in elementary or alternative schools, standardized achievement test scores were the prevailing quantitative indicators of student outcomes. Attendance appeared to be a little higher than in public schools, but because at the elementary level all attendance rates are high, it was hard to make a clear comparison.

In terms of achievement tests I concluded, after repeated permuta-
tions of data and models, that there were no differences in achievement
gains in either reading or math between Choice and MPS students. I
further argued that although there was a Choice advantage in math in
comparison between Choice and Reject students after four years, the
comparison was unfortunately invalid. Nonrandom attrition from the
Reject sample and the extremely small Ns led to the differences being
based on literally a handful of Reject students who may well not have
completed the math test.

All of these results are bolstered by the fact that no one who has
looked at these data has found any statistically significant differences in
reading. Over large populations in the United States, math and reading
standardized tests are correlated in the .6 to .7 range (Witte, 1992). The
researchers who claim dramatic math gains need to explain why there
would be such dramatic gains in math and none in reading. My answer
was that the math gains were fictitious — they resulted not from gains by
Choice students but by aberrant scores for a small set of Reject students
who happened to be still taking tests in the public schools four years
after they were rejected from the Choice program.

Attrition (not counting students in alternative choice schools) was 44
percent, 32 percent, 28 percent, and 23 percent in the four years of the
program. Estimates of attrition in MPS were uncertain, but it appears
that attrition from the Choice program was comparable to the range of
mobility between schools in MPS. Those who left the program had
lower prior test scores, lower scores in the private schools, and lower
change scores than students who returned. Not surprisingly, the parents
of attrition students expressed lower levels of satisfaction with the
Choice schools. Based on followup surveys and interviews, we know
that approximately half of the students returned to MPS schools, with
most of the rest going to other private schools.

## Conclusions

My foremost conclusion is to challenge the proclamation that the MPCP
could be the vehicle for reducing the gap between white and minority
students by a very large amount. Even the best evidence (the 10-point
math miracle) is so fragile that throwing out seven students makes the
finding statistically insignificant. Second, the myriad of selection problems with both groups indicates the evidence may well be totally spu-
rious. Third, even if the evidence held up, we have little idea to whom it
would apply. Clearly the Choice "miracle" would not carry over to even
the low-income students in MPS. They do as well as the Choice students

on math, perhaps slightly better on reading, and they overwhelm their Reject classmates. All of these factors suggest the need for caution and moderation in generalizing these results.

But even if the "miracle" were true, what is it about these private schools that produced the miracle? Our analysis of these schools found them to be initially stressed, with several operating on the brink of financial disaster. Other than the fact that they had very high levels of staff turnover, very low pay, and poor resources, they tended to look much like public schools in terms of their class structure, curriculum, and pedagogy. They did stress discipline and were able to pressure parents and students with nonadmission or expulsion. Several had unique specialties, but those specialties also existed in the public schools.

Thus what I concluded in chapter 5 was that the private schools were very admirable schools, struggling against the same types of forces affecting public schools in Milwaukee. Neither I, as the official evaluator of the program, nor private school administrators ever claimed they could perform some dramatic educational miracles. It would seem to me that other researchers professing such results have a major responsibility to outline the causal mechanism by which these miracles are to be accomplished. Is it only their private school status? Is it only competition? Because, if it is something they do differently and better, those of us who have devoted many years to studying inner-city education in America would like to know exactly what it is.

Rather, I suspect these schools are similar to the public schools—some excellent, some mediocre, and some poor—with very few miracles in sight. Does this necessarily mean that the program was a failure? I believe not. The MPCP provided an opportunity for an alternative education for poor families who were not satisfied with public schools and whose children were not excelling in those schools. Subsequent parental satisfaction increased. In addition, some students did very well, while on average Choice students achieved about as well in terms of national standards as where they began. Further, the subsidies to the private schools allowed several schools to survive and later flourish.

This does not mean, however, that this program should serve as an endorsement for a full-scale, unlimited voucher program. None of the Milwaukee research can legitimately be generalized to that type of program. That has not prevented the evaluations and research reports on the program from being used in national debates over a universal voucher program. And they have contributed to expansions of the program that will inevitably challenge the current interpretation of the First Amendment. Why and how that has occurred is the subject of the next chapter.

# Appendix to Chapter 6 _____

## Modeling Selection Bias

THIS appendix offers the reader yet another method of modeling value-added achievement gains, and it provides further estimates comparing Choice students with only low-income MPS students. However, its primary purpose is to describe tests and alternative estimations to control for selection bias.

The modeling approach used in tables A6.1 and A6.2 includes simple treatment effects, parallel to the Choice indicator variable in the chapter, but only including low-income MPS students. However, also included are two trend effects, controlling both for trends in Choice students and years in the program for MPS students. The first trend for Choice is as a continuous variable; the second uses indicator variables to break the trend into years as was done in the main body of the chapter.

The basic results are contained in table A6.1 for both SRDB control variables and for the Full Variable Set that included variables obtained from surveys. As in the chapter, the sample sizes decline considerably for the latter. For parsimony, the results in the table do not include the coefficients for the control variables.

The basic conclusions from table A6.1 mirror the results presented in the chapter. There were no differences in math and no significant differences in reading until the Full Variable Set of control variables was included. When included, the negative coefficient on reading became significant, indicating Choice students did worse than MPS (as in the main analysis in the chapter). A slight difference from the results of the chapter was that the negative impact of reading was traced to both of the first two years. In the chapter, the first-year estimate was negative, but not significant (see table 6.4).

Because there was potential for selection bias both entering and leaving the program, I conducted several tests on all the relevant samples. Selection into the program was difficult to model because the normal instrumental variables did not work in this context. The two most often used and cited variables as instruments for school selection are school distance (Kane and Rouse, 1993, for college enrollment) and religion (Hoxby, 1996). This program, being nonsectarian, nullified the latter, and the court-ordered busing program in Milwaukee nullified the for-

**TABLE A6.1**

Ordinary Least Squares, 1991–94, Choice (Treatment) and Low-Income MPS Students ($b$, std. Error of $b$)[a]

| | SRDB Only | | | | | |
| --- | --- | --- | --- | --- | --- | --- |
| | Reading | | | Math | | |
| | (1) | (2) | (3) | (4) | (5) | (6) |
| Treatment | −.55 | −.47 | — | −.17 | −.47 | — |
| | (.47) | (1.15) | — | (.51) | (1.15) | — |
| Treat*Yrs | — | −.07 | — | — | −.07 | — |
| | — | (.47) | — | — | (.47) | — |
| YrsInPrg. | — | −.35 | −.35 | — | −.35 | −.33 |
| | — | (.20) | (.20) | — | (.20) | (.22) |
| TreatYR1 | — | — | −.36 | — | — | −1.17 |
| | — | — | (.89) | — | — | (.93) |
| TreatYR2 | — | — | −.98 | — | — | −.29 |
| | — | — | (.69) | — | — | (.81) |
| TreatYR3 | — | — | −.26 | — | — | .96 |
| | — | — | (.94) | — | — | (.93) |
| TreatYR4 | — | — | −1.05 | — | — | −.43 |
| | — | — | (1.23) | — | — | (1.57) |
| $R^2$ | .39 | .39 | .39 | .44 | .44 | .44 |
| MSE | 12.48 | 12.48 | 12.48 | 13.68 | 13.68 | 13.68 |
| Reading: N = 4,019 | | | | Math: N = 3,967 | | |

| | Full Variable Set | | | | | |
| --- | --- | --- | --- | --- | --- | --- |
| | Reading | | | Math | | |
| | (1) | (2) | (3) | (4) | (5) | (6) |
| Treatment | −1.75* | −3.77* | — | −.07 | −2.05 | — |
| | (.71) | (1.63) | — | (.81) | (1.94) | — |
| Treat*Yrs | — | .87 | — | — | .86 | — |
| | — | (.66) | — | — | (.78) | — |
| YrsInPrg. | — | −.61 | −.61 | — | −.55 | −.55 |
| | — | (.38) | (.38) | — | (.45) | (.45) |
| TreatYR1 | — | — | −2.37* | — | — | −1.07 |
| | — | — | (1.24) | — | — | (1.47) |
| TreatYR2 | — | — | −2.71** | — | — | −.60 |
| | — | — | (1.00) | — | — | (1.12) |
| TreatYR3 | — | — | −.98 | — | — | .89 |
| | — | — | (1.31) | — | — | (1.32) |
| TreatYR4 | — | — | .21 | — | — | 1.08 |
| | — | — | (1.62) | — | — | (2.05) |
| $R^2$ | .41 | .41 | .41 | .46 | .46 | .46 |
| MSE | 12.06 | 12.06 | 12.07 | 13.72 | 13.72 | 13.73 |
| Reading: N = 1,320 | | | | Math: N = 1,311 | | |

***Probability that $b = 0 < .001$

**Probability that $b = 0 < .01$

*Probability that $b = 0 < .05$

[a]Standard errors are robust using White/Huber estimation procedures to account for clustering. Also included in the *SRDB* equation are prior tests for reading and math, test grade, and race and gender indicator variables. In addition to the *SRDB* variables, the *Full Variable* set adds log income, mother's education, employment, educational expectations, and marital status.

mer. Inclusion of various models with Inverse Mills ratios in the first-order selection equation had no effect once the other control variables were included. In part this may be due to the requirements of value-added assessment. Prior tests, in combination with other control variables affecting both Choice and achievement, could offset any potential Choice selection effects.

I was more successful in modeling selection out of the program, defined in any year as not having a posttest. However, the results of the corrections were modest. The absence of test data for Choice and MPS students occurred in a number of ways. First, as indicated in the chapter, for Choice students there was a high and sustained attrition from the Choice schools. In addition, some students in private schools were not tested because they were in kindergarten or first grade or because they were absent. The chapter analyzed attrition from the Choice sample over the four years of this study. The conclusion was that the better Choice students were likely to stay the course into the third and fourth years of the program.

Attrition from the MPS sample was due either to moving out of the system or not being tested in a given year. The latter was much more prevalent in that Milwaukee only tested all students in the second, fifth, and seventh grades. However, in compliance with Chapter 1 of the Primary and Secondary Education Act, students qualifying for Chapter 1 aid were required to be tested every year. Because Chapter 1 is means-tested, poor, minority students were more likely to be included in MPS testing. Combined with the upward SES bias of those students leaving the MPS system, missing tests could introduce selection biases in the Choice/MPS comparisons. The dual effects of retaining the better students in Choice, while over-testing and retaining the weaker students in MPS, would suggest that the combined biases would work to the disadvantage of MPS students.

One test of the general problem of missing data from the model is provided by using two-stage Heckman correction models to model missing data and then reestimate the achievement model using maximum likelihood estimates (Heckman, 1979). That procedure worked well, with first-stage results (available from the author) indicating that more treatment group tests were available than MPS tests, and that black and Hispanic students from lower-income, less educated families were more likely to be tested.

However, the effects on the reestimated models, given in table A6.2, were modest. The one effect of note was that the reading results that favored MPS students in the Full Variables model were no longer significant (lower panel, columns 1–3, table A6.2). Thus the adverse selection out of Choice may have been offset by the fact that almost all students

**TABLE A6.2**

Heckman Two-Stage Results, 1991–94, Choice (Treatment) and Low-Income MPS Students ($b$, std. error of $b$)[a]

| | SRDB Only | | | | | |
| | Reading | | | Math | | |
| | (1) | (2) | (3) | (4) | (5) | (6) |
|---|---|---|---|---|---|---|
| Treatment | −1.06* | −.95 | — | .45 | −1.14 | — |
| | (.51) | (1.25) | — | (.57) | (1.38) | — |
| Treat*Yrs | — | −.09 | — | — | .70 | — |
| | — | (.51) | — | — | (.57) | — |
| YrsInPrg. | — | −.40 | −.40 | — | −.35 | −.36 |
| | — | (.21) | (.21) | — | (.24) | (.24) |
| TreatYR1 | — | — | −.91 | — | — | −.53 |
| | — | — | (.92) | — | — | (1.02) |
| TreatYR2 | — | — | −1.41 | — | — | .13 |
| | — | — | (.78) | — | — | (.86) |
| TreatYR3 | — | — | −.77 | — | — | 1.63 |
| | — | — | (.92) | — | — | (1.01) |
| TreatYR4 | — | — | −1.68 | — | — | .64 |
| | — | — | (1.46) | — | — | (1.62) |
| Chi-Sq. | 198.60 | 200.96 | 203.09 | 184.20 | 186.39 | 188.24 |
| Lambda | −8.51 | −8.51 | −8.51 | 8.09 | 8.11 | 8.10 |
| Reading: N = 4,116 | | | | Math: N = 4,132 | | |

| | Full Variable Set | | | | | |
| | Reading | | | Math | | |
| | (1) | (2) | (3) | (4) | (5) | (6) |
|---|---|---|---|---|---|---|
| Treatment | −1.34 | −3.15 | — | −.33 | −2.49 | — |
| | (.87) | (1.81) | — | (1.19) | (2.13) | — |
| Treat*Yrs | — | .75 | — | — | .92 | — |
| | — | (.69) | — | — | (.79) | — |
| YrsInPrg. | — | −.59 | −.59 | — | −.56 | −.56 |
| | — | (.39) | (.39) | — | (.45) | (.45) |
| TreatYR1 | — | — | −1.94 | — | — | −1.45 |
| | — | — | (1.37) | — | — | (1.66) |
| TreatYR2 | — | — | −2.18 | — | — | −.90 |
| | — | — | (1.16) | — | — | (1.47) |
| TreatYR3 | — | — | −1.02 | — | — | .69 |
| | — | — | (1.30) | — | — | (1.63) |
| TreatYR4 | — | — | .57 | — | — | .75 |
| | — | — | (1.92) | — | — | (2.31) |
| Chi-Sq. | 646.52 | 648.32 | 650.34 | 588.11 | 590.17 | 592.20 |
| Lambda | 2.02 | 1.77 | 1.77 | −1.08 | −1.29 | −1.32 |
| Reading: N = 1,566 | | | | Math: N = 1,570 | | |

***Probability that $b = 0 < .001$

**Probability that $b = 0 < .01$

*Probability that $b = 0 < .05$

[a]The *SRDB* equations include prior tests for reading and math, test grade, and race and gender indicator variables. In addition to the *SRDB* variables, the *Full Variable* set adds log income, mother's education, employment, educational expectations, and marital status. Distance to present school is included in the first-stage model.

in Choice were tested every year. The fact that employing this common selection correction eliminated the significance of the reading difference adds further evidence to my conclusion that none of the numerous models or approaches indicated any consistent evidence that Choice and MPS students differed in terms of achievement.

# 7

## The Politics of Vouchers

EDUCATIONAL VOUCHER ADVOCATES consistently tout the educational advantages of voucher programs. In the context of American experiments with vouchers in Milwaukee and Cleveland, advocates emphasize the benefits for poor, minority students. Those opposed also cast the arguments in educational terms — the advent of vouchers leading to the demise of public education by draining resources of public school systems. But neither argument may be genuine. Voucher programs are likely to have immediate and direct impacts that have little to do with educational outcomes. The battle and politics over vouchers may have more to do with money and with the allocation of power than with education.

Many years ago Harold Lasswell in a wonderfully short monograph defined and explicated politics as "who gets what, when, and how" (Lasswell, 1958). More complicated theories could be brought to bear on explaining the politics of vouchers. However, with one addition — "why?" — this simple and basic set of questions frames the issues quite well.

There are interests that will benefit from various voucher programs. Some families benefit and others do not. There are also institutions that benefit and perhaps others that will lose. So "who gets what" is clearly relevant.

The "when" is also crucial and provides a fascinating example of policy patience and incremental decision making. In the past, incrementalism was often associated with powerful elites forestalling or vetoing governmental actions that challenged their dominant position and ideological justifications (Lindblom, 1979). The voucher case is different. While one set of powerful actors plays this reactionary role, other elites are proactive and use their power to keep the issue alive and moving forward. The irony is that most of the proactive elites who use the incremental process in seeking government subsidies are usually thought to be conservatives and tend to be partisan Republicans. Those opposed and clinging to the status quo are often thought to be liberals and are aligned with the Democratic party.

The "how" is also critical to our understanding of public policy formation and change. Voucher policy has been partly a high-pitched debate over the organization and delivery of education. But that debate has operated on multiple levels and in many forms. Those forms have included public opinion polls, policy-elite and legislative debates, and what I will stress—a healthy dose of media influence. My term for the latter is "choice theater," which I find the most appropriate metaphor for explaining the unfolding of voucher politics.

Finally, and most elusive, is the "why?" Perhaps that is why Lasswell excluded it from his famous list. To answer the question "why" invokes scary phenomena for those who profess to be positivists, because the "why" implies delving into strategies, motives, and intentions. And it implies that they matter. But I believe those strategies, motives, and intentions are absolutely essential in explaining the course of voucher policy and in understanding how it should be judged.

The chapter follows these questions by first addressing the long-term politics of vouchers in Milwaukee and Cleveland. Considerable emphasis is placed on how the programs gradually expand, and how the Cleveland program begins at the advanced stage of the Milwaukee program. Thus the programs can be seen as overlapping policy layers, with each layer moving from a more targeted to a more universal program.

The second section of the chapter addresses the question of how the program has been affected by the enormous media attention it has drawn. The third highlights the role of the courts and how they may be affected by the politics of choice and choice theater. I argue that the effects can be considerable given the wide scatter of legal precedents and the nebulous nature of the core concepts the courts have developed in this area of First Amendment law. What this means is that judges can find support for just about any position, thus allowing judgments to be affected by raw politics.

The final substantive section deals with the question "why?" That involves the intentions of key actors, especially voucher advocates. The argument advanced is that the most plausible explanation for the continuity and expansion of vouchers has little to do with aiding poor, minority students, and much more with distributing subsidies to those who now attend private schools, or would do so in the future.

## The Politics of the Voucher Movement

To understand and interpret the politics of vouchers, we first need to understand the stakes involved and the national coalitions facing off on this issue. Because that face-off has produced a stalemate, the politics of vouchers has followed an incremental path. In this scaled-down format,

which has been taken over by state and local politicians, odd combinations of actors, coming from very different perspectives, have been the moving forces — especially in the successful cases of Milwaukee and Cleveland. But against the background of these local political battles, national players loom, and above them the courts.

## Partisan Politics

Despite the rhetoric of choice supporters that the movement for vouchers is a bipartisan issue, generally the evidence indicates that it is not — Republicans support vouchers, Democrats by and large do not. Presidents Reagan and Bush were outspoken supporters of vouchers, as was Robert Dole. Bush's two sons, Jeb in Florida and George Jr. in Texas, made vouchers a central plank in their respective races for governor. Clinton and Dole, agreeing on much about education policy, differed sharply on private school vouchers in the 1996 election. Dole released his proposal for a $2.5 billion voucher program during a visit to Milwaukee in the summer of 1996. The Milwaukee program not only was featured by the press, but also became a point of disagreement in the presidential election debates (*Washington Post*, 19 July 1996, p. A29).

Vouchers have also been a high-profile issue in Congress, where partisan politics has also been the rule. Although Congress has not actually voted on vouchers in many instances, a Senate vote on February 8, 1994, on an amendment to add a voucher demonstration program to *The Goals 2000 Educate America Act*, was defeated 41 to 52 on a highly partisan vote (D: 5–47; R: 36–5). As of this writing, in the latest recorded congressional vote on October 9, 1997, the House approved a voucher demonstration proposal for Washington, D.C., by a bare 203–202 majority. On that vote, of the 202 negative votes, only 11 were Republicans. The bill failed to pass only when the Senate refused to stop Senator Kennedy's filibuster on a 58–41 vote.

Partisan support for statewide and local initiatives has also been important. To date, Republican governors have headed all the movements for private school choice. That has been true of the legislative efforts in Wisconsin (Thompson), Ohio (Voinovich), Pennsylvania (Ridge), Minnesota (Carlson), New Jersey (Whitman), Michigan (Engler), Texas (Bush), and Connecticut (Rowland). The one exception was Republican Governor Pete Wilson, who failed to support the California referendum in 1993. He stated that he felt it would be potentially too costly given the budget crisis in California at the time. Although a number of Demo-

cratic governors have supported public school choice proposals, none
have supported, or worked to introduce, private school vouchers.[1]

## National Coalitions

The groups forming opposing coalitions at the national level generally
follow these partisan divisions. Groups normally associated with the
Democratic party are usually staunchly aligned against voucher proposals — both in the legislative arena and in filing court cases. In a *Washington Post* article cited earlier, Milton Friedman clearly identified the
opposition: "No one has succeeded in getting a voucher program system adopted, thanks primarily to the political power of the school establishment, more recently reinforced by the National Education Association and the American Federation of Teachers, together the strongest
political lobbying body in the United States" (Friedman, 1995). Teachers
and other school-based associations (principals, superintendents, administrators, and parents) are often joined by state departments of education, state school boards, and civil rights organizations in opposing
voucher legislation.

Equally as impressive, although not always as consistent, are the
forces moving the voucher movement forward. In alignment with prominent Republican leaders are associated businesses groups, influential
entrepreneurs, and conservative foundations and think tanks. The network of choice advocates includes academics, private sector proponents
(such as employees of the Edison project or Pat Rooney, President of
Golden Rule Insurance Company), and a number of policy research institutes and foundations (such as the Hudson Institute, Landmark Inc.,
the Bradley Foundation, the Reason Foundation, and the Heritage
Foundation). Key people in these organizations know each other and
are often on call when states are beginning to think about choice issues.
These networks provide a degree of commonality in policy formation as
well as continuous promotion of the ideas. Recent studies by Mintrom
and Vergari meticulously analyzed the importance of these networks in
the diffusion of education choice programs between states (Mintrom
and Vergari, 1998).

Business support was initially not as strong at the national level as
might be expected, but has grown considerably over time. Several groups,
the Committee for Economic Development and the Business Round-
tables have endorsed public school choice, but have not supported pri-

---

[1] A letter supporting the first phase of the Milwaukee voucher experiment (without
religious schools) was sent by then-Governor Clinton to Representative Polly Williams.
He later changed his mind during his first presidential campaign.

vate school vouchers, working instead on various public school reform proposals. On the other hand, the day the Wisconsin Supreme Court upheld the MPCP including religious schools in June 1998, a group of national business leaders pledged to raise $200 million for a national voucher program to send 50,000 poor students to private schools (*New York Times*, 11 June 1998, p. 1). Also, as shown below, state and local business groups have been instrumental at critical times in formulating and advancing the voucher agenda.

The other major players involved in the politics of school choice are private school and religious interest groups. In general, private schools and their associations favor vouchers. A recent study by Michael Mintrom found a statisically significant correlation across states between the introduction of choice legislation and the percentage of private schools in the state (Mintrom, 1997). Their support is at times cautious in that they fear state regulation if they receive public funding.[2] Although there are exceptions for specific groups, religious interest groups also generally endorse voucher initiatives.[3] For example, several years ago, the Christian Coalition came out with a major policy statement, "Project Samaritan," advocating vouchers for students in all private schools in our one hundred largest cities (Associated Press, 4 February 1995).

The one more or less constant force in the voucher movement is the Roman Catholic church. In six of the ten states with the largest enrollment of Catholic school students, the movement for school choice has been significant (California, Pennsylvania, New Jersey, Ohio, Michigan, and Wisconsin). The remaining states have been mixed politically or are controlled by Democratic governors (New York, Illinois, Missouri, and Louisiana).[4] In Wisconsin, church leadership was solidly behind the effort to expand choice to religious schools (Archbishop Rembert Weakland, Wisconsin, *Catholic Herald*, 16 February 1995, p. 3). As discussed below, major interest groups connected to the church were also

[2] In all states, because private schools are mostly religiously affiliated and contain religious instruction, the free exercise clause of the First Amendment limits the regulatory powers of states. Thus state regulations of private schools are a fraction of the regulations applying to public schools.

[3] Jewish groups are not of one mind on vouchers, for example. In Wisconsin, Milwaukee Jewish groups stridently opposed expansion of the Choice program (*Madison Capital Times*, 1 January 1995, p. 1). Similarly, when the Wisconsin Supreme Court upheld the program in June 1998, the American Jewish Conference opposed the decision (*New York Times*, 11 June 1998, p. 1). But the opposite occurred in California, where orthodox Jews were leaders in the 1993 initiative effort (*Los Angeles Times*, 18 October 1993, p. 1).

[4] In Illinois, Governor Edgar has pushed several times for choice initiatives, including during the Chicago school reform negotiations (*Wall Street Journal*, editorial, 29 March 1995).

pivotal actors in that expansion. Similarly, in both Pennsylvania and
Ohio, Catholic support for vouchers was overt — and each is a heavily
Catholic state. Governor Ridge's proposals in Pennsylvania were supported by Catholic associations, as were his earlier efforts when the
legislature was split between Democrats and Republicans. This support
is not surprising given the precipitous decline in Catholic school enrollment, especially in inner-city parishes that tend to be increasingly poor
and non-Catholic (see chapter 3).

## Political Stalemate at the State and National Levels

As is often the case when there is direct confrontation over a very controversial issue, and opposing forces are well organized and politically
powerful, the status quo is maintained. In this case, the status quo also
has some advantages for members of both political parties. Although
when the issue comes to a political head, partisan differences emerge,
there is some ambivalence in each party. Liberal Democrats often represent inner-city or ethnic religious voters, both of whom might benefit
from vouchers. But unions also support these Democrats, including
teachers' unions that oppose privatization. Conservative Republicans
would certainly applaud vouchers for furthering privatization, weaken-
ing unions, and putting pressure on education bureaucracies. However,
vouchers would not necessarily benefit their suburban or rural constituents who seem content with their current public schools. Vouchers
could prove costly, while also possibly increasing regulations on private
schools.

Thus a stalemate over large-scale voucher programs results both from
the political confrontation of powerful groups and the political ambivalence of some members of each political party. What has resulted, however, is not retreat on the part of voucher advocates. Rather, a two-
pronged strategy seems to have emerged: (1) keep the pressure on at the
national and state levels; and (2) begin highly publicized voucher experiments at the local level. Such programs can be structured to gain political acquiescence, engender the sympathy of the widest possible audience, and provide the best possible court case for establishing the
constitutionality of vouchers.

## Incremental Expansion of the Milwaukee Program

Expansion of the Milwaukee voucher program occurred in two steps in
the state's budget bills in 1993 and 1995. The results of these changes

are also outlined in figure 3.1. The 1993 changes were modest — consisting of expanding the total number of students from 1 percent to 1.5 percent of the MPS student enrollment (an expansion of about 500 students); and expanding the maximum number of Choice students in any school from 49 percent to 65 percent. Several other nontrivial provisions that had been introduced as administrative rules were also codified in the statute. These included exempting from random selection students whose siblings already attended the school.

Not included in the changes in 1993, despite being recommended by both the governor and the state school superintendent (opposing forces in the battle over vouchers), were recommendations from our evaluations that the private schools (1) meet public school state requirements for testing and reporting data; (2) have the same financial accounting and audit requirements as nonprofit organizations; and (3) have a formal governance structure (Witte et al., 1991; 1992). These conditions were all lacking in the bankrupt Juanita Virgil Academy.

By 1995, the governor and both houses of the legislature were (narrowly) Republican. With the very active support of the Milwaukee business community and religious private schools, Governor Thompson proposed expanding the program. The expansion legislation was drafted in December 1994 by a group of Milwaukee business, private school, and religious interest group leaders. Representative Polly Williams approved the draft with modifications.

The legislation was formally introduced as part of the governor's budget bill, but he made it the cornerstone of his education proposals highlighted in his State of the State address in January 1995. His support for choice and vouchers was very general:

> School choice is more than a program . . . it is a philosophy. It is a belief that parents know best when it comes to their own children. . . . It is a belief that poor parents have the same right to choose that other parents do. . . . It is the belief that parents will choose the best school for their child. That's education serving the public.
>
> We are expanding our Milwaukee private school choice program to include more children and all private schools. If a mother in Milwaukee wants her child to walk to the private school across the street instead of being bused to public school across town . . . she is going to have that choice. If that private school across the street has a religious affiliation . . . she still is going to have that choice. Religious values are not the problem, drop-out rates are. (Thompson, 1995)

The original proposed expansion (1) included parochial schools; (2) allowed all students already in private schools to be eligible; (3) allowed 100 percent of the students in a school to be Choice students; (4) re-

moved the program limit on total students who could receive vouchers; and (5) dropped the annual evaluations. Religious groups and the business leaders involved opposed random selection. The original draft in December 1994 dropped it (Mitchell, 1994), but Representative Williams interceded and insisted that randomization be retained.

To conform to the *Mueller v. Allen* decision, the bill also changed the way vouchers would be paid. In the existing program, which did not include religious schools and thus did not have to worry about First Amendment challenges, the vouchers were paid directly to the private schools. However, since *Mueller* noted that tuition tax credits went to parents, not religious schools, the new legislation stipulated that parents would receive checks that would then be countersigned and cashed by the private schools.

During the redrafting of the bill in the Joint Finance Committee, current private school students were made eligible only if they were in the third grade or lower.[5] After long arguments, the program was limited to 15,000 students, which would have included more students than currently enrolled in all private schools in Milwaukee. With those changes, the bill was approved by the Joint Finance Committee by a vote of 11 to 4. The three opposing Democrats supported the contentions by opposing Republican Dale Schulz. After noting that the voucher program's $26,000 family income limit was close to middle class in his rural district, Schulz stated: "It is inevitable that there will be demands for state-wide expansion," and "I'm warning you—every low-income voter in your district is going to demand to know why they are being treated differently than people in Milwaukee" (Cleaver, 1995; *Wisconsin State Journal*, 12 May 1995, p. 3B).

Whether that expansion will come depends on a number of factors, including the actions of the courts. As summarized in figure 3.1, however, changes in the MPCP have only expanded the program. The shifting coalitions and divisions between coalition members suggest that the intent of the most powerful forces is for a universal voucher program.

*Shifting Coalitions*

The initial 1990 choice legislation was primarily the creation of four people—Governor Thompson, Representative Polly Williams, Dr. How-

---

[5] Because private schools prefer to admit students in lower grades to socialize them early in school practices, this was not the concession it might appear. For example, in the Choice program from 1990 to 1994, over 60 percent of the students were admitted in kindergarten through second grade (Witte et al., 1995). In Cleveland in the first year, with only kindergarten to third grade students eligible, 64 percent were in kindergarten or first grade (Ohio Department of Education, 1997).

ard Fuller, and George Mitchell. Fuller was a black activist turned government administrator who was raised on Milwaukee's North Side and
had joined with Williams in battles with white-run MPS. When he was
appointed to the cabinet of Democratic Governor Tony Earl in 1982, he
conceived the idea of a governor's study commission on Milwaukee education. His immediate goal was to put pressure on MPS to release data
on racial differences in achievement, which he surmised correctly were
considerable. Mitchell, then a Milwaukee businessman, was appointed
chair of the commission. I was appointed Executive Director of the
commission. Later Mitchell supported Williams and Fuller in their effort to create an all-black school district in the middle of Milwaukee
(centered around Fuller's old North Division High School). Ironically,
Fuller was appointed in 1992 as Superintendent of MPS, but by that
time Williams, Fuller, and Mitchell had become staunch choice supporters.

The Milwaukee business community, other than Mitchell, was not
very involved in vouchers before 1990. Through an organization of
large company CEOs, the Greater Milwaukee Committee (GMC), business leaders had created and funded the Education Trust, which was
dedicated to reform and support for the public schools. The attitudes of
the business community, however, and the influence of the GMC changed
radically after passage of the 1990 voucher program. At the center of
the change were two organizations—the conservative Bradley Foundation,[6] headed by Michael Joyce, and the Metropolitan Milwaukee Association of Commerce (MMAC), directed and chaired by men who became staunch voucher supporters. Joyce was instrumental in using his
position and access to the Milwaukee business community to convert
many of the most influential business leaders to the voucher cause. He
was very forthright about his beliefs in interviews in 1994 on the role of
business in educational reforms:

> What you have now in the business community is a contest between those
> who prefer moderate incremental status quo oriented reforms which turn out
> to be failures . . . (and those) who are more interested in providing greater
> accountability to the consumers, to the parents and who are questioning the
> degree of political organization that exists with respect to the unions and the
> like. (Rigdon, 1995, chapter 5)

---

[6] The Bradley Foundation funds a policy institute, the Wisconsin Policy Research Institute. Over the years, in addition to funding a number of very pro-choice papers, it also
produced papers attacking public schools, papers on the liberal Wisconsin welfare system,
and a number of papers on crime and prisons that argued for longer jail terms, more
restrictive parole, and privatization of prisons. The Foundation also was a major supporter of Charles Murray after he was asked to leave the Manhattan Institute and while he
was writing *The Bell Curve*.

Joyce's role in converting the business community, and using the very significant funds of the Bradley Foundation to support private vouchers, institutes, and lobbying groups supporting choice, was confirmed by both supporters and opponents of choice. One staunch choice supporter, Quentin Quade, who with Bradley Foundation help, created an institute to support educational choice and vouchers, acknowledged Joyce's role: "Michael Joyce at the Bradley Foundation has always been a strong educational choice advocate and he has strong links to the business leadership in the community. Therefore, he became a force, arguing with his councils to think more about educational choice" (Rigdon, 1995, chapter 5). An important civic activist and proponent of public school reform succinctly described the conversion of Milwaukee business and Joyce's role in that conversion:

> Independent of the leadership group that set up the [GMC Education] Trust was a group that was becoming much larger and more vocal saying that public schools were beyond saving. They defined the (education crisis) in various ways, one of which was to put competition and choice into the public school system. It was spearheaded by Michael Joyce and the Bradley Foundation. He was not alone. He was reflective of a group of business people here who found that to be a compatible message. . . . This group developed an ideology . . . and would not listen to anything about helping the public schools. (Rigdon, 1995, chapter 5)

The most important organized business group, which in 1995 led the move to expand the program, was the Metropolitan Milwaukee Association of Commerce (MMAC). Although the MMAC also included many CEOs as members and leaders, the organization was much broader and more inclusive than the GMC. Quentin Quade, a retired vice president of Marquette University, had started, with the help of Bradley funds, the Blum Center for Parental Freedom in Education at Marquette. He, along with Joyce, was instrumental in making vouchers a lobbying priority of the MMAC. Rigdon writes:

> Over the past three years [1991–94], Dr. Quade has succeeded in gaining the support of several influential members of Milwaukee's business community including John Duncan, executive director of the MMAC for over 20 years, his successor Tim Sheehy, Bob Foote, chairman of Universal Foods, Tom Hefty Vice President of Blue Cross, and Bob O'Toole, chairman of A.O. Smith. John Duncan was so swayed by the arguments offered by Dr. Quade, that he became a board member of the Blum Center and then left his post at the MMAC to start Parents Acquiring Choice in Education (PACE), a lobbying group devoted to expanding choice statewide. (Rigdon, 1995, chapter 5)

The conversion of MMAC members and its dominance in the choice debate became clear as early as 1993, when a survey of its membership

found that over 80 percent of its members believed it was important for the MMAC to be directly involved in expanding educational choice options (Metropolitan Milwaukee Association of Commerce, 1994). They quickly became very involved. In late 1994, MMAC hired consultant Susan Mitchell (wife of George) to draft legislative changes that expanded the program to include religious schools, drop random selection, and so on. That proposal, included in a memorandum addressed to Sheehy and a number of other business and religious leaders, was the basis for the governor's proposal in 1995 (Mitchell, 1994). As *Education Week* later reported: " 'Business actively told legislators that this kind of change has to occur as a matter of economic survival for the city,' said Susan Mitchell, a consultant on school choice issues for the Metropolitan Milwaukee Association of Commerce" (*Education Week*, 12 July 1995). When her legislation reached the Joint Finance Committee, MMAC Chair Robert O'Toole (CEO of A.O. Smith, Inc.) testified supporting the legislation by endorsing vouchers without specifying any limits (Wisconsin Joint Finance Committee,1995).

The second leg of the 1995 coalition consisted of religious-based private schools and the Catholic Archdiocese in Milwaukee. From the beginning there were close links between the private schools, the church, and the business community — often with Bradley money covering expenses. The first step in this alliance was the creation of a privately funded voucher program in 1992. The program, Partners for Advancing Values in Education (PAVE), grew out of the Milwaukee Archdiocesan Education Foundation, directed by Dan McKinley, who subsequently resigned to direct PAVE. The inspiration came from business members of the Education Foundation's Board. These members, who were CEOs of three of the largest companies in Milwaukee — Northwestern Life Insurance, Johnson Controls, and Wisconsin Power and Light — had heard of the program recently created by the Golden Rule Life Insurance Co. in Indianapolis. As Don Shuenke, CEO of Northwestern Life, later recalled:

> We started the PAVE program because we felt that the state choice program was underutilized, hard to get into, and disallowed schools with religious affiliations to participate. . . . The time had come in the community for an opportunity to raise funds that would cross the barriers that prevented people and organizations from contributing money to parochial schools in the past. . . . We raised a great deal of money to pay for that program. (Rigdon, 1995, chapter 5)

Indeed they did, with each company pledging $100,000 annually for five years. This was more than matched by a $500,000 per year contribution by the Bradley Foundation. From the beginning, however, the program was slated to run for only five years ending in 1997, by which time supporters were certain the state voucher program would be expanded to include all private schools. As Schuenke later stated: "When we started raising money we wanted a five-year commitment from each donor so that these students could have some kind of permanence. We also told them that we wouldn't ask them for any more than that because we weren't going to run this program forever. We want to demonstrate that (the scholarship approach) can work and then we expect the state to change their policies" (Rigdon, 1995, chapter 5). As the five-year deadline approached, PAVE, in concert with MMAC and with the lobbying support of PACE and the Marquette Blum Center, constructed the legislation and lobbied successfully for the 1995 expansions.

Throughout this process, until just before inclusion in the governor's budget, the black community was only tangentially involved. The business/private school/church coalition, which was composed almost exclusively of whites, led the effort. The Choice program had seemingly outgrown the poor, nonwhite community and clearly, with parochial students and schools included, many more white students would benefit.

Although in 1995, Williams and Senator George went along with expanding the Choice program, other black leaders including Representative Spencer Coggs and then Senator Gwendolyn Moore did not. Williams very quickly changed her mind, and began attacking the business-run coalition. Coggs, being on the Joint Finance Committee, was the first to voice his concerns and vote against the expansion. In the committee markup sessions, he said:

> There are two ways to look at religious school choice: Before the current choice program, there were schools like Urban Day and Harambee that were facing financial ruin and the choice program helped them. It could do the same for religious schools. That is the pro. But the con: it may be unconstitutional. There is a recent court ruling which casts serious doubt on the constitutionality. [A] church elder (this one from the South) told me that he feared this program would be a forerunner to nationwide religious school choice that would harken back to segregated academies in the South. (Cleaver, 1995)

As early as November 1995, Williams had changed her mind and was on a new course, independent of the business coalition. First, in the wake of two private Choice schools going out of business in mid-year 1995–96, and with those principals under criminal indictment, Williams went to the state Department of Public Instruction and requested administrative rules requiring essentially what they and the governor had requested in 1993. Then in 1996, she introduced a bill, which was subsequently thwarted by the Republicans, to rescind the 1995 changes and go back to the 1993 law (Wisconsin Department of Public Instruction, 1995). By the fall of 1996, she was supporting Dane County court rulings which eliminated religious schools from the Choice program (Williams, 1996). By the summer of 1997, after once again introducing changes that would rescind the 1995 expansions, she was openly attacking the business-religious coalition. In an interview following a public hearing on April 22, 1997, she stated: "When I formed a coalition with Tim Sheehy [Director of MMAC] and the Catholic Archdiocese and all those people who say they support us, I did so because it was a way of helping my parents. I knew all along they didn't care about my children. They cared about their agenda" (*Rethinking Schools*, Summer 1997, p. 10). And then she went further: "Powerful interests such as the MMAC have no moral authority in our community. If they really cared about our community the way they say, we would not be in such dire need right now. They have all the power and money in their hands. They could help make the conditions better in our community. But they don't" (*Rethinking Schools*, Summer 1997, p. 10). This was matched by Senator Gwendolyn Moore, who had opposed expansion in 1995, and stated at a legislative conference in 1997:

> I'm really stunned and it's really laughable what other people regard as the "black agenda." I think it's laughable that somebody thinks that a new baseball stadium is part of a nationalist strategy, or that school choice is part of a nationalist agenda. . . . The focus is wrong. Public education has been the only way lower income and minority students can receive an education in our country. (Moore, 1997)

By 1997, the only significant black political leader left who supported vouchers was Howard Fuller. Having resigned as Superintendent of MPS following a school board election won by a slate opposing Fuller's choice initiatives, he was awarded a chair at Marquette University — funded primarily by the Bradley Foundation. Senator George had become silent on the issue and was threatening the Democrats with switching parties. A black judge in Madison, Wisconsin had ruled the program unconstitutional as it began its journey to the Supreme Court.

Voucher politics in Milwaukee have been complex, but the direction of change and the shift in coalitions has been consistent. Changes have expanded the program, pushing constantly toward a more inclusive program. The coalition supporting that expansion has grown from the core of black supporters representing poor, minority constituents to include the white political, business, and religious community. The process has marginalized black leaders, many of whom have withdrawn support for the newly formulated program.

These patterns came together in a dramatic way on August 5, 1998, when the white Mayor of Milwaukee, John Norquist, proposed that income limits be raised to a $100,000 household income, and favored

eliminating limits altogether. Norquist, a prior state senator, was suc-
cinct in describing the political forces behind voucher expansion: "As
choice expands, the dissatisfaction with this income limit is going to
become very acute. This is something when legislators hold town hall
meetings, people are going to come and yell about" (*Milwaukee Journal-Sentinel*, 5 August 1998, p. 5a). Representative Polly Williams was
again outraged, stating: "This is what you call hijacking the program.
There are people in the coalition who never intended to help low-
income children" (*Milwaukee Journal-Sentinel*, 5 August 1998, p. 5a).

On the other hand the reactions of several key Republican politicians
were favorable, including Speaker of the Assembly Scott Jensen and
Milwaukee Senator Roberta Darling. The Wisconsin Association of
Nonpublic Schools (a combined association of Catholic, Christian, Lu-
theran, and Independent schools) took advantage of Norquist's proclamation and their jubilation over the June 1998 Wisconsin Supreme
Court approval of the program to clarify their goals. They wrote in
their September 1998 *Update* newsletter: "The struggle to allow parents
*of all income levels* to have a say in their children's education is
far from over" (Italics added). Thus forces for shifting to a universal
voucher program are certainly poised to move quickly. With the U.S.
Supreme Court declining to review the case, a significant obstacle to the
expansion has been removed.

### The Cleveland Voucher Program

The story of the Cleveland program is remarkably similar to the Milwaukee program, but it began at a more advanced stage. Republican
Governor George Voinovich, a long-standing school choice advocate,
was the moving force. Democratic majorities in the legislature defeated
his proposals until 1995, when the Republican legislature passed the
bill. In 1994 a Democratic, inner-city Cleveland Councilwoman, Fannie
Lewis, joined Voinovich and his chairman of the Commission on Educational Choice, David Brennan, in supporting a voucher program for
Cleveland. Brennan, an Akron businessman and strong Catholic school
supporter, was co-chair of "Ohio's Children," a pro-voucher group,
when Voinovich appointed him as chair of the Commission on Choice.
That commission recommended voucher programs in eight Ohio cities.
This was the governor's original proposal, which was cut back in the
legislature to include only Cleveland. Lewis, frustrated with the Cleveland public schools, had declared: "We're looking at the voucher system
as an alternative to public education. We're willing to be a pilot here to
show what can be done" (*Cleveland Plain Dealer*, 15 October 1994, p.

1B). In December 1994, in the lobbying buildup to the bill, Lewis was joined in support of the choice legislation by Wisconsin's Polly Williams (*Cleveland Plain Dealer*, 14 December 1994, p. 1B).

Religious private schools were even more overtly supportive than in Wisconsin and they openly lobbied for vouchers. Since Ohio is a heavily Catholic state, the Catholic church was especially prominent. St. Adalbert, an inner-city Cleveland Catholic school, was featured in numerous media events leading up to passage of the voucher bill. Principal Lydia Harris and her mostly black students were featured in stories in major Ohio newspapers and "appeared in local forums and on television championing the $5.5 million state-funded pilot program that will give 1,500 Cleveland children vouchers worth up to $2,250 to attend private and religious schools next year" (*Cleveland Plain Dealer*, 31 December 1995, p. 1B).

As in Wisconsin, the voucher bill was passed as part of a comprehensive budget package, without a separate vote on the measure. Unlike Wisconsin, none of the black legislators voted for vouchers. As noted in chapter 4, the legislation included religious schools, students already in private schools were eligible, and there were no income limits on families. Consequently, most schools in the program were religious and over 80 percent of the voucher students attended those schools in the first three years of the program (see chapter 4, p. 77).

The program was immediately challenged in court. The initial county court ruling was in favor of the program, denying it violated church-state separation clauses in either the Ohio or U.S. Constitutions. That ruling was overturned on May 2, 1997, by a 3–0 vote of the appeals court. Unlike Wisconsin, while court actions were being appealed, children were allowed to enroll in private nonsectarian or religious schools. Although the governor's proposal in 1997 to go statewide with the program was not accepted, the court ruling did not prevent him from expanding the program to include more students for 1997–98 (*Akron Beacon Journal*, 14 May 1997).

Thus both the Milwaukee and Cleveland programs exemplify an incremental policymaking process. Cleveland borrowed from Milwaukee, picking up at a later stage. There appears to be a determined march toward universal voucher programs in both states. I return to that issue after discussing the role of the media and the courts in voucher politics.

## Choice Theater

One of the intriguing aspects of the voucher movement, and the politics of that movement, is that the programs that have been put in place are

extremely modest in terms of the numbers of students and schools and
the relative amount of state money being spent. Despite this, however,
the media attention on the programs has been nothing short of phenom-
enal. Why that has ocurred is an interesting question. The answer, I
believe, is at least threefold. The first has to do with the nature of education policy. The second and third involve what I will call "choice
theater" and how that theater plays perfectly in a political world of
symbols and news bites that need to be translated quickly and simply.

Education policy in all states is big business. It involves large chunks
of state budgets and concerned voters in their role as parents, employers,
or taxpayers. It also involves interest groups that are often among the
most powerful state lobbying groups. But it is also often perceived as
boring. Despite innovative forms of schools and practices, most education of most children occurs in a very similar manner to that received by
their parents. Coverage can highlight controversies that emerge, or
showcase innovative or unusually dedicated teachers or administrators,
but the day-to-day operation of schools is routine and not particularly
good copy. Often the innovations, such as new curriculum standards,
are very complex and hard to communicate to nonexpert audiences.

Enter school choice. As outlined in detail in chapter 2, choice provides a truly radical departure from education as usual. For those concerned with the course and quality of education now or in the future, it
challenges the basic framework of the policy regime. It also focuses attention on parents as critical actors in a system where they are often
neglected or relegated to quite subservient support roles. Finally, if
packaged properly, it invokes deep value structures revolving around
the twin poles of freedom of choice and the unjust denial of equal opportunity. In the case of the Milwaukee Parental Choice Program, that
packaging fit perfectly, and there was an explosion of media attention
once the program was enacted.

The initial Choice program began as an almost textbook case of policy entrepreneurs initiating a modest, experimental program. It did
not remain that way for long, and part of the explanation for the transition was the role of the media. Once enacted, the supporting cast grew
quickly to incorporate national actors and important state and national
interest groups. As national actors became involved, this further expanded media coverage in a synergistic upward spiral.

When the bill passed in 1990, business organizations quickly began
lining up behind vouchers. The *Wall Street Journal* latched onto the
issue with a vengeance, attacking opponents such as the State Superintendent of Public Instruction Bert Grover as "Blocking the School
House Door" (*Wall Street Journal*, 27 June 1990, editorial page). Over
the years the *Journal* has published more than a dozen supportive sto-

ries and editorials on Milwaukee. In Wisconsin, the most powerful state business organization, the Wisconsin Association of Manufacturers, also supported the program, stating, "We think it is absurd to tell people like Representative Polly Williams and concerned parents that their ideas lack merit" (Wisconsin Association of Manufacturers, August 14, 1990).

The program was also highlighted in all forms of media and relentlessly used by national politicians, usually Republicans. From 1990 to 1995, major daily newspapers in almost every large city in the country ran stories on the program. *CBS 60 Minutes* ran two favorable shows, and *MacNeil/ Lehrer Newshour*, *NBC Nightly News*, and *Nightline* ran feature stories. *Forbes* Magazine also lauded choice and the Milwaukee and Cleveland programs in a lengthy cover article (*Forbes*, 2 June 1997). Milwaukee Choice schools were visited by President Bush and Vice-President Quayle, several times by Education Secretaries Lamar Alexander and William Bennett, and by 1996 presidential nominee Robert Dole. Polly Williams was twice honored at the White House, appearing with President Bush and Governor Thompson. Her travels were so extensive after the enactment of the MPCP that she went from having almost nothing in terms of outside honoraria and speaking fees to being by far the number one beneficiary of such funds in the Wisconsin Legislature (*Madison Capital Times*, May 19, 1992, p. 3A).

I employ a theatrical metaphor to explain this phenomenon because the media presentation of the program much more closely followed the form of a play than a policy debate. What is implied is that the images, symbols, characters, and dramatic flourishes are just as or more important than legislative and administrative details, votes, or budgetary considerations. They certainly are more important than policy evaluations, especially when such evaluations provide complex and mixed findings.

Theater characterized both visual and print media. The original *60 Minutes* program was a perfect case in point, but so were literally dozens of newspaper articles, including articles in publications usually quite favorable to public schools (Ruenzel, 1995). Daniel McGroarty's sensationalized depiction of the "Choice miracle" in Milwaukee (entitled "Break These Chains") also followed the genre format to the letter (McGroarty, 1996a).

The play opens with a tragic set of circumstances, depicted visually in pathetic education scenes (such as deteriorating buildings and metal detectors) and a small but poignant set of statistics demonstrating public school failure (usually test score comparisons to national averages or dropout rates). Once the scene is set, the tragedy becomes real by introducing one or two families—usually single-parent families living in poor economic conditions, yet struggling against long odds so their children will be able to escape. The conditions and the families are quickly put together by highlighting the poor performance of the children and the anger of parents at the public schools.

Following this introductory act, the heroines and heroes are introduced, often quite literally with words such as "enter Polly Williams," or "enter Tommy Thompson." They are portrayed as individuals, unconnected to external organizations, and usually doing battle with powerful organized forces embodied in the public school establishment. Their ideas are fresh and radical, challenging an order that has failed. The contrast in the Williams-Thompson alliance is either explicitly or implicitly noted: black, inner-city former welfare mother and Democrat who supported Jesse Jackson for President compared to white, male Republican from small-town Wisconsin.[7]

What follows is a short description of the program, often with a quick visual, because the details detract from the play. Then the focus shifts to the resolution in the school. Again, to keep the drama focused (and to keep to time limits), usually one school is highlighted, with perhaps a quick cut or photos of another school, usually to display a different race of students. The focus on the school almost always highlights differences from the public schools — discipline, school uniforms, a sense of belonging and community, dedicated teachers and staff, and so on.

The longer productions are able to add delightful touches of caring and difference. Perhaps the most dramatic was the *60 Minutes* broadcast which showed an eighth-grade black male student weeping, while being comforted by his white teacher, her hand gently on his shoulder. We are told that he has just been informed that he would not graduate and would have to repeat the eighth grade. The sequence adequately portrayed the style of the teacher, who was actually a nun still teaching in the school. I had met both teacher and student some weeks before;

[7] Heroes are also presented in losing causes related to the program. For example, McGroarty wrote an article about the program eligibility fight of Messmer High School, which was run by Catholic Brother Bob Smith. The school had been Catholic through the mid-1980s when the Church pulled its support. A wealthy benefactor and very hard work on Smith's part saved the school. By 1992 it had enrolled more than 200 students. When they applied for the Choice program, they were challenged by the Department of Public Instruction on religious grounds. The McGroarty article depicts the losing battle that ended in a hearing examiner deciding against Messmer. Throughout the article, Smith is portrayed in heroic terms, fighting the well-funded and powerful education establishment. This is symbolically captured in a cover portrait of Brother Bob, who is black. He is presented in his collar and coat, smiling with a broad yellow aura surrounding his head. The portrait follows the classic representation from paintings of the Middle Ages in which the Catholic church required inclusion of circles of light around the heads of revered holy figures (see McGroarty, 1996b).

the student was one of the most engaging, outgoing, and playful students I have ever met. Thus my reaction on viewing the program was that the tears may have been added for effect. Regardless, the dramatic effect was successful. The contrast with the image of public school mass indifference toward students and performance did not need to be spelled out.

The dramatic resolve of these plays takes different forms. "Is the program working?" "Are these schools the answer?" For those taking strong pro-choice stands, such as McGroarty, or the *Wall Street Journal* or *Forbes* articles, the results are clear and unequivocal. These schools, they say, work miracles — breaking chains — and the market model will revolutionize American education. Others try to fight their way through the mixed results and interpretations, but in as brief a fashion as possible, because the complexities are not susceptible to theater or to easy visual encapsulation. In good dramatic style, however, most presentations end not with the complexities, but again with individual families or schools. "For [Rita Alvarez] the program has been a success, and [Raul] is doing much better than in his prior public school."

Choice theater serves not only media needs, but also political needs. Just as Ronald Reagan learned it was good business to highlight heroes, the Choice program allows politicians to highlight crusaders like Williams, Thompson, or Brother Bob Smith and courageous families fighting long odds, and schools working as independent, caring innovators. All of these heroes are fighting against a Kafkaesque public school bureaucracy. The Choice solution is concise and simple, and has the added advantage, at least in one interpretation, of being costless or even saving taxpayers money.

I discovered a print-media representation of those conditions in a cartoon in a Colorado Springs newspaper (figure 7.1). It was published several days after the release of the Greene, Peterson, and Du paper on the eve of the Republican national convention in 1996. Presumably for Senator Dole, the Milwaukee stones will simply and quickly slay both candidate Clinton and the education forces aligned behind him. The sequel, ostensibly featuring Clinton's severed head, was never drawn.

In terms of political television, choice theater provides a perfect format: quick talks on camera with a parent; a highlighted school exterior or corridor; over-shoulder shots of the politician working with or being shown something by a student (with computers the preferred backdrop); and then a serious proclamation about the program's success and the politician's undying support for it. The politician comes across as personal in a personalized setting, caring, involved at the grass roots, and dealing with an issue of interest to almost all voters.

**Figure 7.1** ASAY'S VIEW. Source: *Colorado Springs Gazette Telegraph*, August 15, 1996. Reprinted by permission of Chuk Asay and Creators Syndicate.

Even noncampaigning politicians, such as then Whitewater Special Prosecutor Kenneth Starr, who was among the counsel representing the Choice schools, followed the format on his obligatory visit to the schools. In an effort to get to know the families, he visited one school and discussed the program and schools with several Choice families. It has subsequently been reported that his firm billed the state (at $390 per hour) through March of 1998 for $387,693. However, $344,000 was paid for by a grant from the Bradley Foundation (*Milwaukee Journal Sentinel*, 4 March 1998).

Did choice theater affect the policy decisions made in the MPCP? The more appropriate question is how could it not have? Politicians and their staffs read newspapers, watch television, and catalogue and file the results. Witnesses appearing before both the Joint Finance Committee and other committees reviewing various aspects of the program relied either on the media accounts or on similar theater of their own construction. This included on numerous occasions, especially before the courts, galleries loaded with small minority children dressed in cleaned, pressed blue and white uniforms.

On the other hand, by 1995 the political forces were also well lined up to advance the Choice program to the next stage. The business community was presenting a united front, even if it did not incorporate all business leaders. Those who were not advocates did nothing to oppose the expansion. The partisan forces were also in place. The Republicans controlled the governor's office and both houses of the legislature. Thus while choice theater played well for those advocating expanded choice, it served primarily to reinforce and provide useful ammunition for a battle already won on the basis of sheer political power.

## The Role of the Courts

The role and actions of the courts in the educational choice debate is extremely important. Despite the apolitical image of the judicial branch, in the case of educational vouchers courts were clearly an object of choice theater and politics. The Choice program was from the beginning of considerable interest to the legal community. And there is substantial evidence that the structure and changes in that program have been made with one eye focused on the type of case which might best be brought before the courts. Although voucher programs that include religious schools will be challenged as violating the First Amendment, the cases may not get that far if they are shown to violate state constitutional provisions. Many states, including both Wisconsin and Ohio, have more explicit provisions against aiding religious schools than the First Amendment. The U.S. Supreme Court will accept or reject these cases, depending on how they interpret the state constitutional protections of religious rights.[8]

The Choice program was challenged in 1990 as violating prohibitions in the Wisconsin constitution for not fulfilling a public purpose and for using public monies for private purposes. The Department of Public Instruction, the Wisconsin Education Association Council (teachers' union), and the Wisconsin NAACP brought the original suit. Defense of the program was provided by the state and a private attorney, Clint Bolick, brought in from Landmark Legal Foundation of Kansas City. The Wisconsin Supreme Court decided in favor of the program on a 4–3 vote in March 1992. The swing vote in an otherwise politically predictable outcome was Justice Day. The majority, especially Day, cited the targeted and modest size of the program and its "experimental" nature. In keeping with the metaphor of choice theater, one of the more

---

[8] The U.S. Supreme Court is unlikely to review a case in which it decides that a state constitution provides greater protection of rights than current interpretations of the U.S. Constitution provide. In the case of vouchers to religious schools, whichever way the state court decides, the U.S. Supreme Court must decide whose rights are being extended and restricted by the law. Choice opponents will argue that religious freedom is extended by prohibiting vouchers for religious schools, while proponents will argue that such a prohibition in fact limits religion and discriminates against religious practice.

enthusiastic justices (Ceci) ended his brief opinion with a popular slogan of the voucher movement: "Let's Give Choice a Chance!" (Wisconsin Supreme Court, March 12, 1992).

When religious schools were added in 1995, much as the politics had escalated, so did the court case. Believing that the case was destined for the U.S. Supreme Court, in an unprecedented action both parties agreed to send the case immediately to the Wisconsin Supreme Court. Given the impending importance of the case, and to build media attention, both sides went to national organizations to bolster their legal teams. Thompson (using a Bradley Foundation grant) brought in the law firm of Kenneth Starr, who presented oral arguments in Madison on February 27, 1996. Starr was supported by Bolick, then of the Washington-based Institute for Justice, and attorneys from the Landmark Legal Foundation. The opposition brought in national counsel from a well-known Washington civil rights law firm and lawyers from the ACLU, Americans United for Separation of Church and State, and People for the American Way Action Fund (Wisconsin Supreme Court, 1995).

During oral arguments two justices, clearly questioning expansion of the program, cited the dramatic nature of the changes, with Chief Justice Day questioning how this could any longer be viewed as an experiment. Justice Bablitch was even more emphatic on the actions that would result from a positive vote: "This is the case, right? This one opens it up. If we say this is O.K., there's nothing to stop the legislature from going all the way" (*Wisconsin State Journal*, 27 February 1996).

On March 29, 1996, the court split 3–3 with Day switching his vote from 1992 and joining Bablitch and Abrahamson, who had both voted against the original program. One justice, Bradley, had recused herself because she had received campaign money from the state teachers association. The three favorable justices noted: "This court concluded that the program was experimental in nature and served to advance the goal of improving 'the quality of education in Wisconsin for children of low-income families'" (Wisconsin Supreme Court, 1995, p. 3; *Wisconsin State Journal*, 30 March 1996, p. B1).

The result was that the case was sent back to the county court level. The governor then attempted but failed to have county judge Paul Higginbotham removed, charging he was biased against choice (*Wisconsin State Journal*, 20 April 1996, p. 38). Judge Higginbotham ruled the expansion unconstitutional in January 1997 and restored the 1993 legislation during appeals. The appeals court upheld that decision on a 2–1 vote on August 22, 1997. Both lower courts questioned whether the program was still experimental and limited. Both sides vowed to appeal all the way to the U.S. Supreme Court. The appeals court, however, limited its decision to violation of the Wisconsin constitution and did not address First Amendment concerns. If that were to remain the basis for reversal of the decision by the Wisconsin Supreme Court, it would have been much harder to get the U.S. Supreme Court to review the case, and thus provide the definitive test voucher supporters seek (*Milwaukee Journal Sentinel*, 23 August 1997).

But that was not what the Wisconsin Supreme Court did in June 1998. The 4 to 2 favorable decision went well beyond the Wisconsin constitution and directly addressed First Amendment concerns:

> "We conclude that the amended (choice program) does not violate the Establishment Clause because it has a secular purpose, it will not have the primary effect of advancing religion and it will not lead to excessive entanglement between the state and participating sectarian private schools," wrote Justice Donald Steinmetz for the court majority. (*Milwaukee Journal Sentinel*, 11 June 1998, p. 1; [*Jackson vs. Benson*, Wisconsin Supreme Court, 97-0270, 10 June 1998])

This obviously provides grounds for appeal, which must have been a deliberate action on the part of the court majority. The dissenting minority opinions were very brief and limited to Wisconsin constitutional issues.

Oral arguments before the Wisconsin Supreme Court in each of three instances were the object of the theatrics of educational choice. The sessions in the ornate chambers have all been attended by overflowing crowds, with observers standing in the doorways and proceedings piped to loudspeakers in adjacent corridors. Although television cameras are not allowed in the courtroom, private school supporters used a wonderful tactic which each time garnered the rapt attention of the justices and was duly reported in the print media—in some cases with court drawings included. Seats in the Wisconsin Supreme Court hearing room are given on first-come, first-served basis. The private schools, led by Urban Day School, secured first-row seats in which they sat silently, elementary school students immaculately dressed in school uniforms. An interesting tactic was begun during the first oral arguments in 1991. Ostensibly to give more children a chance to see the proceedings, every few minutes the row of children silently got up and walked out, often hand-in-hand, to be replaced by their classmates. All eyes of the court followed each transition.

The role of the courts also exemplifies the intricacies of using and manipulating an incremental policy approach. Going immediately to a full-fledged, unrestricted voucher system would amount to a direct frontal assault on state and federal constitutional provisions providing separation of church and state. With a limited, targeted, and experimental program, the courts, in sympathy with the plight of inner-city children, may let the "experiment" proceed. But in so doing, they may also establish an unassailable precedent that can then be cited as justification for statewide voucher efforts. The Milwaukee program was designed and redesigned to maintain this limited effect and to give state monies first to parents — both stipulations of the *Mueller v. Allen* decision.

Whether this was part of the Milwaukee and Cleveland strategies from the beginning is a matter of conjecture. What is not conjecture is how the lawyers for the private schools have viewed the program. As Clint Bolick, the attorney defending both programs, noted: "The program places the decisions in the parent's hands and is a remedial program for low-income children. It is a great program to defend against legal challenges" (*Education Week*, 2 January 1995, p. 11). Later Bolick was equally as straightforward about the intent and purpose of the program: "We are very anxious to get a case up to the Supreme Court as quickly as possible to remove the constitutional cloud once and for all" (*Wall Street Journal*, 31 July 1995, p. 3B).

But Polly Williams's effort to go back to the 1993 legislation dropping religious schools had the business-religious school coalition very concerned. At a very heated 1997 public hearing on her bill to rescind the 1995 changes, Williams indicated how her program was used in the courts: "The Republicans and conservatives needed a credible base upon which to push and legitimize this issue." Equally candid was the response by the Executive Director of the Metropolitan Milwaukee Association of Commerce, Tim Sheehy, who had done so much to expand the program in 1995. He said, "The [Williams] bill changes state law while that law is still in the courts," and he argued that if that occurred, the issue before the court would be moot — the implication being that the carefully prepared court test would not occur (*Rethinking Schools*, Summer, 1997, p. 10).

The U.S. Supreme Court let the Wisconsin court ruling stand, thus leaving in place the first U.S. program providing private parochial schools with vouchers. Were they affected by the Choice politics and theater? It is difficult to know, and the game is hardly over. The Cleveland challenges are still in the system.

The mix of precedents and the amorphous construction of the legal tests to be applied suggest considerable political latitude is possible in courts deciding the voucher issue. Courts could choose to remain with *Nyquist* (1973), arguing it is the most directly applicable case. Or they could overrule *Nyquist*, as the Wisconsin Supreme Court majority did, and side with the string of less direct, but cumulative cases easing the court toward approving vouchers [(*Mueller v. Allen* (1983); *Witters v. Washington Department of Services for Blind*, (1986); *Zorbest v. Catalina Foothills School District* (1993); and *Agostini v. Felton* (1997)].[9]

[9] See chapter 2 for case citations.

Will the tripartite test as laid out in *Lemon v. Kurtzman* (1971) decide the case? The tests certainly will be cited, as will the selected precedents. But to side here with intellectual traditions I rarely promote, the *Lemon* tests seem to me to be a postmodernist wonderland of multiple meanings. What does it mean for voucher programs to have a "secular purpose"? Education in a Catholic or Christian school, even if it requires attendance at religious services for one-seventh of the day and has a curriculum imbued with religious texts and lessons, may still teach students reading, math, or constitutional law. Who is to say what the purpose is? Religious . . . yes. Secular . . . yes.

The second *Lemon* test may be even more vague. Does a voucher program have a "primary effect of either advancing or inhibiting religion"? The question can easily be converted to an empirical hypothesis. However, testing the hypothesis would be very difficult for an explicit program and it seems prima facie absurd to consider the impact of such programs in advance of implementation. But since the court must decide before there is any experience with the programs, the idea of empirical tests is irrelevant. The court could of course fall back on legislative intent, but that seems to be a discretionary swamp under even the best circumstances. A serious attempt to infer the legislative intent of voucher supporters in terms of their desires for advancing or inhibiting religion must rely on scattered and selective quotation that offends even the weakest standards of evidence and common sense.

Finally, do vouchers create "excessive entanglement" between government and religion? This test broaches the very serious policy issue of whether government subsidies may lead to regulation of private and parochial schools. Might this regulation include curriculum, thus affecting religious instruction and perhaps even religious practices in schools? Apart from the constitutional import of these questions, I will return to the policy implications of this issue in the last chapter. But again, the concept seems vague and variable, allowing multiple definitions of "excessive," "entanglement," and even "religion." Can a curriculum, for example, teach about religious beliefs and practices, without promoting religion? And if regulations say no, is that excessive entanglement? Finally, as with the other tests, regulatory aspects of voucher programs will evolve over time and probably face long legal battles the outcomes of which are difficult to predict.[10] But the court must decide first.

What this means is that the latitude of interpretation by judges

---

[10] Since court approval of the MPCP in June 1998, there has been a pitched legal battle between the Department of Public Instruction and the private schools in the expanded Choice program over regulation of schools in terms of civil rights and disability statutes. Three months into the school year, most vouchers have not been paid pending court action on regulatory issues.

is enormous. Although the pages devoted to the constitutional issues on voucher policies would undoubtedly fill large rooms, there is every reason to believe that politics will govern these court rulings. And that may well have been the primary impetus behind the politics of vouchers and choice theater.

## Intentions

Choice politics and theater are critical for understanding the voucher movement in America. Their impact, however, and the ultimate impact of educational vouchers, depends on the underlying intentions of those at the center of the movement—both for and against. But intentions are difficult to analyze. They are like tracks in a snowstorm—fleeting images, quickly covered. I will offer my interpretations, but as with the outcomes of the MPCP, readers may reach different conclusions.

For voucher opponents, who couch opposition to choice in "the best education for all" rhetoric, one must consider that the intention may rather be simple obstruction, by whatever means, of vouchers for private schools, and further that the underlying motive could be simple monetary and political self-interest. Educational choice potentially threatens the education establishment. It means more power to parents, a different form of accountability, and potentially very different personnel policies for schools. Vouchers for private schools must be viewed, at least in the short run, as a windfall for private, mostly religious schools, and this may lead to less resources for public schools.

Those opposed to vouchers are unlikely to stress power or monetary losses as their principal arguments. However, some of their actions can be interpreted in that light. Unions and other educational organizations have lined up in every state and at the national level to oppose private school vouchers. Their opposition has been seen in the legislatures, on referendums, and in the courts, and they are willing to commit considerable resources to the fight. The last time a statewide voucher movement appeared on an initiative ballot was in California in 1993. Organizations opposed to Proposition 174 outspent pro-voucher forces by six to ten times (*Wall Street Journal*, 4 November 1993, editorial page). The result was a devastating defeat of the initiative by over two to one. The margin may have been enough to convince pro-voucher groups that referendums are not the way to go. No others have emerged, and the movement in California appears dead at least for the present.

On a less malevolent note, as described in chapter 3, national educational organizations have considerably modified their opposition to almost all other forms of educational choice over the last decade. The organization previously most opposed to choice, the National Education Association, now, at least rhetorically, not only supports all forms of public school choice but is also promoting charter schools (National Education Association, 1997). Teachers' unions in general have been much less oppositional when it comes to charter schools than to vouchers. Depending on the state, charter school legislation may cut to the core of power relationships education groups hold dear. These can include changes in bargaining rights, personnel hiring, teacher assignment and rewards, and accountability systems for Charter schools (Wohlsetter, 1995; Maughs-Pughs, 1995; Vergari and Mintrom, 1995). One could view this as a strategy to accept choice concessions to head off vouchers, but that ignores the possibility that these forms of choice may incrementally lead to vouchers.

For voucher advocates, two potentially duplicitous sets of intentions are possible. The first is an incremental shift from targeted programs intended to provide increased educational opportunity for poor families to one subsidizing all private schools — most of which are not attended by poor students. The second is a strategy to use limited vouchers to bring before the courts the decisive First Amendment case on the best grounds possible.

What do the facts say? Facts are not intentions, but several facts suggest that expansion of the Milwaukee program to all private schools was the intention of many voucher supporters. First, the legislation initially proposed by the governor in 1988 was much broader than what he finally settled for. Second, each legislative action since 1990 has produced a more expanded program, and initial proposals for expansion were usually more radical than what was finally enacted. That was true for program limits, income restrictions, random selection, inclusion of private school children, and the range of schools involved.

It was also clear that for some groups the intention was and always has been universal vouchers. That is clearly the position of many of the private and religious groups and most of the key business elite in Milwaukee. The National Catholic Education Association, while declaring their concern for the poor, admonished both national parties in 1992 to include in their platform vouchers for all students and schools (National Catholic Education Association, April 21, 1992). At their conference in 1996 they reaffirmed that position. Frank Savage, the national Director of Administrators of Catholic Education, was quoted: "I do believe we will have vouchers in a large number of places by the year 2000." Robert Guerra, director of secondary schools for the National Catholic Education Association, proclaimed in support of vouchers: "We're not going to give up the fight for public policy change" (*Wisconsin State Journal*, 13 April 1996, p. 1C).

Similarly, the business community in Milwaukee got involved and worked to accomplish that explicit end, stopping short only out of political and legal necessity. Both the leaders of MMAC and the business leaders who started PAVE spoke unconditionally of the value of vouchers. Further, as Representative Schultz noted, it is going to be difficult in the long term to distinguish between the poor in Milwaukee and elsewhere, and then between the poor and middle-class families paying for their own private schools. In other words, regardless of intentions, politics may overwhelm the opposition — a result pleasing to some current voucher supporters, but clearly anathema to others (such as Williams).

What are the intentions of voucher sponsors concerning the courts? Initially the court case was probably a minor part of the overall strategy. Making a case in Wisconsin courts would have had modest effect nationwide. But once the program was established, subsequent changes were made consistent with bringing the best case possible before the U.S. Supreme Court. The changes were designed to provide vouchers for parents, rather than the previous method of paying schools directly. Initially, every effort was made to preserve the image that the program was an experimental effort to aid a modest and needy population.

All pretense of the Milwaukee program as being a modest experiment seemed to vanish when the Wisconsin Supreme Court upheld the program as including religious schools in June 1998. The principal defense attorneys, obviously elated, expounded on the national importance of the case. Speaking on the eve of the decision, Clint Bolick seems to have lost his experimental and targeted rhetoric: "What is about to happen in Milwaukee is a huge story everywhere. The Milwaukee program is the largest functioning school choice program. As a result, all eyes are on the court to see what they decide" (*Milwaukee Journal-Sentinel*, 10 June 1998). The president of Bolick's Institute for Justice was even more emphatic when he spoke to the *New York Times* after the decision was released:

> "Today's decision will help school choice spread like wildfire across the nation," said Chip Mellor, president of Institute for Justice, a Washington-based conservative public policy law firm and one of the major litigators. "The court's careful analysis of the constitutional issues provides powerful insight that voucher programs are fully compatible with the principles of the First Amendment." (*New York Times*, 11 June 1998, p. 1)

The opposition attorneys, such as the NAACP attorney Jeffrey Hall, also indicated the general importance of the case. He said, "This will play a significant role in how this whole thing plays out nationally" (*Milwaukee Journal-Sentinel*, 10 June 1998).

When the U.S. Supreme Court declined review in November 1998,

Bolick was very direct in terms of his intent for future programs: "This is a green light for other states to proceed with the most promising education reform on the horizon" (*USA Today*, 10 November 1998, p. 1).

The intentions, as well as the linkages between business, religious groups, and the courts, were highlighted in comments by Michael Joyce and actions of the Bradley Foundation, which he runs. Joyce was characteristically candid when he announced a $2 million donation from the Bradley Foundation to PAVE for the 1997–98 year after the circuit court injunction preventing students from enrolling in private schools while appeals were heard.

> "We can't just keep doing this as a matter of charity," Joyce said. "Getting kids to the school of their parents' choice is a matter for public policy, not charity," he said. Joyce said he believes 1998 will be an important year in the school-choice movement because of the pending state Supreme Court decision. "There is good reason for us to hope that we won't have to keep our children afloat in a lifeboat again next year," Joyce said. "August of 1998 in Milwaukee may see the beginning of an historic new era in American education." (*Milwaukee Journal-Sentinel*, 29 August 1997, p. H5)

Earlier he had underscored the importance of the court by providing the $344,000 grant to the state to pay for the legal services of Kenneth Starr's law firm.

However, even if the intentions of voucher supporters are as described, the purpose may still be benevolent. Given income limits, it could be that the system that emerges will be designed to help all children by increasing access for the poor to current private schools and by requiring private schools to give up their current selection and expulsion rights. Obviously, advocates around the country will vary in their attitudes concerning this prospect. The incremental slide to remove program limits has been described and will be discussed further in the final chapter. However, I have repeatedly pointed out in this book the inclination for schools to maintain selectivity and not give up expulsion rights. This was true of both public and private schools when the opportunity arose.

Two further pieces of evidence, very close to the current voucher debate, support this contention. Clint Bolick provided one in a memorandum to Choice Supporters on providing legal counsel for a 1997 Washington, D.C., voucher proposal by Representative Richard Armey and Senator Daniel Coates. Bolick addressed the questions of selection and exclusion in the broadest terms:

> Dick Komer and I met with representatives of the Catholic Conference, who urged that the bill contain the full panoply of federal civil rights regulations,

including Title IX (gender) and disabilities provisions. We argued strongly against those regulations. We are pleased to report that the final bill contains only a general antidiscrimination requirement and expressly provides that schools are not "recipients of federal funds." (Institute for Justice memorandum, Sept. 22, 1997)

One could interpret this quote differently — that the (misguided) Catholic Conference did not favor exclusion. But if so, they lost. And the eliminated regulations would have been key legal tools that would enforce open access.

A second incident is even more troubling in that it directly indicates what the selection practices would likely be of private schools in Milwaukee under an expanded voucher program. In a number of chapters, I noted how selection was important to schools and how difficult it was to monitor the selection process. The subtlety of screening students and families was revealed in a new context with parochial schools in the summer of 1995. By August, many students had already applied and been accepted into previously excluded parochial schools for the upcoming 1995–96 school year. Those schools, facing the immediate influx of a large number of unknown students, were worried about the selection process and some of the requirements from the Department of Public Instruction concerning compliance with required state laws. In response, a meeting of private school administrators was scheduled in Milwaukee, under the leadership of Dan McKinley, the director of the PAVE program and a leading figure in expanding the Choice program.

In preparation for that meeting, McKinley wrote the memorandum presented as figure 7.2. The PAVE selection process, which relied on schools to admit students, was described in chapter 4. It is very clear from the highlighted sections that McKinley is providing instructions on how screening can also occur under the Choice program. Obviously he is recommending that the "final enrollment interview," *to be conducted after random selection*, should be used as a screening interview. Depending on the circumstances, that interview would probably be conducted under conditions in which the rights of parents were not well known to them. In addition, he is providing the simple means for enrolling existing students and their siblings. All schools needed to do was amend their policies if they did not already contain provisions allowing automatic admission of parishioners' children and siblings of existing students.[11] Thus McKinley is offering a roadmap indicating how to encourage the appropriate families, discourage those who might not fit with school expectations and requirements, and how to favor those al-

---

[11] The inclusion of parishioners' children was not allowed by statutes, and a memo issued by PAVE in the following year dropped the reference to "children of parishioners."

What does random selection mean? "Random" can be defined as "designating a sample drawn from a population so that each member of the population has an equal chance to be drawn."

The nonsectarian schools participating in the original choice program all agreed to a common random process. Your school can design its own process, and set one or more dates for the random drawings to occur. A few observations and suggestions:

1. Hold a random drawing early in August and schedule another later in the month if all available seats are not filled.
2. Once applicants for each particular grade have been assigned a number in the random drawing, then final enrollment interviews can take place. *Many parents may choose not to complete the enrollment process once they learn what is specifically required by your school.* In any event, you begin with applicant #1 and proceed down the list until all seats are taken. *Your school may be able to offer siblings or children of parishioners priority placement if that is part of your stated policies.*
3. Finally, remember that the key to making this whole program work is to make sure that the parents are informed about the policies and expectations of your school prior to enrollment. We all want parents to make good choices.

Kee up your great work! Keep the faith!

*Source:* Memorandum from PAVE Director Daniel McKinley to School Administrators, August 4, 1995.

[Italics added by the author; underscore in the original.]

Figure 7.2 Memorandum from PAVE Director Daniel McKinley to School Administrators, August 4, 1995

ready in or committed to the school. This is not an indictment of the PAVE program, which over a five-year period provided thousands of scholarships to needy children. But it is an admission that schools will naturally want to select "appropriate" students.

## Conclusions

In terms of who gets what, when, how, and why, the "who gets what" in the future remains the great question for educational vouchers in America. We know a lot about the "how" and "when" of voucher politics. We know that the progress of voucher policy has been the result of powerful forces contesting a high stakes policy issue. That has led to stalemate in some places, incremental expansion in others. The media and the courts continue to play crucial roles. If the courts finally approve programs in either Milwaukee or Cleveland, a major obstacle to expanding vouchers will have been lifted. The issue then returns to the ultimate intentions of decision makers and the political pressure to universalize the benefits of voucher programs.

While a considerable amount of material has been covered in this chapter, each of the distinct sections, I believe, points to the troubling prospect that voucher programs may end up not being what they were originally advertised. Moreover, there is reasonable suspicion that the intentions of many involved were to use the original, limited programs, under the favorable cloak of aiding the children of our poorest families, to gain political acquiescence and support in the media and the courts for a much larger program.

Who will benefit if these programs expand into universal voucher programs? That depends on a number of assumptions that will be reviewed in the final chapter. However, given the religious nature of private schools in America and enrollment in the privately funded voucher programs we have reviewed, the current private school population provides an approximate answer at least in the short term. For Wisconsin, that answer is quite clear. A study using 1990 census data compared families with children in private and public schools in the state of Wisconsin and in its five largest cities. The results were consistent with national samples looking at the same demographics. For example, in the city of Milwaukee, 84 percent of private school students were white, compared to only 33 percent white in the public schools. In terms of income, the private school children came from families with incomes over $42,000, while the income of public school families was only $25,000 (Witte and Thorn, 1995, table 6).

But will expanded voucher programs lead to subsidies for existing private schools and families? Evidence in chapter 5 based on a number of programs indicates that the answer is yes. However, evidence from the first year of the "new" MPCP is also instructive. As of June 1998, of the 112 schools certified as eligible for the 1998–99 MPCP, 81 were religious schools (*Milwaukee Journal-Sentinel*, 8 June 1998). Two-thirds of the 6,199 students enrolled in the fall of 1998 attended parochial schools. Only 23 percent of the total in Choice were transfer students from MPS. The rest were students already in private schools but not previously in Choice (37 percent); continuing Choice students (22 percent); and students not in school in the prior year (18 percent).[12] Thus

[12] Data provided by the Wisconsin Department of Public Instruction, October 15, 1998.

a program originally intended to aid poor, minority families in Milwaukee's inner city seems to be subsidizing what we may infer to be primarily white families. If the income limit is removed, as the mayor proposes, the subsidy will go primarily to the white, upper-middle class.[13]

[13] Getting accurate data on even the race, let alone the income, of future Choice students may be impossible. When the legislature removed the evaluation from the legislation in 1995, administrative rules requiring schools to report students by race and gender were terminated. No data on families, schools, or student outcomes are being collected.

# 8

## Implications and Conclusions

THIS STUDY has implications for American education policy, policymaking theory, and the use of experimental policy designs. Because I wish to end with the choices we face in thinking about the future of education in America, I will begin with the more general implications of voucher policies and politics for the broader questions of policy theory.

### Implications for Policymaking Theory and Design

In recent years there has been a flurry of interest in what Kenneth Bickers and Robert Stein have termed "the universalization hypothesis." That hypothesis says simply that government programs often start with targeted populations and programs limited to those with a specific need, but then expand to include more people and the less needy. The mass of statistical evidence that has been accumulated to show that this occurs with regularity is impressive (Stein and Bickers, 1994a, 1994b). Educational vouchers provide an in-depth look at how that occurs and how the policymaking process allows, and is used, to secure that end.

#### Policy Rhetoric, Process, and Evolution

The Milwaukee voucher program began with a set of political goals. Representative Polly Williams was determined to do something for her constituents and, at the very least, to make a point with the public schools. Governor Thompson's motives are less clear. The rhetoric strongly points to aiding poor children in Milwaukee, whom he felt were not being well served by the public schools. Both spoke poignantly about equal opportunities. But initially the political forces were not strong enough to create a radical program, thus a modest and targeted program was enacted after several failed attempts. As the voucher program matured and evolved, the process seemed to follow naturally the universalization course we have witnessed in other policy arenas. How was this accomplished? How does it fit with the broader voucher movement across the country?

In Milwaukee as in other states where vouchers have been proposed, when the more radical initial proposals were defeated, the resources

were still available to create more modest alternatives. This by itself kept the issue on the agenda and supporters throughout the country encouraged. Once those alternatives were created, they drew considerable media attention. Because of the targeted population, the stories were usually favorable. In addition, the mere presence of the program serves as a form of legitimization. Milwaukee and Cleveland have become the demonstration projects repeatedly proposed in federal voucher legislation.

Voucher programs also provide the best assault on a very significant constitutional limitation. There is evidence that educational vouchers and the evolution of voucher policy were part of a larger strategy to affect much broader issues circumscribed by current First Amendment precedents. The ultimate goal of some very powerful advocates may not be to "break these chains," as McGroarty rhetorically stated, but rather to break the wall between church and state in the United States.

The politics of educational vouchers are not the bully politics of employers controlling jobs and making commensurate demands on the community (Lindblom, 1977). Nor are they the politics of the wealthy crudely buying political access through election donations. Rather, vouchers exemplify a subtle politics that uses a social problem to gain advantages for people well beyond the parameters of that problem; and proponents do so by understanding and successfully manipulating the incremental and pluralist nature of our system. Thus in some ways it is a much more impervious form of power. It occurs slowly, continuously taking advantage of inattention and the inability of opposing groups to maintain constant counterpressure.

How should this evolving, incrementally induced policy shift be judged? That depends on one's point of view of the policy, the attitude of citizens toward that policy, and how one believes an ideal democratic policy process should work. Those committed to vouchers as a rational and clearly positive educational reform may care little about how that result is achieved. The same may be true for those convinced that the policy is evil—they may not care how vouchers are stopped. Citizen attitudes on this issue are complex, and varying studies have shown that how one asks the question makes a great deal of difference (Witte, 1996). On one of the most straightforward questions asked by a Gallup survey, only a minority support vouchers for private schools, but supporters are increasing over time.[1] When statewide programs have been proposed, they have all been defeated either at the ballot box or in state or national legislative bodies.

---

[1] The question read: "Do you favor or oppose allowing students and parents to choose a private school to attend at public expense?" The favorable responses have been: 1991 = 26 percent; 1993 = 24 percent; 1995 = 33 percent; 1996 = 36 percent (*Phi Delta Kappan*, September 1996).

There is also, however, the question of process. Some might view this shift in policy purpose and focus as normal and routine, and to be expected with a policy as controversial as vouchers. On the other hand, I share the view that it is duplicitous and fundamentally perverse for a democratic process to enact a policy with the rationale of helping a population in need, but ending with a policy that in all likelihood will do the opposite. Even if it does not harm that targeted population, it will transfer public cash benefits directly to a population that is considerably better off. That would be the result of statewide voucher programs in Wisconsin or Ohio or other states.

### Experimental Approaches to Public Policy

The political problems with evolving policy regimes raise concerns for the broader issue of experimental public policies in the American setting. Some of these problems are technical and some structural. I deal with the major structural problem first because in a way it overshadows the technical issues.

A major structural problem, in its most general form, arises from the shift in the format of voucher programs over time. The intellectual idea behind vouchers was to create a *substantive program* to improve education. That meant that analysis of that program focused on understanding parent choices, the operation of schools, and outcomes for children. Or, put simply, who would participate, in what type of schools, and with what achievement effects?

However, if I have judged the trajectory of the voucher movement correctly, vouchers appear to evolve quickly into a *distributive program*. In that event, the evaluation issues should focus on the subsidy and on eligibility and inclusion rather than on what the program does in terms of education or achievement. As with similar distributive programs, little attention would be directed to outcomes other than subsidy amounts and the efficiency of delivering the checks with the least intrusive regulations. With the expanded voucher program, those are the types of issues that are currently being debated in Milwaukee as this book goes to press.

Obviously this shift has considerable impact on doing evaluations at all. Early in a program there may be an attempt to provide some process and outcome information, which will be expensive to acquire, and, if Milwaukee and Cleveland are guides, may produce mixed messages. But as the program shifts to a more broad-based distributive program, the theoretical and political need for such evaluations wanes. This does not mean, however, that what one learns about targeted voucher pro-

grams is necessarily useless. The precise relationship between evaluating targeted and universal programs is discussed below.

Technical problems with experimental designs aggravate the policy problems—at least in education research. The technical problems with low-income voucher experiments involve difficulties with random assignment, selection biases, and tracking and monitoring students and outcomes. Experimental designs begin with selection of a sample to which one later hopes to generalize results. Even without the problem of incremental movement toward universalization, for voucher programs it is difficult to apply randomization in an adequate manner. The reason is that to avoid selection effects, assignment for a sample population cannot be voluntary. In the case of MPCP, we were also very interested in which families would volunteer for vouchers. That was because we wanted to understand who would benefit from a voluntary program, and who would be attracted to private schools. The fact that choosers were so very different from nonchoosing MPS families was a very important finding, but it also suggests a selection problem in estimating achievement outcomes (see chapter 4). Ideally, a random sample of the entire low-income MPS population would have been selected, with an appropriate proportion; then assigned to attend private schools. That, of course, was not politically feasible, and will not be for most programs and experiments in education.

A further problem with selection effects occurs because we cannot force selected or rejected students to continue in their respective treatment groups. And again, we saw that those who left the program were hardly a random sample of those who began. I highlighted the specific effects of that attrition on the set of rejected students and on those who left Choice schools. This problem in education is further exasperated because often the schools themselves are involved in the decision to retain a student. Because the schools were the experiment, the right of schools not to readmit students confounds the selection problem with the treatment. Although there are statistical means of correcting for some of these problems, they in themselves are controversial, and become even more so when multiple problems exist at one time.

Finally, there are practical problems with enforcing and monitoring selection, retention, and testing and in tracking students and families over a number of years. With adequate funding and lead time, some of these problems may be overcome. However, careful monitoring in the schools, of both processes and records, requires a degree of intrusion that raises ethical questions, and that would need to be built into legislation and administrative rules. No choice or voucher legislation that I know of has contained such provisions.

Are these technical problems relevant to other social policy experiments? That depends on the policies and the government's relationship

to the target populations. Prison experiments may be easier than education experiments. Income maintenance, job training, and other welfare experiments may come closer to the experimental ideal because client benefits are conditional and government has more leverage over the clients. However, as those trying to make sense of the latest wave of welfare reform programs have attested, there remain very serious issues of take-up rates, selection into and out of programs, and tracking those who leave the programs (Institute for Research on Poverty, 1997).

Voucher experiments also exemplify and perhaps accentuate the political problems with social policy experiments in general. There are three types of problems. The first is the problem of evaluation. As is very clear from the MPCP, evaluations become political tools in that they are used selectively by opposing sides in controversial policy experiments. Given the complex and mixed results of the Milwaukee experiment, selective use of data may have been more prevalent than in policy fields where outcomes are simpler, e.g., job placement and training programs.

A second political problem results from pressure to produce quick and often premature evaluation results. Meaningful educational change takes time. To expect students to react immediately to new environments, especially when much of the old remains, is nonsensical. But often education programs are expected to produce immediate or short-term improvements. For high-profile experiments, first-year or even more immediate results are eagerly awaited and zealously reported. But by the third year, the media is very likely to have lost interest. Given the short tenure of big city superintendents, a new regime may already be dismantling the program or adding a new one of their own design, regardless of the outcome of the previous program.

The Milwaukee Choice program was something of a luxury in this regard. Four years of continuous data were compiled and analyzed, and the trend effects have become an important issue. Annual reports had to be filed, however. That was unfortunate because they took time away from data collection and analysis, and early reports were given undeserved importance in setting the tone for longer-term conclusions. But a great deal of data were collected and made available to the public. At a crucial point of change in the program in 1995 (when parochial schools were added), the evaluations were removed from the legislation altogether, which seems to me to be a critical error.[2] Evaluations inevitably

---

[2] My role in the process was by that time not considered neutral by some politicians and activists on both sides of the debate. But I would not have continued as evaluator in any event. Given the current legislation, there will be no further data even on the race or socioeconomic status of those enrolled in private schools, let alone on outcome measures. That seems irresponsible by any standard given the suspicions raised in this book concerning who may benefit from an expanded program.

become part of the political process in controversial policy fields, but that does not mean that they should either be eliminated or subject to little more than a battle of hired consulting firms, each producing a version of the true results. Managing the process of evaluations is critical to the use of policy experiments. Perhaps the MPCP will serve as a useful example of both success and failure.

The outcome of that process suggests a final issue for experimental public policies — generalization of evaluation results. The temptation to generalize results is very strong. The internal temptation to provide grandiose conclusions is natural because evaluators spend a great deal of time and effort at their tasks. The right politicians will gladly accept such extrapolations as the result of "their program." Thus the results of a modest, targeted program may be extended to encompass broad population differences, such as the differences in achievement between white and black students in America. To some degree, however, all of us fall into this trap, and it is therefore necessary to point out that what we have learned about vouchers from Milwaukee is conditioned on the program and its constraints.

What one learns from a single case study is always suggestive. That is true of the MPCP. But one of the tests for whether the suggestions are worthy of further followup is how reasonable they appear to the observer and how well they conform to other similar experiences. In relation to that test, the Milwaukee and Cleveland voucher programs provide reasonable conclusions both in terms of policy process and policy design. I would argue that the incremental progression of the politics of vouchers is both reasonable and quite predictable. Why would most private school families and institutions delivering those services not favor vouchers? Why would the business community not support a policy moving toward free markets, and against admittedly powerful unions and public bureaucracies? Why would we not expect threatened public school employees to resist the imposition of vouchers? Finally, do the underlying partisan divisions really surprise us? The case of vouchers fits with other programs that have experienced incremental expansion.

Similarly, the lessons and inherent difficulties for experimental policy designs seem straightforward. There are limits in educational and other social policy settings to enforcing the strict experimental trial protocols that are commonplace in medical and drug experiments. Identifying and randomly assigning target populations, tracking subjects, and restraining schools from expelling subjects are not problems exclusive to voucher experiments. Perhaps more manageable under better circumstances are the political problems associated with expansion, evaluation, and generalization of experimental results. However, those problems are also hardly unique to education or voucher experiments (Weiss, 1972).

## Implications for the Design of Voucher Programs

The MPCP was a targeted voucher program, limited by income and geographic eligibility. The details of what we know of that program are confined to that population. However, there is every reason to believe that the intentions of voucher advocates are much broader and that powerful political forces are pushing toward universal voucher programs. Thus a critical issue is whether we should evaluate a targeted voucher program in the same way we would evaluate a universal voucher program, which would offer all students vouchers to attend private schools. Or put another way, should we consider a targeted program as merely the experimental trial of a universal program? My answer to both questions is no. But there is also a further issue — do policy differences matter at all? There is an argument that must be taken seriously for why it may not.

### Targeted Versus Universal Voucher Systems

The problems of transferring knowledge from a targeted to a universal voucher program are by this point obvious and deserve but the starkest review. Our data on who chose to participate in the MPCP was consistent and very robust — low-income families with children having trouble in the public schools were the primary recipients of vouchers. But those data were contingent on three significant constraints: (1) low-income eligibility; (2) nonsectarian schools; and, (3) residence in the city of Milwaukee. All three clearly affect the population of choosers. Considerable data from other choice programs and current private school students indicated that without these constraints, choosing families were much more likely to be white, have higher incomes and more educated parents, and be attracted to private schools for religious reasons. Similarly, as was clear from privately funded voucher programs, the Cleveland experience, and enrollment in the revised Milwaukee program, if sectarian schools participate, they would overwhelm nonsectarian private schools and enroll most voucher students.

But how large are the differences between targeted and universal programs likely to be? If we assume that under a universal program most of the students would be similar to students currently attending private schools, we can estimate magnitudes by comparing private and public school student populations. In terms of race, chapter 4 indicated that researchers studying the PAVE program, which also had an income limit, were happy to report that only 46 percent of the recipients were white because "the Catholic school population in Milwaukee was 92 percent white." Data reported in the last chapter confirmed that in Wisconsin and Milwaukee, the vast majority of private school students are white and their average family income is considerably above the average income of public school families (Witte and Thorn, 1995). Thus if either the Catholic school population or the population of students attending all private schools are used as guides to who would benefit from a universal voucher program, it is clear that the effects would differ dramatically from those who benefited from the targeted MPCP.

Given different students and schools, we must assume the outcomes of targeted programs are also likely to differ considerably from universal voucher programs. Based on numerous studies of student achievement, we know that parent education, family income, and other measures of socioeconomic status are key variables explaining the variance in both test scores and educational attainment. Those studies are inconsistent on the effects of other variables on achievement (class size, school effects, family choice). However, those variables clearly explain less variance than socioeconomic status variables (Hanushek, 1986; Witte, 1992, 1996, 1997).

Does this mean that what we have learned about Milwaukee, and to a much lesser extent Cleveland, is of little value? The answer is no, but generalizations must be limited. What generalizations seem warranted? Although people may differ in their interpretation of the mix of outcomes described in chapter 6, I concluded that the MPCP did what it set out to accomplish. It provided an alternative opportunity for families who needed it and could not afford private schools; and it provided support and improvement for private schools, some of which would no longer exist without the program. Thus I concluded that states can offer limited voucher programs, which will provide opportunities and some successes for families unhappy with their current public school options. These programs, in conjunction with existing magnet and charter schools, and districts contracting out with private schools, offer a substantial set of nontraditional school options for families in inner-city school districts.

More problematic may be the effects of the politics of choice and choice theater in insuring that the limits on voucher programs are upheld. I interpreted the expansion of voucher programs as unwarranted. However, there is another perspective on that issue.

## Do Policy Differences Really Matter?

When confronted with the arguments above—that targeted voucher programs will inevitably become universal and the beneficiaries will then change substantially—Dr. Howard Fuller responds that he is willing to take the chance. And I take Fuller seriously. He began as an activist critic of Milwaukee public schools, then became superintendent of the district, and now is again a critic and also an overt voucher supporter. From my long, friendly, and respectful relationship with Fuller, I can guarantee that his interests are not in providing subsidies to middle-class white families. Thus he differs from many voucher advocates in Milwaukee and the state.

Fuller also acknowledges the possibility of the expansion of the program from a targeted to a universal program. What then are his arguments? In his words, "Choice is like a bomb that needs to be thrown into a system that is so bad, so rotten, that nothing else will work."[3] Fuller has argued for the fifteen years I have known him that the public school systems in our inner cities are producing continuously more uneducated, mostly minority youths who he says "are piling up out there each year." The results of that failure are not only tragic for the kids involved, but also for society. Again in his words, "Choice was a natural outgrowth of a struggle about what was happening to our children." In an article published on the eve of the June 1998 court ruling favoring vouchers, "he [Fuller] said he remains convinced that choice would be 'a very key lever in the overall effort to create learning environments for kids'" (*Milwaukee Journal-Sentinel*, 8 June 1998).

Confronted with my scenario concerning the expansion of vouchers, he admitted, "What this is about is money. The only people who tell you money doesn't matter are those who have it." And, "I am not so naïve as to realize that most government programs end up benefiting those who have that money." But, and it's a big but for Fuller, "We have to take the chance, and we will deal with that problem when it comes. For now we need an inside-outside strategy. We need pressure from the outside."

As was noted in the last chapter, not all black leaders in Milwaukee share his opinion or are willing to take those chances. Representative Williams, Fuller's friend and often ally, has shifted her view and is trying to reverse the expansion of the Milwaukee program. The remaining black members of the legislature opposed expansion earlier than Williams. All of the black members of the Ohio legislature voted against the Cleveland program.

In some ways, Fuller's position is very similar to that of Milton Friedman (1955), John Chubb and Terry Moe (1990), and others who see a radical shift to a market approach as the necessary spark to reform

---

[3] Unless otherwise cited, the quotations and arguments are from a speech in which Fuller and I were introduced as representing different perspectives on the MPCP (Business Roundtable, Education Committee Conference, May 22, 1997, Washington, D.C. Notes available from the author on request).

American education—especially for those who are most consistently failing in the current system. But again we cannot overlook who that radical change is likely to benefit most. Friedman's theories are not specific on that issue. Fuller believes resources can be conserved or limited in some way to keep them within the poor communities that need them most. I disagree, but we are all predicting courses of policies that are not determinant, and which are yet affected by debate and argument.

I hope if nothing else this book is testimony to the importance of those arguments. What is at stake is the general direction of education policy in America. Vouchers are a concrete manifestation of a larger issue, of a potential watershed in American education. To that end we need to consider outcomes of a radical shift to a market approach to American education.

## Choice and the Market Approach to Education in America

Is choice and the market approach the appropriate direction for educational reform in America? To analyze that question it is first necessary to distinguish between choice and a market approach. In economic theory these two concepts are inextricably linked in that market models begin with preference orderings or preference bundles for individuals or households. Obviously the same applies to education. So why is the distinction necessary?

The reason is that one can conceptually separate the idea of choice from a full market model for the delivery of educational services. Nothing in this study, or the logic of education, suggests that family preferences for education are unimportant. I discussed why people attend private rather than public schools, and why families might choose unique types of schools. And I have argued how critical choice is as a normative justification in our country. I have also underscored that choice in public schools was facilitated by residential choice. One way to interpret expanding public school choice is as a retreat from rigid residential school assignment systems.

But if moving to expand school choice seems to be positive, why not advocate a full market model of education services? The general answer is that other values also influence policy decisions. I argued in chapter 2 that the choice debate was enduring because it brought two cherished values into direct conflict—freedom and equality of opportunity. To best understand this conflict, I want to move the discussion beyond proposals for publicly funded vouchers, to consider the question of why government should be involved in education at all. If the market produces efficient results in terms of the expenditure of national resources, why not go all the way and simply argue that families are responsible for funding education from current and borrowed resources?

The language of economic theory is useful for the analysis. On the demand side, individual consuming families would choose the type of education they desired and how much to spend on education. On the production side, schools would be similarly autonomous. With the exception of rules limiting a very few schools that may educate in ways obviously destructive to the commonweal, schools would be unconstrained in their actions. Differences in tuition, student admission policies, teaching approaches, organization, and operational approaches would create a product mix offered to families. Theoretically this system would improve efficiency in terms of both resource allocation and delivery of services and would have the added advantage of being fairer to childless couples or even small families. But if the logic is so compelling, why have we adopted a system so very far removed from a pure market?

Ironically, the original education system in America was probably close to that model—surely closer to the pure market model than the public system that has developed since. Beyond a very modest level of public education in some states, family income dictated who went on to postelementary schools and colleges. One of the most instructive views of this system comes from a famous "radical" reform proposal by Thomas Jefferson for the state of Virginia. He offered for enactment a "Bill for the More General Diffusion of Knowledge" in 1779 and again in almost identical form in 1818. Both times it failed to pass. The bill has generally come to be viewed as a model of foresight and radical thinking on the organization and funding of education. However, on closer examination, the modesty of the proposal indicates the state of education at the founding of the republic.

Although Jefferson proposed a common education for all through the third grade, beyond that level parents were responsible for funding further education. The exceptions were to be based exclusively on merit. To fulfill the education through the first three grades, approximately seven hundred schools were to be paid for by public funding. In each school, one student would be selected to attend at public expense one of the twenty-five grammar schools in the state. After two years, one student from each of those schools would be selected to go on for four more years. Thus only twenty-five students in the state would be publicly educated beyond grade 5. As late as 1818, the proposal was considered too radical and too expensive (Henderson, 1890; Hellmers, 1995).

The remarkable transition in the latter nineteenth and twentieth centuries initially turned on the drive for a "common" education. It was unclear what that meant in practice other than a slowly growing set of standards of compulsory education and increasingly common curriculum through the introduction of reading and math books in nationwide series. As the required standards grew, the funding of schools also became mostly communal. Because most families could not have afforded to pay for the required years of education for their children, funding was extended across the community and across generations. Compared to free market allocation, this clearly meant a distorted oversupply of education.

The communal nature of funding combined with compulsory years of education led to communal control over school systems. Because of the American reluctance to centralize power, that control, more than in most other industrialized nations, was vested at the most decentralized level—the township, town, or city. Thus, unlike the private school systems that grew up in parallel at the end of the last century, both the supply and demand for education were collectively controlled. Although in every state that control was ostensibly democratic, in reality power was wielded by a combination of professional administrators, increasingly with elaborate forms of job protections, and less expert citizen representatives on thousands of local school boards. If anything, in the latter half of the twentieth century, control was increasingly centralized as state-level bureaucratic and political institutions became relatively more powerful in education policy.

Nearly every aspect of this system should repulse a true believer in economic markets. Consumers are forced to accept services they might not have purchased on their own. Households are forced to pay for services they might not receive. Families are given incentives to produce children they may not want. Producers are constrained in the products they offer. The whole system is guided neither by efficiency nor equity. The democratic impulse of school board members to win reelection, and administrators and teachers to retain their jobs and increase their salaries through collective and political actions, are not linked to the products they produce—children's education.

So how does one defend this system against a market model? Certainly not on purely economic theory grounds. A pure market model would clearly produce other results. But thinking about those results, what the free market picture of education would produce, is critical in the continuing policy debate over market model alternatives to public education in America. The question must be: Are the results of that market model what we want in this country?

What would a pure education market produce? On the demand side, with families paying full costs, the total investment in education is likely to fall and, given various estimates of willingness to mortgage future incomes, fall substantially. Second, with demand being heavily dependent on income (which also conditions ability to borrow against future income), investment would be uneven between families and highly correlated with income.

The supply side picture is difficult to predict in all relevant parameters, but it seems obvious that elite schools would flourish — elite at least in the sense that schools would attempt to attract the highest income students with the promise of the best education for them. How would schools convince parents of their quality? It could be based on results, and in this case the correlation between family socioeconomic status and achievement discussed above would be an overriding factor. But it may also be, as Peter Cookson and Caroline Percell observed in their excellent study of elite schools, that parents judge quality by the company their children keep — that is, by the families attending the school. This requires much less emphasis on actual outcomes, which are time consuming and tricky to analyze. Rather it requires an understanding of where classmates come from in terms of social class, education, or barring that, simply address. As they noted, prep schools and elite private colleges have worked that terrain for hundreds of years (Cookson and Percell, 1985).

Would there be a mass market for middle- and low-income students? Yes, because there clearly would be demand. But relative economies of scale and cost controls would be put in place. As with the current differences between wealthy districts and public and private schools, poorer schools would have larger class sizes, lower teacher salaries, and fewer resources to accommodate the lower price for services. Thus just as the market stratifies consumption patterns by income for hundreds of other products, it will also stratify the purchase of education.

Would there be greater diversity in schools, more innovation, and quicker response to changing family desires for education? Probably. In terms of diversity and innovation, all that is required is to assume that schools not governed by collective actions are likely to develop in more diverse ways than those created and maintained through an ongoing community-selected board. Would they be more responsive to parent desires? Again, probably, but the image of parents shifting schools continually in search of the optimum school for their children is constrained by geography and the whining of children. Would they be more responsive to changing technology and pedagogy? That would appear to depend heavily on the funding level. New technology and organizational flexibility cost money, and the higher priced schools could adapt much more easily.

How do these pictures add up in comparison with the current system? First, on the demand side there would be less investment. Should we cut back on overall investment in education? People who argue that many of the higher order skills taught in college and even advanced high school classes are often not used in the workplace might say yes. However, anyone following the technology revolution, which America is clearly leading, may sense that investing less is a mistake and even that the reverse is desirable.

Should a child's education be correlated with current and past family income? That depends on a host of values and beliefs about the relationship between ability and past family success, about opportunity, and about life successes unconnected to educational ability. If, as *The Bell Curve* (Herrnstein and Murray, 1994) seems to argue, there is a relatively tight connection between innate ability and financial success, one might agree that market sorting by income level is appropriate. One might overeducate a few rich dullards and undereducate a few poor geniuses, but on average the system would work quite well. On the other hand, if one views those relationships as highly permeable, then one might err on the side of mass education. One might also arrive at that view if one assumes even a modest connection between educational achievement and life successes in outcomes other than income (e.g., happiness, civility).

Regardless of the outcomes of education, one could still support mass education, possibly at quite a high level, based simply on equality of opportunity in a democratic society. We know that education is viewed by many as a stepping-stone to success. Therefore, in a country that claims equality for its members, all should be given some degree of opportunity to receive an education without regard for the financial success of their parents. The equal opportunity argument may also be premised on the assumption that opportunity creates incentives. If one knows that coming from a poor home makes going to college nearly impossible, why work in high school?

The pure market model also has not-so-subtle racial implications. By design the system would free up individual choices of schools. The Milwaukee voucher experiment offers modest evidence on what might occur. The MPCP probably led to more segregated schools than would have occurred without it. However, the unique set of schools and circumstances involved may have produced that result. The longer view, based on attempts since 1954 to integrate schools in America, is probably more telling of the types of market choices consumers would make. Regardless of one's beliefs or hopes, the overwhelming social fact of the integration movement was white flight from our cities. It is difficult for me to see how a market model of choice would do anything but accelerate the growing racial balkanization of our schools and country. Whether that result will be class or racially motivated, is in one sense irrelevant given the correlation between the two.

Is the supply side of the picture desirable? Granting that the current system already stratifies educational opportunities and that there may be more diversity and choice between different types of schools under a pure market model, we must also assume that a pure market model would produce greater inequality between schools. Unless I have completely misread the existing incentives for selection on the part of schools, under a pure market model there would be an increasing stratification of schools from elite to mass institutions. The former would take students further and teach at higher levels. The latter would spend less per pupil, with inevitably lower standards, expectations, and results.

Although it is easy to dismiss stratification of schools as unacceptable, that does not face the reality of the inequities we have always had in American education. The issue comes down to the trade-off between mass education and elite education. Mass education can open up vistas for students and families, creating opportunities at the highest levels of our society within a single generation. But elite education also plays an important role for our best students. For high-achieving students, working with a highly selective set of students and faculty has inestimable rewards in terms of training, intellectual discourse, motivation, and independent thinking. Both have roles to play and hopefully both can coexist.

But two points are critical. First, mass institutions touch many more lives than elite ones — and numbers may well count, especially in a world where the type of intellectual environment of elite schools is spreading through technology and more equal resources across schools. Second, in contrast to *The Bell Curve* assumption, to provide educational advantages, access to elite schools cannot be based on wealth but rather on stringent achievement criteria. Otherwise, they provide access to power and continued economic privilege, but do little to advance the benefits of education.

One of the great changes in post–World War II America was that both our public and our most elite private colleges and universities opened their doors to women and the nonrich. For the private schools this meant that many of the new students and faculty were high achievers usually selected from the very large middle-class pool. Education historians may point to these two facts — a dramatic increase in access to college and basing that access more on achievement than family wealth — as two of the most important phenomena in explaining the success of post–World War II college and postgraduate education in America.

Perhaps then we can justify elite educational institutions if they are based on merit. That would break what many would argue is an inappropriate link between parental income and wealth and educational access. It may also fulfill some people's criteria for equal opportunity — falling back on Jefferson: those who among the many succeed, deserve to go on. Even so, however, public policy may still need to balance support for mass versus meritocratically elite institutions.

A number of factors affect where that balance should be placed. Meritocratic elite schools provide incentives for students and families to excel and achieve. In addition, society may disproportionately benefit from the students educated in those elite schools. Offsetting these factors, however, is the fact that mass education raises the overall level of education in society and, as a consequence, allows many more students to enter the selection zone for higher, elite education. One would applaud the first result if one believes, as I do, that increasing general education is by itself a key to individual and communal advancement in the future. If one believes an educationally advanced elite is also a significant benefit, mass education may be viewed as enlarging the selection pool. It allows more students the time to mature and excel and to enter the selection zone for further education.

Any recommended balance point between mass and elite education will be based on a combination of individual conjecture and values. But note that the critical assumption of a meritocratically selected elite is one important step removed from a pure market model of education. The market responds to a cash nexus, which may or may not be related to educational achievement in schools. The necessary link is that school achievement levels will be known and translated into the supply price. Those with the resources would purchase quality education for their children, measured by the achievement success of their fellow students. Several problems may interfere with this result, however. The most important are that many of the highest achievers may not be able to meet the price (Ivy League schools without financial aid), and that there is an enormous profit incentive on the part of schools to allow rich dullards to buy in (the prewar status of Ivy League schools?).

Thus, my view challenges the supply-side market structure on two levels. First, I doubt that merit would override income as the key to the more stratified schools that I foresee as inevitable. And even if it did, I place much more faith in educating large numbers than in focusing resources on those few predicted to be gifted.

## Market Models and Voucher Policy Proposals

Throughout this book, I have asked readers to make reality checks. Therefore it seems perfectly reasonable to ask if what has just been laid out is little more than a philosopher's trick — a hypothetical model or situation, carefully designed to reach a predetermined conclusion. In this case, that would be imposing the pure market model as the standard of reference against which to judge voucher proposals.

I do not believe, however, that is the case in this instance. Why? First, as Henig has pointed out, the market metaphor is pervasive and often as extreme as I have described it (Henig, 1994). It seems reasonable to require those who casually advocate market approaches to defend them in their pure form. If proponents do not believe in the pure form, then it is incumbent on them to detail how their positions deviate from that ideal, why, and with what consequences.

Second, and more important, universal voucher programs—open to all without contingencies for income differences and with no constraints on schools—move close to the pure market model. All families would be given a set amount with which to shop for education. Assuming the voucher is set close to current expenditure levels, that would create a much greater demand for mass education than under the pure market model in which families pay their own way. Overall demand could be manipulated—lower voucher prices and demand goes down. Thus the degree of mass education would not drop as severely as under the pure market model.

What of stratification? The connection between income and level and quality would be partially mitigated. However, schools could still select students and could set tuition levels, which would mean add-ons that would discriminate based on income (see Witte, 1993). Thus while the same tendencies as in the pure market model would effect demand, the extremities of the results would be less.

Supply would also follow the same course as in a pure market model, but also with less extremes on both ends. More money spread across all incomes would produce more schools for lower-income families and they would probably run on higher budgets than pure market mass schools. But the quality of those schools would hardly be insured. In the end people will need to spend their vouchers somewhere. Usually that will be in their neighborhood, or close by, and that will mean schools will more or less match neighborhood incomes.

What of new schools? Voucher advocates often emphasize the creation of new schools as the competitive market heats up. The incentives to create elite schools under vouchers will hardly be diminished relative to the pure market model. They will attract better students who are less difficult to educate, from families with higher incomes, and thus be more likely to be white. That will mean better working environments, smaller class sizes, more resources, and a more stimulating intellectual environment for students, staff, and parents. Or to summarize, if given the choice, why would one open a school in the ghetto? Some will, out of altruism, desire for religious instruction, or because one is a member of the community. But one will not if the motive is profit, or tradition, or to produce the best school.

Perhaps the most predictable outcome of universal vouchers will be their effect on parochial schools. Some parochial schools remaining in the inner city will be saved. But as noted in chapter 3, as Catholics moved from city to suburb, they often failed to build or expand parish schools. They understood the parish subsidies involved, appreciated the quality of suburban public schools, and were under less stringent dictates from the church to send their children to religious schools. Vouchers will change the financial disincentives and that will mean building schools or expanding older, smaller schools. But where will this take place? The geographic dispersal of the largesse going to parochial schools is not simple to predict. But the current demographic makeup of parochial school students will probably be a conservative estimate of how much money will go to inner-city schools and students. Thus while the pure market model provides an extreme case of stratification, universal vouchers will clearly increase current stratification and subsidy upward in the income stream.

Does this mean that targeted voucher programs such as the original Milwaukee program should not be supported because they begin the slippery slope to universal vouchers? Again these issues need personal attention and thought. My answer is no. Why? First, Fuller has a point — some type of bomb is probably needed in our inner-city districts. The problems of American education have been exaggerated considerably over the last decade. Those attacks have led to an equally exaggerated defense (Berliner and Biddle, 1995). The outcomes of American education, which seem to defy almost any changes or media presentations of the system, are quite consistent over time. Most Americans are generally satisfied with the public education system, and the closer the survey questions get to home, the more satisfied they are (*Phi Delta Kappan*, 1996). The objective measures are consistent with this stable evaluation. While highly publicized trends in national standardized test scores dipped from the mid-1960s to the late 1980s, these were college entrance examinations scores, and the population of students taking those tests also increased to include many lower-income students as the access to college increased (Berliner and Biddle, 1995). Most critics unfortunately fail to note this changing base and the independent positive implications of the change. The rebound in test scores since 1989 has been considerable, with the major increases among minority students. This includes both college entrance examinations and the National Assessment of Educational Progress.

Attainment, as measured by year of completed education, improved consistently since 1950, leveled off in the late 1970s, but again accelerated in the 1990s. Controlling for socioeconomic status differences, those levels are very high by international standards. In addition, after 1960 the attainment of poor and minority students continued to increase as the population numbers reached a plateau (*Digest of Education Statistics*, 1997).

What this adds up to is that American education has overall either improved or stayed about the same since 1950. At the same time, however, there is also clear evidence that in poor school districts — rural and urban — despite recent gains, many students continue to fail. Perhaps the great tragedy of American education is that we know exactly where those students are, and where they are likely to be in ten years.

Thus the need for Fuller's bomb. But are vouchers the bomb that is needed? I doubt it. If the bomb requires a universal voucher program, I believe it will backfire for poor districts. The money will simply go elsewhere and once it is being routinely spent in the suburbs and selective inner-city schools, it will never be retrieved. If most of the money ends up in the suburbs or private schools, and inner-city students cannot follow the money, what is the incentive to improve inner-city schools?

A targeted program, on the other hand, may not provide a bomb, but it will serve as a constant reminder and even irritant for those systems. It will also serve as a policy alternative for some families, aid private schools as needed alternatives, and perhaps increase cooperation between the public and private school sectors. This may have the further desirable result of integrating these sectors in inner-city environments. Private schools may have to accept more regulation, while public schools may acquire more flexibility.

But what of the politics of vouchers and the slippery slope from targeted experiment to universal voucher programs? In 1995 I gave my first and only formal testimony before the Wisconsin legislature on the MPCP. I testified about that slippery slope, and the argument at least quieted a noisy room. Ironically I felt it was the Republican voucher supporters, among them Committee Chair Senator Peggy Rosenzweig, who listened most closely. None present argued for abandonment of public education, and all present understood the cost implications of a universal voucher program. Thus that slope may not be quite as slippery as I first thought and testified. The slope is long and the political and legal hurdles are numerous. Although voucher supporters are reveling in the Supreme Court decision not to review the Wisconsin case, what they did in actuality was to throw the issue back on the constitutional provisions of individual states. For many states, that may mean substantial changes in their constitutions before universal vouchers could be enacted (Kemerer, forthcoming).

While the incremental forces to expand voucher programs are strong, I sense that there is a leap from targeted programs to pure market models that will yet be substantial. It may occur, but if it does, a substantial shift in people's attitudes toward education will need to occur first. I do not think the logic of the arguments in this chapter and throughout this book are complex or surprising. In other words, I cannot see people abandoning public education in the coming decades.

The more likely outcome is that eventually some state will either expand a limited voucher program or, using Milwaukee or Cleveland choice theater as a rationale, enact a universal voucher program from scratch. The interests supporting that result are powerful and not about to go away.

The challenging question then will be, will anyone be asked or able to adequately evaluate the results of such a program? Who will benefit? How much will it cost? What will be the short- and long-term results, and for which students? What will be the impact on schools? And perhaps most important, what will be the impact on communities and their willingness to support education and a high standard of educational access for all students? This book stands as a pessimistic note that such studies are unlikely to be done, and if they are, they will fail to have much impact on the expanding politics of educational choice.

# References _____

Archbald, Douglas. 1988. *Magnet Schools, Voluntary Desegregation, and Public Choice Theory: Limits and Possibilities in a Big City System.* Unpublished Ph.D. diss., School of Education, University of Wisconsin, Madison.

Beales, Janet, and Maureen Wahl. 1995a. *Given the Choice: A Study of the PAVE Program and School Choice in Milwaukee.* Los Angeles, CA: The Reason Foundation. Policy Studies Paper no. 183.

————. 1995b. "Private Vouchers in Milwaukee: The PAVE Program." In *Private Vouchers.* Edited by Terry Moe, 41–73. Stanford: Hoover Institute.

Berliner, David, and B. J. Biddle. 1995. *The Manufactured Crisis: Myths, Fraud, and the Attack on America's Public Schools.* Reading, MA: Addison-Wesley.

Blank, Rolf. 1990. "Educational Effects of Magnet High Schools." In *Choice and Control in American Education. Vol. 2: The Practice of Choice, Decentralization and School Restructuring.* Edited by William S. Clune and John F. Witte, 77–110. New York: The Falmer Press.

Bridge, G. 1978. "Information Imperfection: The Achilles Heel of Entitlement Plans," *School Review,* vol. 86:504–29.

Bryk, Anthony, Valerie Lee, and Peter Holland. 1994. *Catholic Schools and the Common Good.* Cambridge, MA: Harvard University Press.

Bryk, Anthony S., and Stephen W. Raudenbush. 1992. *Hierarchical Linear Models: Applications and Data Analysis Methods.* Newbury Park, CA: Sage Publications.

*Budget of the U.S. Government, Fiscal Year 1999: Historical Tables.* 1998. Washington, D.C.: Government Printing Office.

Buetow, H. A. 1970. *Of Singular Benefit: The History of U.S. Catholic Education.* New York: Macmillan.

*Catholic Schools in America.* 1995. Montrose, CA: Fischer Publishing Inc.

Choy, Susan P. 1997. *Public and Private Schools: How Do They Differ?* Washington, D.C.: National Center for Education Statistics.

Chubb, John and Terry Moe. 1990. *Politics, Markets and American Schools.* Washington, D.C.: The Brookings Institution.

Cleaver, Mary Jo. 1995. Wisconsin Bureau for Policy and the Budget. Memorandum to Faye Stark, May 15.

Clune, William S., and John F. Witte, eds. 1990. *Choice and Control in American Education,* Vol. 1 and 2. New York: The Falmer Press.

Cookson, Peter W., Jr., and Caroline Hodges Percell. 1985. *Preparing for Power: America's Elite Boarding Schools.* New York. Basic Books.

Cookson, Peter W., Jr. 1994. *School Choice: The Struggle for American Education.* New Haven: Yale University Press.

Coons, John E., and Stephen D. Sugarman. 1978. *Education by Choice: The Case for Family Control.* Berkeley, CA: University of California Press.

———. 1992. "The Scholarship Initiative: A Model State Law for Elementary and Secondary School Choice." *Journal of Law and Education* 21, no. 4 (Fall): 529–67.

———. 1993. *Scholarships for Children.* Berkeley, CA: Institute for Governmental Policy Studies.

Cuban, Larry. 1990. "Reforming Again, Again, and Again," *Education Researcher*: 3–12.

*Digest of Education Statistics.* Respective years. National Center for Education Statistics. Washington, D.C.: Web Site or Government Printing Office.

Fliegel, S., and J. MacGuire. 1993. *Miracle in East Harlem: The Fight for Choice in Public Education.* New York: Times Books.

Friedman, Milton. 1955. "The Role of Government in Education." In *Economics and the Public Interest.* Edited by Robert A. Solow, 123–44. New Brunswick, NJ: Rutgers Press.

———. 1962. *Capitalism and Freedom.* Chicago: University of Chicago Press. Chap. 6.

———. 1995. "Public Schools: Make Them Private." *Washington Post* (February): 19.

Funkhouser, Janie E., and Kelly W. Colopy. 1994. "Minnesota's Open Enrollment Option: Impact on School Districts." Washington, D.C.: Policy Studies Associates.

Gamoran, Adam. 1996. "Student Achievement in Public Magnet, Public Comprehensive, and Private High Schools." *Educational Evaluation and Policy Analysis* 18 (Spring): 1–18.

Gleason, P. 1985. "Baltimore III and Education." *U.S. Catholic Historian* 4: 273–306.

Governor's Study Commission. 1985. *Better Public Schools: Commission Report on the Quality of Education in the Metropolitan Milwaukee Public Schools.* Department of Public Instruction. Madison, WI.

Greeley, Andrew M. 1977. *The American Catholic: A Social Portrait.* New York: Basic Books.

———. 1989. "My Research on Catholic Schools." *Chicago Studies* 28:245–64.

Greene, Jay, W. Howell and Paul Peterson. 1997. "An Evaluation of the Cleveland Scholarship Program." Unpublished manuscript. Cambridge, MA: Harvard University.

Greene, Jay, Paul Peterson, and Jiangtao Du. 1996. "The Effectiveness of School Choice in Milwaukee: A Secondary Analysis of Data from the Program's Evaluation." Paper given at the American Political Science Association Annual Meeting. San Francisco, CA. August 29 to September 1.

Hanushek, Eric. 1986. "The Economics of Schooling: Production and Efficiency in Public Schools." *Journal of Economic Literature* 24:1141–77.

Heckman, James. 1979. "Sample Selection Bias As a Specification Error." *Econometrica* 47:153–61.

Heise, Michael, Kenneth D. Colburn, Jr., and Joseph F. Lamberti. 1995. "Private Vouchers in Indianapolis: The Golden Rule Program." In *Private Vouchers.* Edited by Terry Moe, 100–119. Stanford: Hoover Institute.

Hellmers, Jeffrey N. 1995. "The Connection Between Democracy and Education in the Thought of Thomas Jefferson." Unpublished manuscript. Madison, WI: University of Wisconsin, Madison.

Henderson, John C. 1890. *Jefferson's Views on Public Education*. New York: P. G. Putnam and Sons.

Henig, Jeffrey. 1994. *Rethinking School Choice: Limits of the Market Metaphor*. Princeton, NJ: Princeton University Press.

Herrnstein, Richard J., and Charles M. Murray. 1994. *The Bell Curve: Intelligence and Class Structure in American Life*. New York: Free Press.

Hill, Paul T. 1995. "Private Vouchers in New York City: The Student Sponsored Partnership Program." In *Private Vouchers*. Edited by Terry Moe, 120–35. Stanford: Hoover Institute.

Hirschman, Albert O. 1970. *Exit, Voice and Loyalty: Responses to Decline in Firms, Organizations, and States*. Cambridge, MA: Harvard University Press.

Hoffer, Thomas, and James Coleman. 1987. *Public and Private High Schools: The Impact of Communities*. New York: Basic Books.

Hoffer, Thomas, Sally Kilgore, and James Coleman. 1982. *High School Achievement: Public, Catholic and Private Schools Compared*. New York: Basic Books.

Hoxby, C. 1996. "Evidence on Private School Vouchers: Effects on School and Students." In *Holding Schools Accountable*. Edited by Helen Ladd. Washington, D.C.: The Brookings Institution.

Huber, P. J. 1967. "The Behavior of Maximum Likelihood Estimates Under Non-Standard Conditions." *Proceedings of the Fifth Berkeley Symposium on Mathematical Statistics and Probability* 1:221–33.

Institute for Research on Poverty. 1997. "Evaluating Comprehensive State Welfare Reforms: A Conference." Madison, WI.

Kane, Thomas J., and Cecilia E. Rouse. 1993. "Labor Market Returns to Two- and Four-Year College: Is a Credit a Credit and Do Degrees Matter?" Cambridge: National Bureau of Education Research Working Paper.

Kemerer, Frank R. 1995. "The Constitutionality of School Vouchers." *West's Education Law Reporter*. (August 24): 17–36.

———. "State Constitutions and School Vouchers." Forthcoming in *West's Education Law Reporter*.

Kemerer, Frank R., and Kimi Lynn King. 1995. "Are School Vouchers Constitutional?" *Phi Delta Kappan* (December): 307–11.

Knickerman, James, and Andrew Reschovsky. 1980. "The Implementation of School Finance Reform." *Policy Sciences* 12:301–15.

Lankford, Hemp, J. S. Lee, and James Wykoff. 1995. "An Analysis of Elementary and Secondary School Choice." *Journal of Urban Economics* 38:236–51.

Lankford, Hemp, and James Wykoff. 1992. "Primary and Secondary School Choice Among Public and Religious Alternatives." *Economics of Education Review* 11:317–37.

Lasswell, Harold. 1958. *Who Gets What, When, How*. Cleveland. Meridian Books.

Lee, Susan, and Christine Foster. 1997. "Trustbusters." *Forbes* (June 2): 146–52.

Levin, Henry. 1990. "The Theory of Choice Applied to Education." In *Choice and Control in American Education. Vol. 1: The Theory of Choice and Control in Education.* Edited by William H. Clune and John F. Witte, 247–84. New York: The Falmer Press.

———. 1991. "The Economics of Educational Choice," *Economics of Education Review* 10:137–58.

———. 1998. "Educational Vouchers: Effectiveness, Choice and Costs." *Journal of Policy Analysis and Management* 17:373–92.

Levin, Henry, and Cyrus Driver. 1997. "Costs of an Educational Voucher System." *Education Economics* 5:265–83.

Lieberman, Myron. 1993. *Public Education: An Autopsy.* Cambridge, MA: Harvard University Press.

Lindblom, Charles E. 1979. "Still Muddling, Not Yet Through." *Public Administration Review* 29:517–26.

Manski, Charles. 1992. "Educational Choice (Vouchers) and Social Mobility." *Economics of Education Review* 11 (December): 351–69.

Martinez, Valerie, Kenneth Godwin, and Frank Kemerer. 1995. "Private Vouchers in San Antonio: The CEO Program." In *Private Vouchers.* Edited by Terry Moe, 74–99. Stanford: Hoover Institute.

Martinez, Valerie, Kenneth Godwin, Frank Kemerer, and L. Perna. 1995. "The Consequences of School Choice: Who Leaves and Who Stays in the Inner City?" *Social Sciences Quarterly* 76:485–501.

McGroarty, Daniel. 1993. "School Choice Slandered?" *The Public Interest* 17: 94–111.

———. 1996a. *Break These Chains: The Battle for School Choice.* Rocklin, CA: Prima Publishing.

———. 1996b. "The Trial of Brother Bob." *American Spectator* (March): 34–39.

Metcalf, Kimberly K. 1998. "Advocacy in the Guise of Science." *Education Week* (September 23).

Metcalf, Kim K., William J. Boone, Frances K. Stage, Todd L. Chilton, Patty Muller, and Polly Tait. 1998. "A Comparative Evaluation of the Cleveland Scholarship and Tutoring Grant Program." Bloomington, IN: School of Education.

Metropolitan Milwaukee Association of Commerce. 1994. Internal document and newsletter. "Question by Question Analysis." Milwaukee.

Milwaukee Public Schools. 1998. "District Demographics and Enrollment Analysis: 1992–2002. Mimeo. Milwaukee, WI.

Mintrom, Michael. 1997. "Policy Entrepreneurs and the Diffusion of Innovation." *American Journal of Political Science* 41:738–70.

Mintrom, Michael, and Sandra Vergari. 1998. "Policy Networks and Innovation Diffusion: The Case of State Education Reforms." *The Journal of Politics* 60:126–48.

Mitchell, Susan. 1994. Memorandum to Timothy Sheehy, (MMAC), et al., with attached draft legislation. (December).

Molnar, Alexander. 1997. "The Real Lesson of Milwaukee's Voucher Experiment." *Education Week* (August 6):76.

Moore, Donald R., and S. Davenport. 1988. "The New Improved Sorting Machine." Madison, WI: National Center on Effective Secondary Schools.

Moore, Gwendolyn. 1997. Mimeo fact sheet. Madison, WI: Senator Moore's Office.

Murnane, Richard. 1986. "Comparisons of Private and Public Schools: The Critical Role of Regulations." In *Private Education: Studies in Choice and Public Policy*. Edited by Daniel Levy. New York: Oxford University Press.

National Commission on Children. 1991. *Beyond Rhetoric: A New Agenda for Children and Families*. Washington, D.C.

National Commission on Excellence in Education. 1983. *A Nation At Risk*. Washington D.C.

National Education Association. 1997. Center for Public School Choice. Charter Schools Information Sheets, March. Washington D.C.

National Governors' Association. 1986. *Time For Results*. Washington, D.C.

OECD. 1989. *Education in OECD Countries 1986–87: A Compendium of Statistical Information*. Paris: Organization of Economic Co-operation and Development.

———. 1990. *Education in OECD Countries 1987–88: A Compendium of Statistical Information*. Paris: Organization of Economic Co-operation and Development.

———. 1992. *Education at a Glance: OECD Indicators*. Paris: Organization of Economic Co-operation and Development.

Ohio Department of Education. 1997. Program Documents, Cleveland Scholarship and Tutoring Program Office. (April 3). Columbus, OH.

Peterson, Paul E. 1990. "Monopoly and Competition in American Education." In *Choice and Control in American Education. Vol. 1: The Theory of Choice and Control in Education*. Edited by William S. Clune and John F. Witte, 47–78. New York. The Falmer Press.

———. 1993. "Are Big City Schools Holding Their Own?" In *Seeds of Crisis*. Edited by John Rury. Madison, WI: The University of Wisconsin.

———. 1997. "The Case for School Choice." *Harvard Magazine* (May–June). Internet: www.harvard-magazine.com.

Peterson, Paul E., and Chad Noyes. 1996. "Under Extreme Duress, School Choice Success." Unpublished manuscript. Cambridge, MA: Harvard University.

Phi Delta Kappan. 1996. *The 28ᵗʰ Annual Phi Delta Kappan/Gallup Poll*. Bloomington, Indiana.

Plank, Stephen, et al. 1993. "Effects of Choice in Education." In *School Choice*. Edited by Edith Rasell and Richard Rothstein, 115–18. Washington, D.C.: Economic Policy Institute.

*Rethinking Schools*. 1997. Newsletter. Milwaukee, WI (Summer).

Rigdon, Mark E. 1995. *The Business of Education Reform*. University of Wisconsin, Madison. Ph.D. diss., University of Michigan, microforms.

Rom, Mark C., and John F. Witte. 1988. "Power Versus Participation: The Wisconsin State Budget Process." In *State Policy Choices: The Wisconsin Experience*. Edited by Sheldon Danziger and John F. Witte. Madison, WI: University of Wisconsin Press.

Rose, Susan D. 1988. *Keeping Them Out of the Hands of Satan: Evangelical Schooling in America*. London: Routledge.

Rossell, Christine. 1990. *The Carrot or the Stick for Desegregation Policy: Magnet Schools or Forced Busing.* Philadelphia. Temple University Press.

Rouse, Cecilia. 1997. "Private School Vouchers and Student Achievement: An Evaluation of the Milwaukee Parental Choice Program." Unpublished manuscript. Princeton University.

———. 1998. "Private School Vouchers and Student Achievement: An Evaluation of the Milwaukee Parental Choice Program." *Quarterly Journal of Economics* (May):555–602.

Rubenstein, Michael, R. Hamar, and Nancy Adelman. 1992. *Minnesota's Open Enrollment Option.* Washington, D.C.: U.S. Department of Education/Policy Studies Association.

Ruenzel, David. 1995. "A Choice in the Matter." *Education Week* (September 27): 23.

Ryan, Susan P., Anthony S. Bryk, Kimberley P. Lopez, Kathleen Hall, and Stuart Luppescu. 1997. *Charter's Reform: LSCs — Local Leadership at Work.* Chicago: Consortium on Chicago School Research.

Smith, Kevin, and Kenneth Meier. 1995. *The Case against School Choice.* Armonk, NY: M. E. Sharpe.

Stein, Robert M., and Kenneth Bickers. 1994a. "Universalism and the Electoral Connection: A Test and Some Doubts." *Political Research Quarterly* 47: 295–318.

———. 1994b. "Congressional Elections and the Pork Barrel." *Journal of Politics* 56:377–99.

Teske, P., M. Schneider, M. Mintrom, and S. Best. 1993. "Establishing the Micro Foundations of Macro Theory: Information, Movers, and the Competitive Local Market for Public Goods." *American Political Science Review* 87:702–13.

Thompson, Tom. 1995. *State of the State Address.* Madison, WI: Governor's internet site.

Vergari, Sandra, and Michael Mintrom. 1995. "Charter School Laws across the United States." Lansing, MI: Institute for Public Policy and Social Research.

Wahl, Janet. 1994. "Second-Year Report of the PAVE Scholarship Program." Milwaukee: Family Services of America.

Wanat, John. 1974. "Bases of Budgetary Incrementalism." *American Political Science Review* 68:1221–28.

Weiss, Carol H. 1972. *Evaluating Action Programs: Readings in Social Action and Education.* Boston, MA: Allyn and Bacon.

Wells, Amy S. 1993. *Time to Choose: America at the Crossroads of School Choice Policy.* New York: Hill and Wang.

Wells, Amy S., C. Grutzik, and S. Carnochan. 1996. "The Multiple Meanings of U.S. Charter School Reform: Exploring the Politics of Deregulation." Paper presented at the British Education Association Meetings Lancaster, UK (September 12–15).

White, H. 1980. "A Heteroskedasticity-Consistent Covariance Matrix Estimator and a Direct Test for Heteroskedasticity." *Econometrica* 48:817–30.

Wildavsky, Aaron. 1979. *The Politics of the Budgetary Process.* 4th ed. Boston: Little Brown.

Williams, Annette Polly. 1996. Press release. Madison, WI: Wisconsin Assembly, (September 9).

Wisconsin Department of Public Instruction. 1995. Press release. Madison, WI (November 10).

Wisconsin Legislative Audit Bureau. 1995. "An Evaluation of the Milwaukee Parental Choice Program." Madison, WI.

Wisconsin Legislative Reference Bureau. 1990a. Madison, WI. Electronic file LRBs0621/1 (March 8).

———. 1990b. Madison, WI. Electronic file LRBa4204/1 (March 13).

Wisconsin Supreme Court. 1995. Notice of Opinion, No. 95-2153-OA (July 29).

Witte, John F. 1985. "Metropolitan Milwaukee Dropout Report, Report 3." Governor's Study Commission. Madison, WI: Department of Public Instruction.

———. 1990. "Choice and Control: An Analytical Overview." In *Choice and Control in American Education. Vol. 1: The Theory of Choice and Control in Education*. Edited by William S. Clune and John F. Witte, 9–45. New York. The Falmer Press.

———. 1991a. "Choice in American Education." *Educational Considerations*. Vol. 19 (Fall): 12–19.

———. 1991b. "First-Year Report: Milwaukee Parental Choice Program." Report to the Wisconsin State Legislature. Madison, WI: Department of Public Instruction.

———. 1992. "Public Subsidies for Private Schools: What We Know and How to Proceed." *Education Policy*, 6 (June): 206–27.

———. 1993. "Market Versus State-Centered Approaches to American Education: Does Either Make Much Sense?" In *An Heretical Heir of the Enlightenment: Science, Politics and Policy in the Work of Charles E. Lindblom*. Edited by Harry Redner, 235–64. Boulder, CO: Westview Press.

———. 1996. "School Choice and Student Performance." In *Holding Schools Accountable*. Edited by Helen Ladd, 149–76. Washington, D.C.: The Brookings Institution.

———. 1997. "The Milwaukee Parental Choice Program: Achievement Test Score Results." Paper given at the American Economic Association Annual Meeting, January. New Orleans, LA.

Witte, John F., and Douglas Archbald. 1985. "Metropolitan Milwaukee Specialty Schools and Programs, Report 5." Governor's Study Commission. Madison, WI: Department of Public Instruction.

Witte, John F., and Mark E. Rigdon. 1993. "Education Choice Reforms: Will They Change American Schools?" *Publius* 23:95–114.

Witte, John F., Mark E. Rigdon, and Andrea Bailey. 1992. "Second Year Report: Milwaukee Parental Choice Program." Report to the Wisconsin State Legislature. Madison, WI: Department of Public Instruction.

———. 1993. "Third Year Report: Milwaukee Parental Choice Program." Report to the Wisconsin State Legislature. Madison, WI: Department of Public Instruction.

Witte, John F., and Christopher Thorn. 1995. "Who Attends Public and Private

Schools in Wisconsin: With Implications for the Milwaukee Choice Program." Madison, WI: Robert LaFollette Institute of Public Affairs.

———. 1996. "Who Chooses? Vouchers and Interdistrict Choice Programs in Milwaukee." *American Journal of Education* 104 (May):186–217.

Witte, John F., Christopher Thorn, Kim Pritchard, and Michelle Claibourn. 1994. "Fourth Year Report: Milwaukee Parental Choice Program." Report to the Wisconsin State Legislature. Madison, WI: Department of Public Instruction.

Witte, John F., Christopher Thorn, and Troy Sterr. 1995. "Fifth Year Report: Milwaukee Parental Choice Program." Report to the Wisconsin State Legislature. Madison, WI: Department of Public Instruction.

Witte, John F., and Daniel Walsh. 1985. "Metropolitan Milwaukee District Performance Assessment, Report 4." Governor's Study Commission. Madison, WI: Department of Public Instruction.

———. 1990. "A Systematic Test of the Effective Schools Model." *Educational Evaluation and Policy Analysis* 12 (Summer):188–212.

Wohlsetter, Priscilla. 1995. "Charter Schools in the United States: The Question of Autonomy." *Educational Policy* 9:331–58.

# Index

Agostini v. Felton, 22, 180
American education, 4; expenditure on, 18–19; implications of choice on, 27, 52, 199–209; normative conflicts in, 18, 53. *See also* public schools
American Federation of Teachers (AFT), 33, 160. *See also* teacher's unions

Beales, Janet, 76, 77
*The Bell Curve*, 165n.6, 203, 204
Bennett, William, 35, 173
Bickers, Kenneth, 190
Bolick, Clint, 177, 180, 184, 185–86
Bradley Foundation, 160, 165–66, 165n.6, 167, 176, 178, 185
Brennan, David, 170
*Brown v. Board of Education*, 32, 33
Bush, George, 35, 159, 173
Bush, George W., Jr., 159
Bush, Jeb, 159

Catholic schools, 17, 96; closings of, 19; enrollment in, 19, 29–31, 196–97; in Milwaukee, 40, 196–97; and voucher movement, 17, 161–62, 167, 171, 174n.5, 181, 183, 185–86, 207. *See also* private schools
Chapter 220 Program, 79–81, 82
charter schools, 15, 16, 33, 109, 109n.5, 183
choice theater, xiv, 9, 171–77
Christian schools, 16, 30–31, 181. *See also* private schools
Chubb, John, 12, 115n.3, 198
Cleveland voucher program, 45, 81, 158, 192, 197; enactment of, 170–71; selection into, 74–75, 81–82, 164n.5
Clinton, Bill, 159, 160n.1, 175, 176
Coggs, Spencer, 44, 168
*Committee for Public Education v. Nyquist*, 21, 22, 180
common schools, 5, 201
Community Education Opportunity Program (CEO), 75, 78–79

Cookson, Peter, Jr., 202
Coons, John, 12

Dewey, John, 32, 109
Dole, Robert, 159, 173, 175, 176
Du, Jiangtao, 133–34, 175

educational choice: and constitutional issues, 20–23, 32–33, 161, 171, 177–82; why controversial, 11–23; interdistrict plans, 16, 32–33; issues surrounding, 5–8, 18, 23–27; and race, 24–25, 26, 203; selection into, 73–79, 199; theoretical and research issues on, 23–27, 192–96. *See also* Milwaukee Parental Choice Program (MPCP); vouchers
experimental policy design, 120–22, 192–99

Fliegel, S., 113n.1
Friedman, Milton, 11, 34–35, 160, 198–99
Fuller, Howard, 164–65, 169, 197–99, 207, 208

George, Gary, 43, 44, 168, 169
Golden Rule Scholarship Program, 75–76, 160, 167
Greater Milwaukee Committee (GMC), 165, 166
Greene, Jay, 133–34, 175
Grover, Bert, xiii–xiv, xv, 172

Heckman, James, 134, 154, 155
Henig, Jeffrey, 114, 206
Hill, Paul, 75n.10
Hirschman, Albert O., 73

incrementalism, 157, 162–70, 188, 191, 208

*Jackson v. Benson*, 22, 179
Jefferson, Thomas, 200, 204–5
Joyce, Michael, 165–66, 185

Landmark Legal Foundation, 160, 177, 178

Lasswell, Harold, 157

*Lemon v. Kurtzman*, 21, 181

Levin, Henry, 57, 105–6

Lewis, Fannie, 170, 171

magnet schools, 15, 16, 32, 41, 53

market model of education, 10, 11–15, 16, 110, 199–209

McGroarty, Daniel, 173, 174n.7, 175, 191

McKinley, Daniel, 167, 186–87

Milwaukee, 36–37

Milwaukee Metropolitan Association of Commerce (MMAC), 165, 166, 167, 184

Milwaukee Parental Choice Program (MPCP), 3, 8–9; costs of, 103–4, 105–6; and the courts, 20–23, 161, 177–82; enactment of, 43–44; enrollment in, 55–57; and media, xiv, 9, 43, 171–77; and parental involvement, 64–65, 118–19, 131; program defined and changes in, 44–46, 116, 162–70; politics of, 162–70, 182–89; research on, 46–48, 112–14, 192–96; satisfaction with, 117–18; selection into and out of, 54–73, 81–82, 11, 164n.5, 193
— outcomes: for parents, 117–19, 149; for schools, 114–17, 149; for students, 119–49; summary, 149–51;
— schools: curriculum and pedagogy, 95–102, 147–48; failures, 106–9, 111, 116; finances, 89–92, 105–6; governance, 89; history of, 84–87, 96; and MPS 102–3; segregation in, 85, 87, 104–5; staffing of, 92–95, 110, 147–48;
— specific schools: Bruce Guadalupe, 84, 85, 87, 89, 108, 109n.5, 116; Exito, 84, 86, 87, 108; Harambee, 84, 85, 116; Highland Community, 86; Juanita Virgil Academy, 84, 87, 90, 95, 106–8, 163; Lakeshore Montessori, 84; Learning Enterprises, 84, 86, 87; Messmer High School, 84, 174n.5; Milwaukee Preparatory, 84, 108; SER Jobs for Progress, 84, 86; Waldorf School of Milwaukee, 81, 86, 93, 99–100, 106, 107, 108,

116; Woodlands School, 84, 86. *See also* educational choice; vouchers

Milwaukee Public Schools (MPS) 17; attrition from, 144; demographics of, 40, 58–62; and differences from suburbs, 4, 40, 42; effects of vouchers on, 114–16; history of, 37–42; parental involvement in, 64–66; parent satisfaction with, 66, 68; performance of, 41–42, 49–51; racial enrollment in, 37–42, 59, 60; school choice in, 57–58; students compared to Choice students, 122–32, 143–44; students compared to Rejects, 139–44

Mintrom, Michael, 160, 161

Mitchell, George, 165, 167

Mitchell, Susan, 164, 167

Moe, Terry, 12, 115n.3, 198

Moore, Gwendolyn, 44, 168, 169

Montessori schools, 86, 99

*Mueller v. Allen*, 21, 22, 33–34, 180

Murray, Charles, 165n.6, 203

National Association for the Advancement of Colored People (NAACP), 40, 177, 184

National Education Association (NEA), 33, 160, 183. *See also* teacher's unions

Norquist, John, 109n.5, 169–70

parental involvement: and effects on achievement, 131; measurement of, 47, 64–66; and selection into MPCP, 64–65; voucher effects on, 118–19, 149

Partners for Advancing Values in Education (PAVE), 82, 116–17, 167–68, 183, 185; characteristics of students in, 75–79, 196; selection into, 77, 78n.11, 186–87

Percell, Caroline, 202

Peterson, Paul, 133–34, 136, 175

positivism, xiii, xiv

postmodernism, xiii, xiv

private schools, 19; accountability of 13–14; and constitutional issues, 20–23, 177, 179–82; enrollment in, 5–6; family income of student in, 31–32, 188–89, 197; laws and regulations governing, 13–14, 53; organization of, 13–14, 25; performance of, 53. *See also* Mil-

waukee Parental Choice Program (MPCP)
public schools: accountability of, 13–14; choices in 31–33, 41; desegregation of, 32, 40–41; effects of market approach on, 199–205; effects of vouchers on, 205–9; laws and regulations governing, 13–14; and model of education, 11–15; organization of, 13–14, 25; performance of, 207–8. *See also* Milwaukee Public Schools (MPS)

Quade, Quentin, 166

Reagan, Ronald, 34, 35, 159, 175
Reject (non-selected Choice) students, 54, 120–22; characteristics of, 70–72, 136–37; compared to Choice students, 132–39, 142–43; compared to MPS students, 139–43; as a comparison group, 120–21, 132–34, 143. *See also* Milwaukee Parental Choice Program (MPCP)
Ridge, Tom, 159, 162
Rouse, Cecilia, 133–34

Schulz, Dale, 169, 184
selection bias, 113–14, 121, 132–33, 136–37, 144–47, 152–56, 193–94
Sheehy, Tim, 166, 169, 180
Smith, Bob, 174n.7, 175
Starr, Kenneth, 176, 178, 185
Steiner, Rudolph, 13, 99
Stein, Robert, 190
Sugarman, Steve, 12

teacher's unions, 5, 160, 162, 176, 177, 182–83. *See also* American Federation of Teachers (AFT); National Education Association (NEA)
Teske, Paul, 114
Thompson, Tommy, 43, 159, 163, 164–65, 173, 174, 175, 178

Vergari, Susan, 160
Voinovich, George, 159, 170
vouchers, 3; arguments for and against, 18, 53, 114, 182; cost of, 20; and the courts, 21–22, 32–33, 161, 171, 177–82; implications of, 27, 205–9; politics of, 158–62, 190–92, 208–9; referendums on, 35–36, 159, 182; road to, 31–36; targeted, 7, 15–16, 35–36, 190, 196–99, 207–8; universal, 7, 15–16, 170, 188–89, 190, 196–99, 206, 208. *See also* educational choice; Milwaukee Parental Choice Program (MPCP)

Wahl, Maureen, 76, 77
Williams, Annette "Polly," 43, 160n.1, 163, 164–65, 168, 169, 170, 171, 173, 174, 175, 180, 190, 198
Wisconsin Department of Public Instruction, xv, 45, 46, 54, 57, 58, 107, 168, 174n.7, 177, 181n.10, 188n.12
*Witters v. Washington Department of Services*, 21, 22, 180

*Zorbrest v. Catalina Foothills School District*, 22, 180